THE TRANSPORTATION FRONTIER

THE
TRANSPORTATION
FRONTIER

Trans-Mississippi West
1865 - 1890

Δ

OSCAR OSBURN WINTHER

HISTORIES OF THE AMERICAN FRONTIER
Ray Allen Billington, General Editor
Howard R. Lamar, Coeditor

UNIVERSITY OF NEW MEXICO PRESS
Albuquerque

To Ingrid and Eric

FOREWORD

MORE THAN ANY OTHER FACTOR, transportation routes shaped both the direction and the ebb and flow of the three-century-long migrations that peopled the North American continent. New frontiers might beckon with their promises of fertile farm lands, virgin pasturage, and unexploited mineral or forest wealth. Men might be infected with the wanderlust, or they might dream longingly of the opportunities for prosperity, social progress, and adventure that lay to the westward. Yet unless means existed for reaching those promised lands, they must dream in vain. When the gates to the West were opened by new roads or canals or railroads the population tide flowed steadily; when impenetrable mountain barriers or pathless forests and plains blocked access to the interior men remained locked in the eastern settlements, no matter how urgent their bent for change.

Available routes similarly shaped the course of the westward flowing migratory stream. On the earliest frontiers when waterways provided the only access to new lands, Virginians and Marylanders moved westward because the James and the Rappahannock and the Potomac led in that direction; Yankee and Yorkers turned northward to utilize the navigable waters of the Connecticut and the Hudson; and Pennsylvanians were deflected southward along the Great Valley of the Appalachians by the Shenandoah River and neighboring streams. A generation later the Appalachian mountain wall was breached only when pathfinders blazed trails along which the pioneers could march. Kentucky received its first sizable migration only after Daniel Boone laid out the Wilderness Road through Cumberland Gap; western Virginia and Pennsylvania were occupied because Braddock's Road and Forbes' Road guided migrants to the forks of the Ohio. Throughout America's past the routes that pioneers could follow were as influential as the pioneering urge or the location of exploitable resources in determining the direction of the westward movement.

As this process went on, human ingenuity gradually allowed the frontiersmen to improve on the earliest transportation routes that nature had provided. Waterways and the primitive trails that had been laid out by animals and appropriated by Indians soon were supplemented by roads that could be followed by packtrains and eventually by wagons. The nation's first improved highway, the macadamized Lancaster Turnpike built between Philadelphia and Lancaster, Pennsylvania, in the waning years of the eighteenth century, proved so successful that a road-building craze swept the states for a generation. Toll-roads proved suitable for carriages and stagecoaches, but the costs of freight haulage was prohibitive. This was the incentive that launched the "canal era" of American history. The Erie Canal, opened in 1825 between the Hudson River and the Great Lakes, inspired a host of imitators throughout the East and Midwest during the 1830s and 1840s. The nation's transportation problems, people told each other with smug satisfaction, had been solved for all time by the network of turnpikes and canals that blanketed the East by the middle of the nineteenth century.

Artifical waterways and macadamized highways might temporarily care for the needs of the East, but when pioneers ventured beyond the Mississippi they entered a new world where the old rules no longer applied. The Far West was a land of spacious distances, of sparse population, of isolated settlements separated one from the other by weary miles of plains and desert. The Far West was a land of semiaridity where streams were few and where even the largest waterways flowed sluggishly for only part of the year. How could California's remote settlements be reunited with the Mississippi Valley frontier? How could the distant mining camps of the Rocky Mountains and the inland empire be supplied with the necessities needed to keep them loyal to the Union?

These were the problems that had to be solved before the frontier could follow its manifestly destined course to the Pacific. They had to be solved by the use of animal rather than mechanical power, for the new-fangled railroad was not sufficiently improved to span the Great Plains or surmount the towering Rockies and Sierras. To complicate the situation still more, government construction was ruled out by a public opinion that had shied from state-built internal improvements ever since the tragic aftermath of the Panic of 1837. How could private enterprise be persuaded to risk the astronomical sums needed to bridge the "great American desert" where revenue from way-traffic would forever be nonexistent.

The generation that lived during the 1840s and 1850s found the answer in various forms of government subsidies. The slow-moving wagon trains that crisscrossed the West during those decades showed profits only because of fat government contracts to supply federal forts; the swift-moving stagecoaches that thrilled the world by spanning the miles between the Mississippi and the Pacific in less than twenty-five days operated successfully only because they were generously subsidized to carry the United States mails; the railroads that displaced the stage lines a brief generation later were made possible only by lavish federal loans and grants of land, both to a right-of-way and to salable property on either side. Thus did a paternalistic government assure its people the transportation facilities needed for the final conquest of the continent.

This is the exciting story told by Professor Oscar O. Winther on the pages that follow. Professor Winther brings to his task a wealth of knowledge, for his many books and articles on western transportation have long been highly regarded by professional historians and general readers alike. He also brings a realization that the impact of America's pioneer heritage on today's generation cannot be understood by an overemphasis on the glamorous and colorful at the expense of the important and enduring. The reader will find on his pages hair-raising tales of road agents and stagecoach drivers and Pony Express riders, but he will find far more space devoted to the less glamorous steamboats and railroads that truly conquered the West. This is as it should be. Hollywood and television producers to the contrary, the handful of outlaws and "knights of the reins" who captured popular imagination in their day contributed little to the emerging civilization of the United States.

This book is unique in still other ways. It is the first serious study of all aspects of western transportation, from the advent of overland freighting to the era of the automobile. It is the first to recognize that water transportation played an important role in the occupation of the Far West, and to gauge the influence of traffic on the Missouri and Colorado on settlement and military operations. It is the first to carry the reader back to those days of primitive conveyances and allow him to realize the discomforts of a stagecoach ride or the thrill of a journey on one of the luxurious Palace Cars of George Pullman. And, by no means least important, it is the first to allot the now-forgotten bicycle its proper credit in stimulating the Good Roads movement across the nation. Paved highways shrank distances even more than railroads; as they spread across the West the pioneer era in the history of American transportation drew to a close. These contributions correctly suggest that this is a work from which both scholars and the historically curious can gain much in information as well as pleasure.

This volume is one of eighteen in the Holt, Rinehart and Winston *Histories of the American Frontier*. Like the other books in this series, it tells a complete story; it may also be read as part of the broader history of westward expansion told in connected form in these volumes. Each is being written by a leading authority who brings to his task an intimate knowledge of the period that he covers and a demonstrated skill in narration and interpretation. Each will provide the general reader with a sound but readable account of one phase of the nation's frontiering past, and the specialized student with a documented narrative that is integrated into the general story of the nation's growth. It is the hope of the authors and editor that this full history of the most American phase of the American past will help the people of the United States to understand themselves and thus to be better equipped to face the global problems of the twentieth-century world.

Ray Allen Billington

The Huntington Library
January 1964

PREFACE

THIS BOOK has been written to conform to the general framework of the *Histories of the American Frontier* series. As the title indicates, this study deals mainly with transportation west of the Mississippi River from the end of the Civil War to the passing of the American frontier. Due to the fact that pertinent United States census and other data are available only on a state and not on a county basis, Minnesota and Louisiana—the two states straddling the Mississippi River—are necessarily dealt with statistically as belonging wholly to the area with which this volume is chiefly concerned. Also, in order to help meet the over-all needs of the series, some general pre-1865 background material has been included. And to develop certain topics to what seemed logical conclusions, terminal dates in some discussions have been extended to the turn of the century. Chiefly, it has been my purpose to write a brief history of the transportation developments that transpired in an area passing through stages termed the "frontier process," and to relate these developments to American frontier life.

The materials on transportation in the West are voluminous, especially those concerning railroads. In preparing this book I have attempted to combine and make use of both original sources and adequately executed secondary materials. Both types are widely scattered in repositories throughout the United States. The many libraries to which I am deeply indebted for generous services are the Indiana University Library, Bloomington; the Library of Congress, and the Bureau of Railroad Economics Library of the Association of American Railroads in Washington, D.C.; the Newberry, John Crerar, and Chicago historical society libraries in Chicago; the Mercantile and Missouri Historical Society libraries in St. Louis; the Minnesota State Historical Society and the James J. Hill libraries in St. Paul; the Tulane University and the Howard-Tilton Memorial libraries in New Orleans; the Kansas State Historical Society Library, Topeka; the Bancroft Library at the University of California,

Berkeley; the Eugene C. Barker Library, the University of Texas, Austin; The Timothy Hopkins Transportation Library, Stanford University, California; and, most important, the Henry E. Huntington Library, San Marino, California.

Generous awards of a John Simon Guggenheim Memorial Fellowship in 1959, a senior research associateship at the Huntington Library the following year, and continuing support from the Indiana University Graduate School made this book, as well as other work, possible. I was treated with utmost courtesy and generosity by the staffs of all the above institutions. In this respect I am especially indebted to Mr. Carey S. Bliss, Miss Mary Isabel Fry, and Miss Constance Lodge at the Huntington Library. Moreover, I am deeply grateful to the following for their interest and encouragement: President J. E. Wallace Sterling of Stanford University; Dr. Louis B. Wright, director of the Folger Library; and at the Huntington Library: Dr. John Pomfret, director; Mr. Robert O. Dougan, librarian; and Professor Allan Nevins, permanent senior research associate. Unsparing with helpful criticism and giving generously of his time was Professor Ray Allen Billington, general editor of the series. I was greatly helped in varying ways by Miss Marcia Friedrich, Richard A. Van Orman, and Richard D. McKinzie. And, as always, I was given generous assistance by my wife Mary. Finally, I wish to acknowledge the Museum of New Mexico, Santa Fe, for permission to reprint parts of a paper read before the First Conference on Western History and published in *Probing the American West* (Santa Fe, 1962), and also the *New Mexico Historical Review* for permission to use brief excerpts from my article "The Southern Overland Mail and Stagecoach Line, 1857–1861," published in that journal.

Oscar Osburn Winther

Bloomington, Indiana
January 1964

CONTENTS

LIST OF MAPS
AND ILLUSTRATIONS

MAPS

ILLUSTRATIONS

The Transportation Frontier, 1865

*W*hen the Civil War ended, the West, especially the expansive unoccupied areas of that region, once again stirred the attention of a restless American people. Great portions of the area lying between the Mississippi River and the Pacific Ocean awaited exploitation, and the key to such development was transportation. Awesome and endless as distances seemed to be in 1865, the trans-Mississippi West was in no real sense what some called it, a "trackless wilderness." By then the entire region had been extensively explored; a considerable portion of it had become settled; crisscrossing trails had been cut and charted; and in spite of Indian-infested prairies and the forbidding mountain and desert regions of the Far West, an impressive array of roads had either been constructed or were in the making.

A number of these primitive thoroughfares had been trodden by buffalo and Indians and were considered good because they invariably followed the easiest grades and led to water.[1] Still other trails and roads had been established by white trappers, traders, hunters, settlers, and soldiers. From the Spanish had come the oldest "official" road in the

West—*Jornada del Muerto*, hugging the eastern bank of the Rio Grande, the Old Spanish Trail meandering across the Southwest between Santa Fe and Los Angeles and, as well, mission-studded *El Camino Real* in Alta California. British Hudson's Bay Company traders had created well-trodden cavalcade trails across the mountain areas in the Pacific Northwest. American explorers, mountain men, migrants, stagecoach and wagon freight operators, and military and Department of Interior officials had laid out and established most of the main roads that in primarily east-west directions stretched across the trans-Mississippi West. In addition there was a network of crude local roads established mainly under local auspices within the more densely settled areas.[2]

Most important of the routes crossing the great expanse of western prairies and plains before and after the Civil War was the Central Overland Road. First established as a fur traders' trace and subsequently known as the Oregon-California Trail, it continued to be important after 1865 as an immigrant and military road. In the early stages of its development the Central Overland Road began at the Missouri River in the form of numerous feeder lines that converged in the vicinity of Fort Kearny, 197 miles west of Omaha. From this military post the road stretched westward, with cutoffs and bypasses, mainly along the south side of the Platte River, through South Pass to points on or near the upper Snake River. From such places as Fort Hall on the upper Snake River and Soda Springs at the northern end of the Wasatch Mountains, one branch of this road led northwestward into the Oregon country, another, southwestward to California.

By 1865 the role of this nationally familiar road had greatly increased. From it branch routes reached out to Rocky Mountain mining communities and, subsequently, to the Black Hills of (South) Dakota. By then, too, an almost parallel trail on the north side of the Platte, first blazed by Mormons in 1847, had ceased to serve as a more or less exclusive thoroughfare for Utah-bound Saints. By 1865 most migrants had come to regard the trails on the two sides of the Platte as part of a single Central Overland Road. Many travelers, depending somewhat upon their mood, switched freely from one road to the other. One of many guidebook authors depicting the character of this road went so far as to say that by midcentury the north and the south sides were "about equally traveled over."

Changes had indeed been rapid. During the late 1840s and '50s Fort Kearny had been looked upon as a place far out on the "road to Oregon." But by the end of the Civil War this familiar landmark, and not the muddy Missouri, had emerged as the chief jumping-off place for treks to the Far West. By then farms and small trading establishments along the Central Overland Road connecting Omaha and Fort Kearny were, in the words of another guidebook author, "not unlike what they would be in crossing any of our newer Western States. . . . settlements are springing up along the route, and good roads abound. . . ."³

Even the leaving of Fort Kearny for points westward was in no real sense, as one contemporary called it, bidding an "adieu to civilization." At roughly one- to fifteen-mile intervals along either of the two routes bordering the Platte River between Fort Kearny and the Rockies were ranches, transportation stations, and trading posts. Nearly all, including ranches, catered to travelers by offering at various prices camping, grazing, and watering facilities; groceries, liquor, grain, hardware, blacksmithing, hay, wood, and even at one place, ready-baked bread. Guidebooks frequently gave some hint as to charges, and one even warned readers: "RANCHE. Charge exorbitant prices."⁴ This available market for services and goods was by the close of the Civil War stimulating still further settlement along the Central Overland Road. The region through which the road passed was "attracting great attention among those who have the soberer quest for permanent homes."⁵ To be sure, the high plains country farther to the West was sparsely settled, but even through this area travelers observed many signs of human habitation.

Changes were by no means confined to the countryside. By 1865 the Central Overland Road had become in part maintained by the military and was in fair condition. One traveler even asserted that the entire four hundred miles of road from Fort Kearny to Julesburg in the northeast corner of Colorado, and from this junction point to Denver, "was almost as smooth as a table."⁶ Frank A. Root, an express and mail agent, who knew this route well during the 1860s, had but two criticisms to make: that from Fort Kearny west there was a steady uphill grade, and that frequent stretches of sand impeded progress, at least of the stagecoaches.⁷ Perhaps the least reassuring note in the guidebooks of the mid-1860s was a grim reminder such as this one: "Here, a little west of the river, may be seen the grave of Martin Moran, who was killed by the Indians, 18th of July, 1862."⁸

By no means did the Central Overland Road have a monopoly on the vehicle traffic of the plains after 1865. Colorado gold discoveries in 1859 led to the establishment that year of a stagecoach and wagon freighting route named Leavenworth and Pike's Peak Express Road. Taking off from the Missouri River port of Leavenworth and passing through Fort Riley at the confluence of the Kansas and Republican rivers, this road cut across northern Kansas to Denver; the distance, 687 miles.⁹ Its importance as a staging route was considerable; its role as a general wagon route was, however, secondary to that of another Kansas route, best known as the Smoky Hill Road. Traffic fed into the Smoky Hill Road from the river towns of Atchison, Leavenworth, and Kansas City. Roads leading out from these towns converged at the Smoky Hill River, after which the road was named, then wound west as a single thoroughfare to Denver, approximately six hundred miles from the Missouri River. For Kansans going to Denver the Smoky Hill Road was at least sixty miles shorter than the Central Overland Road, and it gained great popularity with staging firms and wagon freighters who made regularly scheduled trips between Missouri River towns and Denver.

The Smoky Hill Road was not without its points of interest. Between Fort Riley and Denver this route passed through no less than thirty-eight small towns. Shortly after the war several of these places emerged as notorious cowtowns, and still others aspired to "cowtown reputation." Not least among these tiny Smoky Hill places were Junction City, Abilene, Salina, and Ellsworth.[10] Stations, undetermined numbers of ranches, and great herds of cattle also dotted the wayside. One traveler who passed over this route at the close of the Civil War observed buffalo "continually in sight."[11] Lieutenant J. R. Fitch, who traveled over this road in 1865, was aware of its richness and general interest. It was "apparent to everybody," he wrote, that this route was not only richer than the Central Overland Road in grass and timber, but it ran through the very heart of the Buffalo country; "... as far as the eye could see," wrote Fitch, "the *hills* were *black* with these shaggy monsters of the prairie, grazing quietly upon the richest pasture in the world."[12] Quite apart from its civilized touches, the Smoky Hill Road lay in the very heart of Indian hunting grounds. For this reason white men using the trail constantly faced danger of attack from the red men.

Also important in meeting the transportation needs of the post-Civil War West was the old Santa Fe Trail. Over this 841-mile link between Kansas City and the capital of New Mexico moved military personnel and huge quantities of army supplies destined for such places as Forts Larned, Lyon, and Union, and the town of Santa Fe itself. During the postwar years this traffic also extended beyond Santa Fe to Albuquerque, a place that had in turn developed into a military distribution point for the New Mexican army posts of Forts Craig, Stanton, Fillmore, and Arizona's Fort Defiance.[13] Although mainly military, some of this traffic was civilian in character. Civilian goods and numerous southwestbound covered wagon immigrant caravans were observed passing over this now famed trail.

The roads thus far noted were the main ones leading across the plains in 1865, but they were by no means the only ones. Various forwarding concerns had blazed wagon roads across scattered segments of the West, and the most notable of these had been laid out by the Butterfield Overland Stagecoach and Mail Company (1857–1858). This route connected St. Louis and Memphis with San Francisco by means of a 2795-mile oxbow course that dipped deeply into the South. The Civil War had disrupted the Butterfield services but the road over which the company's stages had operated continued to serve as a transportation route during the postwar period.[14]

*I*N ONE WAY or another the role of the federal government in western road building and road maintenance was considerable. During the period 1845–1865 Congress, either directly or indirectly, had sponsored numerous military and postal road surveys and construction jobs (see map of wagon roads on page 6). Then as the postwar era began federal lawmakers again enacted legislation calling for the construction of several roads in the northern Great Plains and Rocky Mountain areas for the purpose of facilitating mining operations as well as settlement and communication in those areas. Several of these projects were to involve the use of United States troops, not only in construction operations but in offering a measure of protection to traffic after the roads were built.

One of these new routes was to be known as the [Colonel James A.] Sawyers Wagon Road. It was slated to extend from the mouth of the Niobrara River, Nebraska, via the Black Hills of (South) Dakota to Virginia City, Montana. Well conceived though it may have been, the Sawyers Wagon Road did not turn out to be a highly successful venture. After two attempts at moving Montana-bound settlers through hostile Indian country, this well-intentioned enterprise was abandoned. A second road was scheduled for construction from Sioux City, Iowa, along the north bank of the Missouri River to the mouth of the Big Cheyenne. Due to mismanagement of federal funds actual construction on this project was confined to a stretch of road between Sioux City and Yankton, (South) Dakota. Still another federal enterprise involved laying out a road from Lewiston, Idaho Territory, through the Bitterroot Mountains to Virginia City, Montana Territory. Even though a considerable amount of money and labor was expended on this project, the road across the Bitterroots fell short of completion.[15] It is apparent in retrospect that a major difficulty confronting all federal wagon road projects after the war was that both public and official interests were diverted from road construction to railroad building within the trans-Mississippi West.

Roads, or what passed for such, were not confined to the plains and Rocky Mountain regions. The Pacific coast area had its own road system of sorts, and these in turn were linked with some of the major east-west routes. The Central Overland Road was one of these. By 1865 this thoroughfare had been extended from Julesburg, Colorado, to Sacramento by way of Denver, Salt Lake City, and Carson City, Nevada. In turn this road

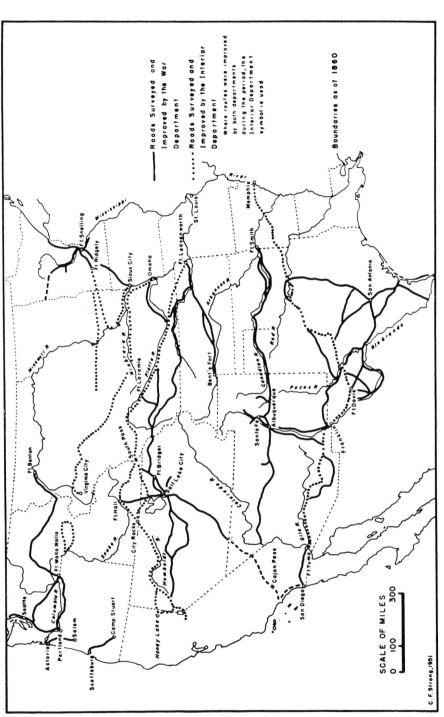

Government Wagon Roads 1846–1869. (COURTESY W. TURRENTINE JACKSON AND PERMISSION OF UNIVERSITY OF CALIFORNIA PRESS)

Roads Surveyed and
Improved by the War
Department

Roads Surveyed and
Improved by the Interior
Department

Where routes were improved
by both departments
during the period, the
Interior Department
symbol is used

Boundaries as of 1860

SCALE OF MILES
0   100   300

C. F. Strong, 1951

was connected with a network of west coast wagon roads, packing trails, or river steamship lines reaching out to towns, farming communities, and mining camps within California and the Pacific Northwest.[16] By and large, roads of the desert Southwest were what nature provided. There the countryside was relatively open and smooth, and, as one guidebook author phrased it, "every traveler seems to take a road to suit himself."[17]

In general, western roads were uneven in surface. "Good roads" were, at best, those that had been graded in places and were reasonably free of deep ruts, rocks, tree stumps, and other impediments, and had a minimum of bridge construction. There were few, if any, hard-surfaced country roads in the trans-Mississippi West in 1865, unless corduroy, plank, and hard pan could be defined as such. Most were simply routes of travel that had been blazed and made passable for wagons either by pioneer civilian migrants and transportation concerns or by such federal government agencies as the Office of Exploration and Surveys of the War Department, the United States Corps of Topographical Engineers, or the Pacific Wagon Road Office of the Department of Interior. Roads built by the government were designated and charted in official publications. The best overview of the road situation comes from the man who probably knew it best, Major General Grenville M. Dodge. As Dodge viewed it from his Fort Leavenworth headquarters in November 1865, the routes that crossed the central plains, those that led up the great valleys of the Platte and the Arkansas and on over the higher table lands, were "the best natural roads in the world." And of all of these, the Central Overland Road (the Platte River route) was "by far the best natural road from the Missouri River to the Pacific Coast." But regardless of relative merit, it was over all of these widely scattered routes, as General Dodge observed, that the supplies for the "mighty empire" then growing up in the Far West had to pass.[18]

The growth of this "empire" was, indeed, impressive. Considered in terms of decades, the Civil War did little more than impose a temporary check upon the westward march. The census of 1860 revealed that settlement had for the first time plunged beyond the west bank of the Missouri River, on toward the middle of Kansas and Nebraska territories, and had protruded far up the Missouri River embankments. The settlement map of Texas then resembled a huge bulbous salient pushed westward between Indian Territory, in modern Oklahoma, and the Gulf to a point beyond the hundredth meridian. At the opposite northern extreme settlements about St. Paul in Minnesota had, according to the Census Bureau, "grown like Jonah's gourd, spreading in all directions, and forming a broad band of union with the main body of settlement down the line of the Mississippi river."[19]

A decade later (1870) the Census Bureau noted what had by then become "a gradual and steady" progression of the frontier line westward across the Great Plains.[20] By that time tillable lands of southern Minnesota and a small portion of southeastern Dakota Territory, practically all of Iowa, and the eastern portion of Kansas and Nebraska—chiefly along the lines of Pacific-bound railroads—had yielded to the settler's plow.

Scattered islands of settlement also lay west of the unbroken frontier line. During the 1840s and '50s settlers had pushed far beyond this line and had established fast-growing colonies in Oregon's Willamette-Puget Sound trough, the Rocky Mountains, and in restless, but constantly tantalizing, California. By the end of the 1860s the population density map showed an amazing proliferation of such "island" groupings. They comprised three major belts: one along the eastern slopes of the Colorado Rockies, the second a much elongated (north-south) Mormon settlement between the Rockies and the Sierra Nevada, and the third the rapidly growing Pacific Coast area. Within these island belts lived the great bulk of those who had ventured beyond the unbroken line of settlement.[21] But like fixed stars and darting particles in outer space, there remained to be accounted for a significant 10 percent of transfrontier population occupying what the Census Bureau called the "vacant spaces on the density map." These vacant-space dwellers were unquestionably the most restless, most mobile of the American people. They were the hunters, trappers, traders, miners, lumberjacks, soldiers, government agents, and cowmen; they were vanguards of migrants en route from old to new locations; they were the packers, teamsters, stage and express men, sutlers, travelers, and floaters of all types. It was estimated that in about 1870 this "floating population" numbered 250,000,[22] and that about a hundred thousand persons traveled either part or all the way across the Plains each year during the decade of the 1860s.[23]

The continued westward march had of course led to an emergence of new states and territories. By 1865 Congress had practically completed its job of subdividing in a political sense all lands between the Mississippi River and the Pacific Ocean. A political map of the trans-Mississippi West for 1865 would show, in order of their admission, the states of Louisiana, Missouri, Arkansas, Texas, Iowa, California, Minnesota, Oregon, Kansas, and Nevada. The remaining portions of this region had become organized as territories to await admission into the Union as states.

More indicative of the solid growth of this region are the population figures for 1860 found on the following page.[24]

An analysis of this population reveals its mobile, westward-moving character. Each state and territory had drawn heavily not only upon other states but upon the human resources of the Germanies, Scandinavia, the British Isles including Ireland, and to a small degree other foreign countries. Missouri claimed 160,541 foreign-born; California, 146,528; Minnesota, 58,728; Texas, 43,422.[25] Other states and territories had correspondingly smaller numbers of emigrants.[26]

States	Population
Missouri	1,182,012
Louisiana	708,002
Iowa	674,913
Texas	604,215
Arkansas	435,450
California	379,994
Minnesota	172,023
Kansas	107,206
Oregon	52,465
Territories	
New Mexico	93,516
Utah	40,273
Colorado	34,277
Nebraska	28,841
Nevada	6857
Dakota	4837
Total	4,524,881

Most of the western states and territories were proud, even annoyingly boastful, of their rapidly growing populations. But they were also fully aware of their "vacant spaces." Viewed within the over-all context of a massive, sprawling, roughly two million square miles of territory, a population density of approximately 2.25 per square mile was certainly not impressive. Apart from the islands of settlement there were, in 1860, only a few tiny west-bank Mississippi regions that could claim forty-five to ninety persons per square mile. Only the eastern portions of Iowa, Missouri, and Louisiana rated eighteen to forty-five persons per square mile on the population map, whereas the balance of the area within the confines of the so-called frontier line could claim but a variable two to eighteen persons per square mile.[27]

*N*UMBER AND LOCATION of people represent only a single view of the trans-Mississippi West. An overview reveals an impressive amount of improved real estate and personal property spread or scattered over a surprisingly wide and diverse area. The 1860 census, for example, accords the area at least 745,595 dwellings.[28] The greatest concentration of buildings, including some fairly impressive industrial and commercial property, formed the three largest and most distinguished cities in the region: the old and vital Mississippi River commercial ports of New Orleans and St. Louis and San Francisco amid the Gold Rush boom. Also on the list of cities and towns that during the quarter century preceding 1865 emerged as important trading, transportation, and, in many instances, outfitting centers, were the Missouri River ports of Atchison, Leavenworth, St. Joseph, Kansas City, Council Bluffs, and Omaha; the Rocky Mountain cities of Denver, Santa Fe, Salt Lake City, and Virginia City (Montana); Houston and Galveston in Texas; and such far western places as Virginia City (Nevada), Sacramento, Los Angeles, Seattle, and Portland.

But this was not all. Notwithstanding Horace Greeley's widely publicized remark in 1859 that the plains were "nearly destitute of human inhabitants" and that they afforded "little sustenance and less shelter to man,"[29] a composite map would reveal, in addition to the places noted, a West possessing a formidable array of villages, military forts, civilian trading posts, stagecoach stations, pony and other express stations, teamster stopping places, ranches, and farms; also cowherd, shepherd, prospector, pre-emptor, and homesteader shacks and soddies; mobile migrant and construction camps; and, of course, an impressive number of permanent and shifting Indian villages and camps.[30]

This region was not, in any sense, static. The West beyond the Mississippi, not unlike earlier Wests, was one of intense movement and change. Not only were people on the move westward with a resultant expansion in settlement but in all sections of the West new towns were being born. And new or old, nearly all such places were expending quantities of printer's ink in promotion and were straining in every way to become metropolitan centers. In a determined effort to achieve such status, most towns tended to overlook their need for better wagon roads. They turned instead to the promotion of locomotive-powered railroad trains.

Without adequate railroad facilities most cities and towns, and even the rural communities, felt at a great disadvantage; and indeed they were. One city that was conscious of transportation was St. Louis. Blessed with a commanding geographical position—centrally located a few miles below the confluence of two great rivers—and a long history intricately associated with transportation, St. Louis' population, in 1865, was estimated at two hundred thousand.[31] More than ten thousand miles of navigable rivers provided passageways to hundreds of skillfully skippered steamboats based on this city's levees, and seemed, as a Scottish visitor phrased it, to go "anywhere—even over the prairies."[32] But in spite of this natural advantage, St. Louis emerged somewhat prostrated from a war that had given rise to a mushrooming rival—Chicago. The question then facing St. Louis was not what this city had been, or was at the moment; it was, as asked by the *Missouri Democrat:*

What Shall St. Louis Be? . . . We have relied upon our position. The development of railroad enterprises has proved that no position is so advantageous that railways cannot flank it. . . . The rivers, once the main reliance of St. Louis, lose importance as steamboats are superceded by railroads.[33]

This newspaper bespoke well the challenge facing not only this great western entrepôt but also that of New Orleans. To be sure, New Orleans was destined to play a continued role in western river trade and even in western migrations and general travel. But it too stood at the crossroads as the war came to an end. In 1860 the "crescent city" had registered a population of 168,675. Physically it had suffered less severely from the ravages of war than had many other cities of the South, but even so New Orleans looked dingy and run down in 1865. In the opinion of one visitor at least, her buildings and streets were excessively dirty, and life there struck him as being somewhat bizarre; it was a city full of contradictions and contrasts.[34] Even the customarily boastful city directories then viewed the trade and commerce of New Orleans not only as prostrated but bound up by numerous regulations. Four years of war had demoralized this city's spirit. The future rested on hope, the possession of a strategic location, the possibility of reviving and realizing its river trade potential, and the consciousness of great plans for railroad extensions from New Orleans into Texas.[35]

In no sense was the lowered morale of New Orleans representative of western cities and towns. By contrast, St. Paul at the opposite and upper reaches of the Mississippi River exuded buoyancy and zest. Not only did the city enjoy its unique position as the headwater port of Mississippi River navigation, as the headquarters of a lucrative overland trade with settlements in the Red River of the North, and as a stagecoaching center, but in 1865 it looked with optimism and enthusiasm toward a new role in railroading. By 1870 no less than seven railroad lines were to converge on St. Paul to make it a rail center of the North.[36]

St. Paul's sanguinary outlook was shared by such Missouri River towns as Nebraska City, Council Bluffs, Leavenworth, and St. Joseph, which, among other towns, had enjoyed renown as jumping-off places for Oregon and California. Omaha City, a relative newcomer, outdid most of its rivals in self-promotion. When in 1854 Postmaster A. D. Jones (Jones carried his mail in his hat) erected a cabin a few miles north of the mouth of the Platte River, Omaha had been considered founded. It at once began to grow, lay out streets, build a levee, and erect homes and hotels. It became Nebraska's territorial capital. By 1860 its population numbered 1883 (exceeded only by Nebraska City's 1922 inhabitants). And when, as happened in 1864, it was designated as the eastern terminus of the projected Union Pacific Railroad, Omaha quickly emerged as a place to which thousands of would-be railroad workers gravitated and where business in general boomed. Omaha's future was assured, a future based squarely upon gigantic transportation developments on the nation's post-Civil War frontier. As one local chronicler remarked: "Omaha owed all she was to the Union Pacific Railway."[37]

Sharing in this youthful vitality was Denver, 589 miles west of Omaha. Colorado's gold strike had given rise to Denver during the winter of 1857–1858, first as a mere tent encampment on Cherry Creek. Shortly it was transformed into a booming shack town that over the course of years rebounded from destructive fires, floods, Indian troubles, and crime to emerge ultimately as the commercial and transportation center of the western plains and eastern slope of the Rockies. Denver, too, had its boastful chroniclers, one of whom looked upon this gold mining city (4749 population in 1860) as one of the great triumphs in the western hemisphere.[38] To this may be added a later comment by the English traveler George J. Holyoake, that for a place making poker its main business and shooting people a pastime, Denver by the 1880s had done well to become a civilized place.[39]

Important too as a link in far-western transportation and trade was Salt Lake City. With a head start of a decade on Denver, the city of Saints reported a population of 8236 in 1860, and a much larger figure, one estimated at eighteen thousand, at the close of the war.[40] By then Salt Lake City had become well established as a trading center and a key point in transcontinental stagecoach operations. Salt Lake City's nearest neighbors to the north were the mining towns of Montana Territory, which by 1865 had attracted approximately thirty thousand floating fortune seekers. Utah-based freighting firms served this northern area, as did also overland freighting and pack-animal outfits from California and Oregon, and, significantly, Missouri River steamboats. The use of the Missouri River, with its navigational head of Fort Benton about two hundred miles away, gave the aspiring Montana mining communities opportunities to claim alternative avenues of communication (grim though they were) with the settled outside world. Helena's *Pioneer Directory* for 1868 reflects this city's confident mood: "We do not think it impossible to construct a water craft below Great Falls, . . . by which Liverpool, Havre de Gras, or any part of the maritime world can be reached. . . ."[41]

If the central and northern regions had their mushrooming river ports, mining towns, and saintly citadels, New Mexico had its historic, almost fabled, Santa Fe (4635 inhabitants in 1860). The Santa Fe Trail trade had long disrupted the once-dreary and somnolent mood of this quaint, Spanish "City of the Holy Faith," with its low, flat, adobe dwellings, dirty, donkey-cluttered streets, and, according to one observer, "lifeless looking women."[42] But never had this pueblo been more alive in commerce and transportation than following the Civil War. Her multiblooded citizenry seemed overawed by reports that in the not too distant future its plaza would reverberate with the thrilling sound of locomotive whistles of a railroad line called the Atchison, Topeka and Santa Fe. Farther to the west was Tucson, which at the close of the Civil War was, in the words of the ubiquitous traveler J. Ross Browne, "a city of mud-boxes, dingy and dilapidated, cracked and baked in a composite of dust and filth," and a place where "Every man went armed to the teeth."[43]

With other Spanish-, Mexican-, or American-born towns of the Southwest things were different. The towns of Texas, linked to be sure by local and overland trails, had long depended upon the Gulf as their main avenue of travel and trade. But with the advent of the railroad Texas towns directed their interests both inland and seaward as efforts were made by such places as Austin, Houston, and Harrisburg to consummate their union with New Orleans. At the end of the war, Galveston, with eight to ten thousand residents, had become the self-proclaimed "commercial metropolis" of the Lone Star State. Steamboats served her bayou environs, and connections by rail and stagecoach brought this port city into daily contact with much of her hinterland, including Houston. The established route of travel between Houston and New Orleans in 1865 was, as a matter of fact, via Galveston. The extreme northern part of Texas remained a portion of the Great American Desert and a place visited, according to one handbook, "only by a few bold hunters."[44]

Not unlike Galveston, west coast cities and towns had sought to play both land and water roles in the transportation operations. Founded by the Spaniards, boomed by the Gold Rush, and nurtured especially by the commercial interests of the East, San Francisco, with a population of 56,802 in 1860, was the undoubted "queen city" of the Far West. By 1865 the onrush of miners had ceased, but the port by the fog-enshrouded Golden Gate and the important river cities of Sacramento and Stockton served as highly important supply depots not only for California communities but for such interior regions as Nevada's Comstock and, in competition with Portland (5819 in 1865)[45] and St. Louis, for the bustling mining towns of Idaho and Montana.[46]

Even though the trans-Mississippi West contained, in 1865, enormous unsettled and unexploited areas, this region—the last of a succession of frontiers—nevertheless possessed a small but widely dispersed population, an impressive array of overland trails and roads, and numerous strategically located cities and towns. It is within this setting that one turns to the specialized transportation developments west of the great river during the final third of the last century.

◁ **2** ▷

The Persistence of the Overlanders

*T*he Civil War had dampened but slightly and temporarily the migratory proclivities of the American people, and cessation of hostilities was, in a way, the signal for a full-fledged resurgence of covered wagon migrations westward. The patterns of these postwar population movements to America's trans-Mississippi West displayed, however, interests and objectives differing from those of *ante-bellum* days. No longer were the principal goals largely confined to Oregon's land-rich Willamette Valley, gold-laden California, or Zion in the Great Salt Lake Valley. Added to these were new and widely scattered mineral regions mainly within the Rocky Mountain ranges and the rich agricultural areas of the Great Plains. The pattern of frontier migration and settlement was altered, not only by these rapidly diversifying goals but also by the westward advance of steam-powered transport.

Clearly, by 1865, steamboats and railroads were in the process of displacing horse-drawn and man-powered transport (except for local services) between the Mississippi River and the frontier of settlement, and on most western navigable streams. Moreover, the decision of the federal government in the mid-1860s to sponsor the construction of Pacific-bound railroads presaged the demise of overland wagon caravans that had long been the grand and stirring symbol of America's westward movement.

As things turned out, the rattling, weatherbeaten, canvas-topped covered wagon that from the early nineteenth century had carried settlers westward demonstrated a remarkable capacity to keep rolling. To contemporary observers the Central Overland Road (and for that matter other western roads) were never more heavily traveled and alive than in the middle and late 1860s. "The closing year of the civil war was immense," declared the observant Frank A. Root, "the larger part of the emigration going into the new gold mining camps being developed in the Northwest."[1] As Horace Greeley viewed the migrations retrospectively in 1869 he was struck, even in this year that marked the completion of the first transcontinental railroad, by the "eager thousands pressing westward overland each summer to the shores of the Pacific" without finding relief from the "shrill but welcome whistle of the fire propelled, floating caravanserai." During the spring and summer weeks they continued as they had two decades earlier "to stalk in dusty, sombre array, beside the broad impetuous Platte."[2]

In an attempt to describe and explain this sudden upsurge in western migration Major General John Pope, writing August 1, 1865, stated that not only had the new gold and silver regions in the territories in themselves "attracted great throngs" of emigrants (their numbers having "tenfold increased by the necessary results of the late civil war"), but that never before had the nation witnessed such an outpouring of restless souls intent upon going to various and sundry places within the expansive trans-Mississippi West. The general alluded in particular to the thousands of disloyal and pro-Southern families who, finding it difficult to reestablish themselves in their old homes, "have left the States of Missouri, Arkansas, Southern Illinois, Kentucky, and no doubt other Southern States, to make their permanent homes in the new Territories."[3] One observer estimated that an average of five thousand teams cross the plains each month during the year 1865.[4]

The sight from almost any given juncture on the Central Overland Road was magnificent to behold. Demas Barnes, who wrote on-the-scene letters during the height of the 1865 spring and summer migrations, was awed by what he saw. "We estimated," wrote Barnes, "from four to five hundred wagons passed [a given point] each day—one day at least a thousand."[5] Also during this good-weather period the far-ranging Colonel James F. Meline reported from Fort Kearny that an estimated one hundred sixty wagons loaded with "Pilgrims" and not freight passed this Platte River post daily.[6] Organized emigrant parties were large; not infrequently individual caravans numbered one hundred fifty or more wagons. Such, for example, was the size of an 1864 party bound over the central route for Idaho.[7]

River crossings over the Central Overland Road (by then generously served by ferries) and campgrounds were the scenes of even greater concentrations of wagons, animals, and people. At one such encampment, or tent-wagon town, on the South Platte Mrs. Sarah Herndon, who traveled West in 1865, estimated the presence of more than a thousand persons. She wrote: "I cannot guess how many wagons and tents.... Oh, for the pen of a Dickens to describe this wonderful scene."[8]

As another traveler phrased it, the Central Overland Road was "only *one* route." Another scene of considerable immigrant traffic was the Smoky Hill Road. It was fed especially by migrants setting forth from the Missouri River landings bordering eastern Kansas and headed for the trans-Rocky Mountain West by way of Denver. During the late 1860s the Smoky Hill Road had its drawbacks. Not only was it considered more exposed to Indian attacks than most other roads but it was extremely rough. Noted one diarist, ironically reflecting upon one day's travel: "not much bad luck. Only broke 2 wagons." And later when in a calmer mood he recorded that "Hardly a day but what we break down wagons."[9]

*B*Y AND LARGE the immigrant traffic over both the Central Overland and Smoky Hill roads had much in common. A large, and possibly the largest, single contingent moving over these two roads were prospective settlers, hopefully on the move from older communities in the East to new homes on the frontier. Government homestead and railroad lands had by then become readily available, and the lush grasslands through which their roads passed were much in demand. Thus in the late 1860s, as in the 1840s, great numbers aboard these wagon caravans were farm families. Not only did they flash banners reading "Kansas (or Nebraska) or bust," but they proudly exhibited in bold letters on their whitish canvas tops the slogans or names ascribed to their respective outfits, such as "Mind Your Business," "Hell Roaring Bill from Bitter Creek," "The Red Bull," "The Sensible Child," and "Cold Cuts and Pickled Eel's Feet." They were a mixed and peculiar lot; some, according to one shrewd observer, lazy and shiftless; others sharp, keen, and enterprising; still others, shabby, genteel adventurers.[10]

There were other differences to be noted between some of these migrants to the plains and their west coast-bound forerunners. For example, those destined for the plains had fewer miles to travel. Accordingly, their wagons and most of their supplies, haphazardly thrown together, came mainly from their abandoned farms. In fact, such prospective emigrants were encouraged by the guide literature to use their common farm lumber wagons for treks either to the western plains or to the Rocky Mountains on the grounds that not only would such vehicles hold up but they would be highly marketable commodities at the mines and in pioneer farming communities.[11]

Immigrants from overseas (increasing markedly in postwar years) were outfitted in whole or in part by well-stocked supply houses that by 1865 were located at nearly all Missouri River ports. Prospective western migrants could, if they possessed cash and disposition, purchase complete outfits ranging from wagons and oxen to frying pans. Outfitting houses vied with one another in bold efforts to capture as much of this market as possible. By 1865 Council Bluffs, for example, regarded itself as a leader among outfitting towns and looked with scorn and misapprobation upon its "paper town" rivals.[12] Then as settlement pushed westward into the plains country, and with it the railroads, there ensued a corresponding westward shift in outfitting enterprises.

Regardless of where or how acquired, a single-family outfit usually consisted of one or two covered wagons, each customarily drawn by four oxen or "plow" horses. Into the wagons were placed such essentials as food, furniture, plows, and seed grains; and often dangling at the wagon sides or ends were some additional pieces of farm equipment. Trailing the wagons were cows, calves, sheep, pigs, and dogs. Projecting through some of the canvas tops were smoking stovepipes, and from cookstoves within came the appetizing aroma of frying beefsteak. Peter Winne, who recounted his experiences in travel to Denver over the Central Overland Road in 1863, remarked: "We have a covered wagon an excellent new one, a good tent (not fully completed)." Winne's family wagon was so constructed that the box projected six inches on each side above the wheels. This permitted passengers to lie crosswise in the box, providing more sleeping room than would have been the case had passengers lain lengthwise. This wagon was also equipped with a stove made of sheet iron. Winne traveled along with a party driving milch cows, so there was always an abundance of fresh milk to supplement their diet. One woman traveling on the Kansas route recalled that her luxury-loving father had a carpet on his wagon floor and that he provided his family with feather beds and an ample supply of comforters.[13]

Those whose destination was the Pacific coast area appear to have been more attentive and exacting in making preparations. For the most part, and especially during the Indian disturbances of 1865–1867, occupants of these immigrant wagons were required by the military to travel as well-armed, self-contained units. On February 28, 1866, General William T. Sherman issued an order requiring that travelers along the central routes form parties numbering not less than twenty wagons, elect captains, be well armed, and comply with instructions issued by military posts along the way. One observer at Fort Kearny indicated how well General Sherman's orders were obeyed when identifying two parties thus:

> June 5—Conductor John Shaum, 23 wagons, 34 men, 34 revolvers, 20 guns, 2 women; bound for Denver.
> June 6— ... Conductor S. M. Scott, 32 wagons, 34 men, 34 revolvers, 20 guns; bound for Salt Lake.[14]

"Every body goes armed in this country," remarked another, "the result being a great deal of unnecessary shooting & killing. ... Men seem ready to shoot on the least provocation."[15]

There were, of course, exceptions to this pattern. Many immigrant parties sought new and more convenient routes to the Far West, and one such wagon trail was blazed in 1862. In that year Captain James L. Fisk, under orders of the War Department, opened a new northern route connecting St. Paul (actually Fort Abercrombie, 250 miles northwest of St. Paul) with Fort Benton, the headwater port on the Missouri River.[16] Captain Fiske's entourage consisted of 217 men and 13 women. Fourteen wagon teams were involved; also 168 oxen, 8 mules, 17 cows, and an unspecified number of dogs. The next year Captain Fiske led a second party over his rough prairie trail and attempted a third expedition in 1864 that was turned back by Sioux Indian attack. During 1865 and 1866 several, and considerably larger, immigrant parties followed the Fiske Trail to Montana. During 1867 only one party, known as the "Captain Davey [Davy] party" passed over the Fiske Trail, and it has the distinction of being the last immigrant group known to have patronized this far northern course. Mail-bearing stagecoaches, however, came in the wake of the wagon trains and as such kept sections of this route alive until displaced by the railroad.[17]

Colonel James A. Sawyers' road-blazing party setting forth along the southern bank of Nebraska's Niobrara River in late June of 1865 was likewise accompanied by wagon-traveling pioneers, and freighters bound for the Montana mines. Sawyers' own escort train numbered 25 wagons; the freighters, 36; whereas only 5 wagons were properly designated by the colonel as "emigrant teams." Since there were over 80 wagons and 143 armed men in the outfit, this caravan must have looked impressive as in single-column formation it moved slowly westward. Colonel Sawyers related that several of the emigrants as well as a number of his hired men turned back in the face of Indian dangers; but in spite of much bad luck and some perfidy the bulk of the party connected with the Bozeman Trail (a trail linking the Central Overland Road with Bozeman, Montana) and ultimately traveled 1039 miles to reach Virginia City, Montana, by mid-October. Sawyers returned to his Niobrara-Missouri River starting point to organize a second expedition the following year, but this one did not involve civilian immigrants. Subsequent attempts to promote the Sawyers Road as a strictly immigrant and freighting route came to naught.[18]

Still another variation in the pattern of overland wagon migrations was one that accompanied the Black Hills gold discoveries in 1876. Argonauts were frantic in their first wild efforts to reach the gold fields centering upon Deadwood. One, Leander P. Richardson, related how in a party of eight he set out from the rail junction at Laramie for Deadwood. The mode of travel was one wagon and one springless coach, best known as a "jerky." Each was drawn by four horses. Richardson was not long in discovering how and why his springless vehicle got its name. This man had many difficult experiences, but most annoying of all was exposure en route to gnats "which darted into our eyes, crawled into our nostrils, buzzed in our ears, and wriggled down our necks in a most annoying fashion." The party traveled at times over the crudest of roads where the "mud was thick and deep, and our progress was far from rapid." The region over which they passed was also Indian ridden, but Richardson found comfort in the theory that no "Injun" could possibly be fool enough to venture out in such weather and over such country as that which this mining party endured.[19] Soon the Deadwood stagecoaches, in conjunction with rails, were to ameliorate somewhat the transportation problems besetting the participants in the Black Hills rush.

The movement of people into the arid and sprawling Southwest presented many distinctive features. An observer there would have been struck more by the goings and comings of troops, small motley groups of cowhands, sutlers, prospectors, government agents, and hunters than by large organized immigrant caravans that dominated the scene along the central routes. Available snatches of information make no clear distinctions between the movement of military and civilian personnel, but traffic —especially over the Santa Fe Trail—was heavy in 1865. During that year at least a thousand wagons, most of them freighters, set out from Fort Larned for Santa Fe. One Kansas newspaper, for example, reported that between May 12 and July 12, 1865, there passed through Emporia 2692 men, 1188 wagons, 736 horses, 2904 mules, 15,855 oxen, and 56 carriages. One traveler over the Santa Fe Trail in 1866 estimated that between five and six thousand ox teams passed over this familiar route during that year.[20]

Even as late as 1870 reports of continued heavy traffic persist. Wrote the freighter P. G. Scott on his observations at Trinidad (Colorado) in that year:

Trains passing and repassing every year, oxen and mules en route to Fort Union. Most were military personnel: "the hardest looking set of soldiers I ever saw, dirty and ragged, their toes sticking through their boots."[21]

Although the bulk of Southwest traffic was at this period military, it was not exclusively so. Many settlers and travelers had trudged not only over the Santa Fe Trail but over scores of other "natural" roads that led into the arable valley of the Rio Grande, west to Tucson, and ultimately to semitropical Los Angeles, where groves and vineyards "meet the eyes at every turn." Even as the rail lines pierced the Southwest desert, small groups of immigrants, as observed by an English traveler, "were wending southward and westward."[22]

*E*VENTUALLY RAILROADS were to usurp most Southwest traffic, but the rate of shift from trail to rail depended upon the advance in track construction. In 1865 the Kansas Pacific Railroad reached Topeka, and thereafter wagon outfitting terminals moved westward with the railhead. Five years later wagon caravans had all but vanished east of Ellsworth and Fort Larned. When in 1878 another railroad, the Atchison, Topeka and Santa Fe, puffed its way over Raton Pass and in 1880 connected with Santa Fe, the death knell of the historic old Santa Fe Trail as a migrant thoroughfare sounded at last.[23]

All population movement of this period was, of course, not westbound. Commercial traffic flowed in all directions. Some settlers like John Milton Johnson simply "gee-hawed" their way to and fro in the West, always looking for a fortune.[24] A considerable number of would-be settlers and miners, betraying the marks of defeat, went back home. Their schooners showed the wear and tear of long weeks on the road. One contemporary noted that the wagons were drawn by half-starved teams carrying bedraggled families and frequently followed by a flabby cow and a mangy pig. One such backtracking family revealed its sentiments in these words painted on its wagon:

> *From Kansas and starvation*
> *To Missouri and salvation.*

Without resort to verse, but betraying utter disillusionment, another traveler returning east exhibited this simple but telling legend: "Back to my Wife's Folks."

From the son of Montana's Justice Hezekiah L. Hosmer comes one of the few diaries of this westward movement in reverse. Hosmer had wintered in Virginia City, Montana, and in view of the hardships encountered there decided to return to the states. The Judge's young son was the diarist of this homebound journey that began September 21, 1865. The family set out from Virginia City in a light wagon, drawn by two horses. They headed first for the Yellowstone, and yet, reads the record, "Not one of us knew where we were going at the time." They camped on the open prairies and all this time young Hosmer feared that his "har might be rized." A Yellowstone rendezvous was safely reached and from there the Hosmers moved downstream by boat. At night they tied their boats along shore where they slept, amidst the hideous cries and howlings of wolves, coyotes, and nighthawks. Young Hosmer reports that happily the family reached Sioux City with "har" on head and just as the ice was closing in (November 20). From there stagecoach and railroad carried them the rest of the way home.[25]

Gradually the pattern of migrations became diversified. With the coming of railroads into all major areas of the trans-Mississippi West the modes of travel tended increasingly to become a curious mixture of the old and the new. The main features of immigrant travel during the remaining third of the century were, curiously enough, very similar to those established by the first Oregon pioneers. Not only did individual parties set forth in prairie schooners and as members of organized caravans but once they moved beyond the area where special accommodations and supplies were readily available, they trudged on in single columns (now over stretches of improved roads) twelve to twenty miles per day. Generally, women and children rode in the wagons. The long-bearded and well-armed men often walked alongside, although some—especially those tending the livestock—rode horseback. After 1865 river crossings had become simplified by the existence of numerous ferries operated as frontier business enterprises. The travelers halted periodically to refresh, water, and graze their animals, with the approach of evening they stopped for encampment. Wagon-made corrals were formed, and again the livestock were turned out to be tended upon the neighboring prairie grasses before being brought within the circle for the night. ". . . see how kindly frontier families take to a roving life," wrote Albert D. Richardson, a passing stagecoach passenger.

> The white-haired children are playing hard by—five or six in number, for these new countries are marvelously prolific. The husband is milking the patient cows, the wife is preparing supper of griddle-cakes bacon and coffee in the open air, at the camp stove, the hens are cackling socially from their coop, while the old family dog wags his tail approvingly, but watches with solicitous care the baby creeping about the wagon.[26]

The scene was picturesque but hardly romantic, and as one wit wryly commented about his trip across the plains: "If there is any human discomfort which is not comprehended in being hauled across the continent by grass-fed oxen in fly-time, I have not rightly studied the wagons. . . ." The discords were many, even among good families, and then as always there were upsets, breakdowns, leaky tents, spilled lard, and horses stepping in the frying pans. All this made traveling by wagon train annoying and extremely difficult.[27]

Diaries and journals for this later period are relatively scarce, but one by Mrs. Lucy Ide chronicles in vivid fashion an 1878 overland trek. The party with which Mrs. Ide traveled set out from western Wisconsin, cut across the southeastern corner of Minnesota, traversed Iowa, and then followed closely the route of the old Oregon Trail into the Washington Territory. Mrs. Ide's diary, if compared with those of the pre-Civil War period, highlights some of the differences that passing years had brought to the modes of overland wagon travel. The ox team had yielded to the horse, herds of cattle had largely replaced the buffalo on the open plains, wagons were no longer burdened down with food and other supplies, and few if any loose cattle trailed the train. There was much to remind one of the "old days." Wagons were still canvas covered and as uncomfortable in 1878 as in the 1840s. Danger of Indian attacks still existed. Weather and disease remained as uncontrolled as before.[28]

Mrs. Ide kept a faithful day-to-day record. The party set forth May 1. ". . . the hardest of all is bidding farewell to your near and dear friends." The route as far as Council Bluffs was through settled parts of Iowa, which she reports had "the appearance of being an old settled country." One notes too the transformations within the Platte River Valley. At Fremont Mrs. Ide goes shopping, and one member of the party "takes the cars for Cheyenne." The weather is favorable and distances in excess of twenty miles per day are recorded. "June 18: Today is pleasant and cool; travelled over clear prairie—nothing but herds of cattle and the Platte River for your eyes to rest upon—such a sameness." And at Ogallala the next day: ". . . they tell us there has been 75,000 head of cattle driven in from Texas, and I should not dispute it, for the broad prairie is one moving mass of cattle. . . ." Across Bridger Pass the party encounters one of many bridges that had been erected over streams on this route. The toll asked is fifty cents per team, "but after threatening to tear the bridge up and cross in the old ford, which they had built the bridge over, they decided to let us pass at the rate of 10¢ per team, so over we go and camp." Through the Snake River region the party encounters hostile Indians, but Mrs. Ide seems reconciled to this danger, saying: "so we get a little supper and lie down to wonder what will come next." Nothing happens and the party moves safely on to its destination, arriving at Dayton, Washington Territory, September 15—"the end of our trials and pleasures for this Four Months' and a half's trip across the plains."[29]

Mrs. Ide's reference to rail service is a vivid reminder, a warning, as it were, that the days of overland caravans were numbered. Nevertheless, westbound wagon trains long remained common sights, even in Indiana where in 1878 a physician reported that he saw literally hundreds of schooners passing his office in a single day—young families flaunting banners bearing Greeley's hackneyed words: "Go West Young Man."[30] Such too were the scenes observed by travelers; some railroad passengers on western trains were moved by the stark contrasts of speeding in comfort across the open plains and seeing from their coach windows the white-topped wagons imperceptibly moving westward.[31] In writing of his frontier wanderings during the 1880s James H. Cook recalled encountering an emigrant train rattling along the old Bozeman Trail. It consisted of Arkansans and Missourians, about fifteen wagons, "bound for the northwest country." Their story was reminiscent of this whole western saga. Children were crying for drink. All were in want of meat. An aged member of the party explained that during the previous night his wife had died in childbirth but that the infant had survived. "They had laid the poor woman to rest by the side of the road that morning," said Cook.[32]

By far the most impressive record of this persistence of wagon migrations comes from James H. Kyner, a railroad contractor for a railroad in Oregon. One day Kyner paused, so he wrote, to see

> an almost unbroken stream of emigrants from horizon to horizon—a distance of not less than eight miles or ten. Teams and covered wagons, horsemen, little bunches of cows, more wagons, some drawn by cows, men walking, women and children riding—an endless stream of hardy, optimistic folk, going west to seek their fortunes and to settle an empire.

Concluded Kyner, "We saw so much of things like that that we thought nothing of it. It was the order of the day...."[33]

When, indeed, the gradual shift from wagons to trains occurred, the process was one that often combined both modes of travel. Many European emigrants, and notably some of the more affluent Mormons, traveled by rail to designated outfitting places from where they proceeded west with animals, wagons, and supplies sorely needed to begin their new life in the West. Delays in the acquisition of such vital equipment were often protracted. According to Mrs. David Eccles of Montana, who recalled the arrival of her family at Union Pacific's North Platte station, they waited a month for an ox-team outfit bought at St. Joseph, Missouri. While suffering this agonizing delay, she found company in her misery: no less than six hundred English and Scandinavian Mormon converts gathered under similar circumstances to form "independent" trains, with Utah as their destination. It was the Eccles'—and doubtless also the Mormons'—first experience with ox-team migration. As Mrs. Eccles recalled, they were not long in becoming experts.[34]

As railroads reached across the plains and to the Pacific, westbound immigrants were provided with a tempting substitute for the lumbering covered wagon. Railroad transportation, however, was expensive and immigrant farm families usually did not possess the necessary cash to buy their own railroad tickets and to pay the freight charges for shipping their wagons, livestock, farm tools, and household supplies that were essential to the establishment of farm operations on a new frontier area. So for at least a decade following the Civil War, native American migrants tended to provide their own means of transit. It was, however, apparent by the late 1870s, with the rise of new towns in the West that served as outfitting places and with the advent and promotion of what was known as the low-fare "immigrant car," that most westbound Europeans and many Americans as well traveled by rail to their new places of abode. By the 1890s railroad trains had practically superseded the covered wagon overlanders. But even then, railroad passengers continued to report having seen from their car windows prairie schooners bound "Westward Ho." These were, as the Englishman Hudson reflected, "the straggling successors of the thousands of bullock-drawn waggons" that went in prerail days.[35]

Teamsters on the Frontier

*B*efore the arrival of the automotive truck, wagon freighting was the chief means by which goods were transported in regions not served by barges, steamboats, and railroads. The large lumbering wagons in which freight was hauled and the teamsters and concerns that carried on the freighting business had their roots in the colonial frontier. Wagon making, for example, was a special contribution of the colonial Atlantic seaboard, mainly of the Pennsylvania Dutch. During the eighteenth century ingenious craftsmen of Pennsylvania's Lancaster County managed to transform the two-wheeled Palatinate cart into a four-wheeled wagon that won renown for serviceability, durability, and beauty. Known as the "Conestoga," the main features of this wagon were a sturdy running gear with out-turned wheels capable of sustaining a two- to three-ton load, a flaring body that helped to hold cargo in place, and a linen top supported by bows in such fashion as to give the *tout ensemble* a jaunty boatlike air. This wagon, pulled by five or more horses, first saw service outside its home base in General Braddock's ill-fated expedition against the French at Fort Duquesne. It was subsequently used on eastern pikes and in the trans-Allegheny freighting business; and even though it was considered too heavy for general use in trans-Mississippi transportation enterprises, most makers of western covered wagons, or so-called prairie schooners, were influenced in basic design by the Pennsylvania Dutch makers of the famed Conestoga.[1]

Animal-powered wagon freighting operations accompanied the advance of settlement westward to and across the Mississippi River, but not until the advent of the Santa Fe Trail trade in 1822 was a pattern developed destined to be widely emulated elsewhere in the frontier West. In pursuance of this trade, individual traders pooled their wagon outfits to form caravans that made round trips annually between Franklin, Missouri (and subsequently other Missouri River towns), and Santa Fe. In spite of vicissitudes, this exchange of goods proved highly lucrative and continued first as a Mexican-American exchange until 1846, and thereafter solely as an American operation until finally displaced by the Atchison, Topeka and Santa Fe Railroad during the post-Civil War period.

The impact of the Santa Fe Trail trade upon the American frontier was far reaching. One important development was the emergence of what became the remarkable firm of Russell, Majors and Waddell, a name which, during the 1850s, literally became the hallmark of western wagon freighting.

In 1853 two partners, William B. Waddell and William H. Russell, both of whom had been directly or indirectly involved in the Santa Fe trade, obtained a government contract to haul military supplies from lower Missouri River ports to Fort Riley on the Kansas River and to Fort Union near the New Mexico end of the Santa Fe Trail. One year later these two enterprising partners were joined by a third, Alexander Majors (also with experience in the Santa Fe trade) for the express purpose of buying and selling merchandise and for carrying on government freighting business on the western plains. For several years their business prospered. It reached its height when Colonel Albert S. Johnston, with twenty-five hundred men, was ordered to Utah to cope with Mormon unrest, and the firm of Russell, Majors and Waddell was awarded a government contract valued at about a half million dollars to haul supplies to the troubled area. During 1858 this firm had in its employ four thousand men, and had on the road thirty-five hundred freight wagons pulled by forty thousand oxen. For a period of about five years Russell, Majors and Waddell's firm dominated the freighting business on the plains.[2]

This pre-eminence did not, however, mean monopoly, and throughout the trans-Mississippi West scores of independent operators (many of whom had expressly entered into the freighting business during the 1850s to meet the needs of western mining communities) were still in operation when the Civil War ended. By 1865 the principal wagon-freighting routes were those leading into the hinterland from such important river and ocean ports as Atchison, Fort Benton, Los Angeles (San Pedro), Memphis, Nebraska City, Omaha, Sacramento, St. Joseph, St. Paul, and Portland; also those extending from constantly shifting, end-of-the-track railroad termini to military posts and fledgling but mushrooming farm communities and mining camps on the frontier. In the post-Civil War era these roads, or what passed for such, were the scenes of intense freighting activities. Foodstuffs, firearms, ammunition, clothing, blankets, and other military supplies transported from major river ports to approximately one hundred widely scattered western military establishments were measured in terms of hundreds of wagons, ten-thousand tons of weight, and millions of dollars. And added to this was the non-military freight consisting of such items as mining machinery, hardware, meats and groceries, liquor, tobacco, lumber, rope, and a host of other items desperately needed by the widely dispersed population. Statistics on the volume of this freight exist, but they are scattered and far from complete, or perhaps, inaccurate. With wagon freighting, as with covered wagon migration, the Missouri River landings functioned as the major outfitting and transshipment points. By 1865 Atchison was not only one of the leading river ports but by then it had also been reached by rail from the East. During the active season from March until November of that year this place received by railroad alone seventeen million pounds of freight. This volume, combined with additional consignments delivered by steamboats, brought Atchison's aggregate shipments for 1865 to about forty-two million pounds—all bound for the "further west." According to an on-the-scene tabulator, moving this mass of freight from the Atchison levees and out of local warehouses involved 1256 men, 4197 wagons, 27,685 oxen, and 6164 mules.[3]

Not only was Atchison the scene of heavy freighting traffic but as one would expect this city was the operating center for leading freighting outfits. Emerging somewhat as a successor to Russell, Majors and Waddell was the ambitious D. A. Butterfield Company, established in Atchison July 4, 1864. Atchison was not only the birthplace of this joint-stock firm but also became the principal place of embarkation for both its freight and stage lines slated to serve Colorado, Utah, Idaho, Montana, New Mexico, and Arizona. During 1865 the Butterfield firm alone dispatched from Atchison four large wagon trains carrying a mighty two million pounds of freight. Before the year was out, Butterfield announced additional plans to place in service twelve hundred ox-drawn wagons and three hundred mule-powered vehicles. This was a gigantic enterprise that required the employment of fifteen hundred drivers, fifty-five wagon masters, scores of warehouse men, herders, blacksmiths, and wagon makers; also twelve hundred mules and ninety-six hundred oxen. Impressive as these figures are, the sum total of Atchison's 1865 wagon-freighting business reveals the employment of 5610 men, 4480 wagons drawn by 29,720 oxen and 7310 mules, and the outgo of 54 million pounds of freight.[4]

Atchison was only one such bustling river port and overland freighting center. Nebraska City, which shipped out forty-four million pounds of freight in 1865, rivaled Atchison in the employment of men and equipment. Other figures available show that, also in 1865, wagon freight shipments out of St. Joseph totaled ten million pounds; from Plattsmouth, three million pounds; and from Kansas City and Omaha, additional millions of pounds. The combined figures are indeed staggering: an excess of one hundred million pounds of freight valued at more than seven million dollars was shipped from these Missouri River ports during 1865; and by combining all points on the Great Plains from which goods were either shipped or reshipped by wagon, the aggregate figures reach an estimated 224 million pounds. Roughly about one half of these goods were shipped by the United States government, mainly to military establishments, and the balance was forwarded to civilians, especially to merchants, throughout the Great Plains and Rocky Mountain areas.

*O*NE STRIKING FEATURE of the overland movement of this huge mass of wagon-borne goods was its singleness of direction—westward. The freighters with their heavily laden trains fanned out toward their respective destinations on the plains and in the mountains, and in due course returned with near-empty wagons to their home bases to repeat the arduous process. Only rarely, and then spasmodically, as in the case of buffalo hide trade, did freighters profit by two-way cargoes in the Great Plains trade. The central roads bore the brunt of this haulage, but much of it, especially that of a military character, passed over the by no means defunct Santa Fe Trail and continued to do so until finally choked off by the Atchison, Topeka and Santa Fe Railroad. Freight thus consigned was usually delivered at Fort Union (east of Santa Fe), where it was reshipped by pack animals to the numerous and scattered military posts within New Mexico Territory.[5] The sight of the long strings of heavily laden wagons crossing the deserts was reminiscent of the early Santa Fe trade. "Since leaving Leavenworth," wrote Colonel Meline, who was traveling by horseback, in 1865, "we have passed on the road, in one week, six hundred and eighty wagons, most filled with freight—some of them with emigrants." And two years later William A. Bell was equally impressed by the great army of white-topped wagons he witnessed in Kansas (mostly driven by Mexicans, so he said) that were headed both for Denver and for New Mexico.

Until railroads finally replaced wagon freighting, the Santa Fe Trail traffic remained important to the panhandle of Texas as well as to New Mexico Territory. During the 1870s Dodge City assumed special importance to Texan panhandlers, not only as a cowtown, but as a place where buffalo hides were gathered from the Southwest plains and then were hauled (on wagons) to market and exchanged for supplies. Greater Texas possessed good ocean harbors, and rail lines appeared early in the coastal area to provide an easy transfer of water-borne goods to inland communities. But on the Texas frontier, as elsewhere on the sparsely settled western plains, wagon-freight commerce assumed importance during the *post-bellum* era. The San Antonio-El Paso route developed immediately after the war; other routes, including the aged Chihuahua Trail,[6] also became active avenues of commerce until they became displaced by steamboats and railroads.

Freight consigned to Denver and the Rocky Mountain area generally passed over the central routes; and as the railroad pushed westward, towns at or near the end of the track served as freight-forwarding depots. A traveler, who made firsthand observations in 1865, reported that the station keeper at Fort Kearny had counted over six thousand freight (as distinguished from immigrant) wagons that had passed this junction point during a brief period of six weeks, nine hundred within one three-day span. Each wagon hauled from two to eight thousand pounds of freight. It was estimated that during 1865 the volume of wagon freight reaching Colorado and ultimately other parts of the Rocky Mountain West exceeded a hundred million pounds. Here, then, was big business, and alert entrepreneurs were well aware of both the fruitful possibilities and risks involved in the carrying trade.[7]

These data are not surprising, for every pound of groceries, manufactured goods, foreign imports, mining equipment, and assorted other necessities, including such items as nails, wagon grease, candles, tobacco, liquor, and glassware, had to be hauled hundreds of miles across the wide expanses of the plains and over winding mountain trails in order to reach the many scattered and isolated communities on the frontier. A Salt Lake City merchant, for example, was supplied mainly with goods hauled in from Missouri River ports, and a one-year hauling bill was reported to have been $150,000. Such figures were due in a large measure to the extremely high freight rates charged. Rates were neither fixed nor regulated, but the going charge was usually one dollar per one hundred pounds for each one hundred miles. In actual practice the Missouri River-to-Denver freight charges for groceries ranged from about nine cents per pound for flour to seventeen cents per pound for crackers. Merchandise could in 1865 be shipped from New York City to Atchison at $2.25 per hundredweight; but it cost on the average $15 per hundredweight to forward the same merchandise from Atchison to Denver. These charges were, of course, passed on to the consumer. Moreover, merchants were seldom worried about mounting inventories, and a one hundred percent markup on merchandise was common practice.[8]

Not all isolated places were served solely by westbound freight trans-shipped mainly from Missouri River landings. The raucous population of sunbaked Virginia City, Nevada, owed its very survival to freighters from Sacramento. All mining equipment and food supplies for the Comstock had to be freighted in from this Sacramento River port over tortuous Sierra roads, and in return some ore from the richly laden mines was hauled out to reduction plants located within California. The volume of trade shifted with fortunes at the mines, but during the mid-1860s approximately three thousand teams or wagons plied this Virginia City-Sacramento route with a net return to operators of about five million dollars annually.[9]

Elsewhere on the far western mining frontier the pattern was similar; goods were conveyed by steamer and rail as far as circumstances permitted at a given time, thence by means of wagon freighters to outlying towns and camps. During an approximate fifteen-year period following the Civil War a considerable bulk of Montana-consigned freight originating at Chicago, St. Louis, and elsewhere was finally discharged at Fort Benton embarkments by up-river Missouri steamers. From there it was hauled by wagon freighters and packers to such struggling Montana mining towns as Helena, Virginia City, and Bannack. The 1866 Fort Benton trade alone had an estimated value of six million dollars, and the means of transport involved the use of no less than three thousand wagons and twenty thousand oxen and mules. Most prominent among the many wagon-freighting firms engaged in the Montana trade were Diamond "R," E. G. McClay and Company, and Garrison and Wyatt. Freight destined chiefly for the Idaho mining camps was, on the other hand, brought in by combined use of both wagon and steamboats from widely separated cities as, for example, San Francisco and Portland, Oregon, over distances that ranged from 1190 to 1283 miles. Upon completion of the first Pacific railroad in 1869, eastern goods conveyed by rail freight to Ogden, Utah Territory, were also transferred to wagons and hauled north to both Idaho and Montana communities.[10]

Wagon freighting was also carried on locally. A farmer who had brought a sturdy wagon and livestock with him to the West often joined with neighbors to engage in seasonal freighting as a means of garnering desperately needed cash. Such operations were especially common in Texas, the Great Salt Lake Valley, the Willamette Valley in Oregon, and in many parts of the Central Plains country. Other farmers who happened to live in the vicinity of projected railroad lines likewise grabbed opportunities to haul freight for construction outfits.[11] Even the completion of the railroads did not, by any means, put an end to wagon freighting. Until rail feeder lines were built, in fact until the advent of the motor truck early in the present century, wagons were needed to haul goods to the rail depots; and in view of the rapid postwar growth of the agricultural West, this business was for a period of a decade or so a thriving and lucrative one for those actively involved. Profits naturally varied with time, place, and conditions. But some measure of return on investments is indicated by reports that under normal circumstances a single wagon unit usually earned four hundred dollars on each round trip between a Missouri River port and Denver. Two such round trips could be and often were made during each dry season and occasionally a single winter trip was managed as well. Some teams were even known to have paid for themselves in a single trip.[12]

Perhaps the most striking variant in the business of vehicular transportation was the employment of two-wheeled carts. Such carts, or *carreta*, had long been familiar sights in the old Spanish Southwest. But at midcentury carts came into prominence on the Minnesota-Dakota frontier as well. There they were used by the *Bois brûlé*, or half-breed, inhabitants of the Red River of the North, for hauling furs and buffalo hides from the Dakota and Manitoba prairies to St. Paul to be exchanged for general merchandise. By 1850 Pembina, a town on the Red River just south of the Canadian border, had become firmly established as the entrepôt for this flourishing cart trade. Goods flowed over a dual four hundred and fifty mile course known as the Red River Trails between the Red River Valley and the headwaters of the Mississippi River steamboat navigation. Each spoke-wheeled cart, made by the half-breeds and priced at about $15, was pulled by an ox or horse. One animal was capable of pulling an eight hundred- to a thousand-pound load for an average distance of twenty miles per day. Scores of carts were driven in caravan fashion on annual summer treks. No lubricants were applied to the wooden axles, and it has been said that the over-all sound emitted by a caravan was wildly cacophonous, due perhaps to the fact that each cart had its individual screech. The total effect, wrote one, was "hellish, horrifying and nervewracking" and "makes your blood run cold."[13] Even though the peak of this cart trade had passed by the end of the Civil War, the fur business alone for 1865 was valued at $250,000. At the height of the trade, five thousand to eight thousand carts were involved, and until the eve of their displacement by railroads during the 1870s approximately twenty-five hundred carts passed annually over the Red River Trails.[14]

Impressive as were these cart operations, the use of two-wheeled vehicles for hauling freight remained the exception on the western frontier. Commonly used in the trans-Mississippi West after 1865 were the four-wheeled wagons. Even though all such vehicles bore some resemblance to their progenitor, the Conestoga, most makers of wagons used in the West gave distinction to their products and they became known to their users by such names as "Chattanooga," "Carson," "Espensheid," "J. Murphy," and "Studebaker."

Particularly reminiscent of the Conestoga was the J. Murphy. Its maker, Irish-born Joseph Murphy, had learned his wheelright trade in St. Louis and he had learned it well. His wagons were fashioned of toughened, well-seasoned hardwoods. Special care was exercised in making the white oak or hickory wheels and axles—in fact, the whole under carriage, or running gear—strong, and in being sure that the iron tires of varying widths and thicknesses were properly and firmly set. Unlike Conestogas, which had a recognizable shape and form, Murphy made his wagons in accordance with specifications of his customers. But all of them bore the hallmark of superior workmanship and on the sides of most was displayed the name of their maker, J. Murphy.

Comparable to the Murphy wagons in soundness of construction was the Studebaker. When the firm Studebaker Brothers of South Bend, Indiana, emerged as a leading wagon manufacturer it made capital of its processes: their seasoning of woods from three to five years, soaking and boiling the running gear in oil to drive out moisture and to add toughness. Axles, read Studebaker catalogs, are the foundations of all wagons, and in their making the firm used Indiana black hickory. Skeins of steel made running easier, and slope-shouldered spokes of white oak contributed sturdiness and durability.[15] Sizes of all wagon makes varied, of course. They ranged from those of two thousand-pound (single-ton) capacity preferred by teamsters intent upon fast service, to large fourteen- to twenty-thousand–pound capacity Carson wagons employed in the California-Nevada mining trade. The most widely used freight wagons on the Great Plains were, however, those made to carry a four- to six-thousand-pound load. The latter had a length ranging from fifteen to twenty-four feet, a width of four and one-half feet, and schooner-shaped boxes of varying heights. Beneath, or on the side or inside the box of each wagon, was a spare axle, a wagon jack, a loaded gun, a shovel, and an axe; also attached to the wagon side was a box that usually held the axle grease and food. Freight wagons had one thing in common; they were invariably tarpaulin covered, a feature, along with body shape, that gave rise to such appellations as "prairie schooners" and "steamboats of the Plains." Wagons were not cheap, for an average-sized one usually cost from five hundred dollars to a thousand, depending somewhat on place of delivery. And such a wagon, plus either a mule team or three to four yoke of oxen normally required for service, called for a capital outlay of four to even ten times this figure.[16]

*T*HE NOT-SO-GENTLE ART of organizing and operating wagon-freight trains was, like the equipment involved, a heritage of earlier frontiers. In many ways operations followed a pattern evolved in the early trans-Allegheny trade, which in turn achieved refinements under the skillful management of Messrs. Russell, Majors and Waddell during the decade of the 1850s. In all large-scale operations, those involving the transport of massive quantities of goods over long distances, individual wagon units were formed into groups or "trains." Trains usually comprised twenty to thirty wagons, each pulled by five to seven yoke of oxen or teams of mules or horses. Some trains, however, did not exceed a dozen, while others in turn were reported by travelers to have numbered sixty canvas-topped schooners. A twenty-six unit train, one unit of which was the mess wagon, was considered a standard and highly maneuverable outfit.[17] Each had its crew, headed by the mule-riding "captain," or wagon master, who usually had an assistant. Depending on the animals used, each wagon was managed by a muleskinner or a bullwhacker. Serving in the humblest capacity was a swamper who managed spare animals, cleared the road, and in other ways made himself useful, and a stock tender or night herder generally known as the "cavvyard."[18]

Relatively little is known about these people as frontier personalities. Some are referred to as youths who drifted into the business, young men seeking experiences in the wild West; others had originally attached themselves to freighting outfits in order to find cheap, relatively secure passage to points further West and then, liking their adventure, stayed on as teamsters. T. S. Garrett, a veteran Wyoming freighter, recollected: "I left Michigan, bound for the Rocky Mountains." He joined with two others, and "As an outcome of this arrangement, the three of us left Lincoln with a four horse team, bound for Wyoming." From then on Garrett was a freighter.[19] But few, like Garrett, left records. Another freighter explains it thus: dangers to them may have been too commonplace to be committed to paper. It might also be surmised that many of these robust teamsters and their subalterns could not write. But thanks to observers who did leave records there emerges the general impression that these far western wagoners were a robust, stout, stolid, and on the whole, vituperative, class of males. For them the dangers, harassments, hardships, and monotonies of their occupation held little terror. By and large they came from farms and as such possessed experience in handling draft animals and wagons. With time they acquired an enviable skill at wielding blacksnakes, or bullwhips; a great propensity for taking the Lord's name in vain; and an uncommon reputation for ability to survive on rugged "grub" and fortified drink.

Sharp social distinctions existed within the trade. The chasm separating the wagonmaster from the muleskinner and bullwhacker was wide, and in turn the teamster looked with no small degree of condescension, if not scorn, upon the swampers and "cavvy boys" attached to freighting outfits. But teamsters as a class were ranked low in the transportation hierarchy, where river pilots were enthroned and stagecoach drivers were regarded as "dukes of the road." A teamster, nevertheless, was, as one of them attested, "a good sport," and he was not lacking in personal pride in himself and his profession. He might even have pointed to a former Yale professor in his galaxy of notables. He took pride, too, in his animals and his wagons as well as in his harnesses, which were frequently adorned with fur-covered hames and jingling bells.

For all that may be said in his behalf, a teamster possessed few of the refinements of life and little of the dash and flamboyance that made other types of frontiersmen legendary figures. He belonged, by and large, to a class of illiterates. A teamster's face, hands, and clothes (including frock pants tucked into jack-boots, checkered shirt, and broad and sloppy-brimmed felt hat) were invariably and indescribably dirty and grimy due to constant exposure to dust or mud and to the back spray of tobacco juice squirted into the prairie winds. Nor was he considered the soberest of men. He drank more than his thirty-five dollar monthly pay with keep would allow. He brawled long and hard before extended trips, and en route he not only patronized saloons where he found them but was even known at times to have raided the liquor in freight. At such times and places he often became involved in quarrels, but seldom in gun fights. A teamster was not gun shy, however. If his scalp or cargo were threatened by marauding Indians, he was adept at marshaling his forces and at returning fire with rifle and revolvers with which he was equipped.[20]

Much as a teamster harbored marked prejudices in matters pertaining to draft animals, decisions as to their use were determined by several considerations. Not least of these were costs and conditions of travel. In any event oxen, horses, mules, and combinations thereof were all employed in the trade. Least expensive of the draft animals were oxen; moreover, they were usually readily available, especially in the great cattle regions of the West. Oxen were looked upon as gentle beasts, tractable, easy to graze, and not easily stampeded. In addition, these animals thrived on prairie grass, green or dry, and feed for them did not have to be carried aboard wagons. And, finally, if disabled, an ox could be slaughtered and served as a most suitable item on any freighter's menu. For these and other reasons the lowly oxen were preferred as draft animals by most freighting proprietors. Texas freighters, for example, used longhorn steers, partly because of their availability but also because Texas teamsters became attached to these sad-eyed, somewhat whimsical creatures.

Mules and horses, nevertheless, had ardent supporters. They moved faster than oxen, and in winter weather this was desirable. Both horses and mules could, like oxen, be grazed along routes of travel, though some supplementary feeding in the form of grain was required. Mules, however, could survive on less grain than horses, and this was important inasmuch as feed of this nature had to be carried as nonpaying cargo. But if it came to a matter of choice between horses and mules, teamsters favored the latter. Mules had many additional advantages over horses. In desert areas where water and vegetation were scarce mules would, as one person wrote, "perform wonders on gramma grass only," could resist saline and alkaline properties of some desert plants (but not without "cathartic effects"), and could survive on one or two waterings per day. In comparison with horses, mules, states the superintendent of the (1860) *Eighth Census*, could do as much work as a horse, be kept at one-third the expense, were more resistant to disease, could bear more ill treatment, be worked a year earlier, and had twice the life expectancy. In any event, if mules were not maltreated, if governed "as you would a woman with kindness, affection, and caresses," wrote the road engineer Captain John Mullan, ". . . you will be repaid by their docility and easy management."

Mules were credited with superior toughness, sureness of foot, and powers of endurance, and in this respect, at least, were preferred to both oxen and horses. Unlike oxen, however, a broken-down horse or mule was considered a complete loss. Teamsters had an aversion to eating horse flesh, and mule meat was at best considered too tough to be devoured. Moreover, said an ardent proponent of the draft horse, this

> thing of using overgrown burros in draggin frat [freight] . . . is not accordin to the Scripters and is not right. In the days of the Bible they rode their mules, but didn't frat them. It never was intended that man should ride behind a mule.

The veteran plainsman Root, however, summed up the relative merits of horses and mules thus: "Horses were all right for mounting cavalrymen and in maneuvering artillery . . . but, simmered down . . . , the mule invariably stood at the front."[21]

Much as mules were admired they, like horses, varied tremendously in quality and price. For example, Mexican mules were generally more favored than native American mules. Mexicans usually offered their buyers a larger selection of animals than did rival Yankee traders. Moreover, a mule from below the Rio Grande had certain educational advantages not possessed by his traditionally stubborn American counterpart. It has at least been reported that a Mexican mule was so well trained that he could recognize his own wagon or cart, and would voluntarily back into position for hitching. In the final analysis, physical factors such as place, time, season, availability, price, and particular service requirements determined the type of draft animals used. One additional generalization: heavy deadweight freight was customarily drawn by sturdy oxen; shipments of high intrinsic value, namely goods that called for quick delivery, were usually shipped in wagons pulled by faster-paced horses or mules.[22]

Muleskinning, as the driving of mules (and for that matter, horses) was called, was a cultivated art. It took an immense amount of skill to manipulate and control long strings of animals hitched in successive pairs or teams by means of harness, whiffle trees, chains, and tongue to heavily laden freight wagons. Basically, muleskinning called for the proper handling of the "lead team." If properly trained, these "leaders" could be controlled in part by the voice, in part by a single "jerk line" extending from the bit of the left front animal through collar rings back to the teamster either riding or walking alongside or seated on the wagon. A stick the size of a broom handle was fastened between the two leaders, thereby causing the right one to coordinate its movements with the one on the left. In order to make a left turn the teamster would make a steady pull; to do a right turn, he would make a series of jerks. The leaders were trained to respond correctly to the respective pulls and jerks. The team next to the wagon, called "wheelers," controlled and steadied the wagon tongue by means of a neck yoke. The team second from the wagon, known as the "swing team," was trained, when a turn was to be made, to step across and then pull in a straight direction on a "swing chain" attached to the end of the wagon tongue. Intervening teams, regardless of number, simply followed the leaders and shared in the pulling. The left side of the team, on which the teamster usually rode or walked, was known as the "near side"; the opposite was the "off side." But wherever his position, the teamster controlled and got the most out of his team chiefly by means of his voice and the skillful use of a blacksnake. It has been said that a good muleskinner could blacken the ears of any one of sixteen mules and if really good, could kill a fly on the head of a leader.[23]

Bullwhacking varied slightly from muleskinning. Oxen were yoked instead of harnessed. The Mexican yoke was lashed to the horns; Americans placed yokes on the shoulders of the oxen. The pulling mechanism and procedures were, however, basically the same. Bull teams, as they were called, were directed by yells of "gee," "haw," and by the same blasphemous supplications and applications of leather that were applied to mules and horses.

But muleskinners and bullwhackers were concerned with more than the handling of their teams. As one Texas pioneer put it, "the old freighter faced death almost daily in the performance of his duties." Teamsters were not at times without danger from marauding Indians and outlaws. They feared and dreaded encounters with the elements: "the terrors of the blazing summer sun, sleeping in snow drifts, blinding blizzards, quicksand, icy water, and spring freshets." There was also danger of becoming engulfed by stampeding buffalo herds. Occasionally teamsters had runaways; also breakdowns far away from repair shops; and they were confronted with the problems of ascending and descending mountainous roads and of extricating their trains from stream beds and axle-deep mud. But most of all they suffered from loneliness and weariness brought on by prolonged, tedious travel over seemingly endless wastes.

Thomas A. Creigh, a Nebraska freighter who in 1866 teamed over the combined 1115-mile Central Overland and Bozeman routes to reach Montana, recorded that his train numbered 52 wagons and 235 yoke of oxen. Over these roads during this dangerous period freight trains were often joined by immigrant caravans, and at one point along the route Creigh stated that as many as a hundred wagons were encamped together.[24] For these and perhaps other reasons teamsters almost invariably traveled in groups, or trains.[25]

There was a touch of the dramatic about the departure of a fully laden wagon train for a long, but standard, forty-five–day, six hundred-mile trek from Nebraska City to Denver. When all was in readiness the wagon master (astride a mule or horse and still groggy from his dissipations) gave the signal to start. In quick response came from all teamsters the resounding cries of "ya," "gee," and "haw," and the gunlike cracks of bullwhips. Then off in single file moved the loudly creaking, crunching wagons—out onto the meandering prairie trail that the teamster knew so well.

*T*HE *RULES* and instructions for travel had been well established by Russell, Majors and Waddell during the 1850s, and with few exceptions they provided an acceptable, workable pattern for later freighting operations. The instructions were rather specific. After the morning start, drive one to two miles; then stop to allow animals to "breathe and urinate." Then drive seven to ten miles (until ten o'clock "more or less") and stop, unyoke stock for two hours of grazing; also at this juncture prepare and eat breakfast. Then, continue the instructions, resume operations for a second seven-to-ten miles, camp again for three to four hours for supper for the men and more grazing for the animals; then carry on for an evening drive until dark. Loaded wagon trains were expected to travel fourteen to eighteen miles per day, empty ones an additional two to three miles.[26]

The teamsters usually messed together, preferably in groups of from six to eight. The process was short and simple. Usually a trench was dug for fire and either wood or *bois de vaca* (cow chips) carried aboard were used as fuel. One man was responsible for getting water, which at many places could be obtained near the camp site. Their food came either from a common "grub wagon" or from supplies stored in individual food boxes in or on the side of each wagon. The fare at best was simple and largely restricted to bacon, crackers, sour dough, beans, dried fruits, black coffee, and dust. Coffee was considered good when it could "float an iron wedge." Molasses served as sugar. Buffalo, antelope, and occasionally other stray animals and fowl provided some fresh meat for an otherwise restricted diet. A water bucket, skillet, coffee pot, tin plate, a one-quart tin cup, knife, and fork met the culinary requirements of a teamster. Everything that could be fried was committed to the skillet, and if no fire could be had, as was frequently the case, meals were eaten cold.[27]

One traveler accompanying a train through Colorado described the cooking as being minimal in fastidiousness. The cook, in this case Mexican, gathered dry dung for a fire and then, without bothering to wash his hands, "was soon up to his wrists in the dough for the 'cakes.'" His Mexican host was, however, the essence of politeness; he apologized for having no plate for his guest. But then after further search exclaimed, "'By gosh, yes, I've found one,'" and proceeded to rub the plate "clean" with his own hands. With his cooking responsibilities thus discharged, the old teamster relaxed contentedly at the campfire while picking lice off his dirt-encrusted shirt.[28] Not all accounts paint such a graphic picture of a teamster's dining formalities, but meals at best, through sheer necessity, had to be kept simple yet substantial.

Much more of a ritual—and an impressive one at that—was the maneuvering of trains into corral formation for night encampment. For reasons of safety it was important to avoid low ground surrounded by hills. Here again, Russell, Majors and Waddell have left specific instructions on the encampment procedure. In simplest terms this action called for one-half of a given train to form a semicircle to the right and for the other half to form the remaining half circle to the left. If a train traveled double file, the process was greatly simplified, but if single file, odd-numbered wagons would circle to the right, the even ones to the left.

Then with teams inturned and with the front wheel of one wagon interlocked with the hind wheel of another, there should be a "long, deep toned 'Whoo'; unyoking in a quiet, easy manner"; directing of the oxen to drink, and, finally, to pasture. At times the animals were hobbled, in times of danger confined within the corral; but if grazing was good and an Indian attack was not in prospect, the long-suffering livestock were allowed to graze and sleep under the watchful eyes of the night herder. Thus encamped within this relatively secure portable fortress, the men got their much-deserved sleep, either on cots or bunks depending on how each man was equipped; at times, too, snug up against the warm body of a steer.

Rising time was dawn. It was the night herder's duty to call the boss, who in turn aroused his men with a resounding knock on a tire of each wagon and accompanied this with the call "turn out." Once the men were up, the animals were immediately brought into position and yoked or hitched to the wagons. With all in readiness the day's routine repeated itself: train following train, as a traveler viewed it, wound "their slow course over the serpentine roads and undulating surface in the distance, ... the effect is poetic, grand, beautiful."[29] When Samuel Bowles, the editor of the Springfield (Massachusetts) *Republican,* toured the West he was awed by the sight of train upon train of canvas-topped wagons. The trains frequently ranged in length from one-quarter to one-third of a mile. "As they move along in the distance," remarked Bowles, "they remind one of the caravans described in the Bible and other Eastern books." In any position, whether on the march or in camp, the teamster trains presented "a picture most unique and impressive, indeed. I have seen nothing like it before. . . ."[30]

Freighting operations were, by no means, limited to a fixed routine. When the going was smooth and easy, two wagons were often coupled or hitched one behind the other, a method known as "tandem." Successful tandem operation necessitated the use of a short tongue on the trailer, or rear wagons, and, moreover, the use of straight-ended wagons rather than Conestogas, which had overhanging tops that interfered with close coupling. The mounting of steep hills, on the other hand, called for quite different procedures, and especially for the cooperation of all hands. In such situations teams were doubly, even triply, attached to one wagon at a time; boulders were held in readiness for blocking backward motion while the teams rested. And then, as all possible exertion was called for, the lash and vocabulary were applied with equal liberality to the straining and usually winded animals in order to inch the heavily weighted wagon upward and onward over the hill. Special contrivances were likewise resorted to in making the descent on steep grades. Huge twenty-inch, well-grooved brake blocks were in such instances applied by means of a long vertical connecting rod which the driver controlled by a rope extended to him astride a "wheeler"; or, if in the driver's seat, by means of a horizontal connecting rod operated by a foot pedal. Dragging logs were at times tied to the rear of wagons, and the rotating motion of rear wheels was on occasion completely blocked by means of chains in order to slow the downgrade advance of heavily loaded wagons.[31]

The exercise of caution in operations could not always forestall difficulties. For example, heavy rains produced mud, and mud invariably caused trouble to freighters. "... have driven thirty miles today," wrote an army officer when crossing Kansas in June of 1866, "passing many wagons loaded with supplies for frontier posts. Some were stuck in the mud with twenty yoke of cattle trying to pull them out." In situations of this kind something would have to give, and usually the freight wagon yielded to this mighty accumulation of animal power.

Teamsters often borrowed trouble, too. They were, for example, reluctant to pay tolls for the use of bridges and ferries. It was difficult enough for would-be operators to secure a charter and necessary funds for the construction of a bridge; it was, wrote a local historian, much more of a task to get a freighter to pay tolls. The alternative course was to ford streams, often with disastrous results.[32] Mountain freighting was most hazardous of all. Occasionally in such areas animals and goods went tumbling over high precipices with tragic loss.[33] Nor were difficulties confined to the Great Plains and the mountains. Freighting in the Southwest posed special problems, not least of which was scarcity of grass and water. "Near all settlements," recalled one teamster, "the grass was nibbled off by the cattle and goats of the natives." And due mainly to this scarcity of forage, the teamster concluded that he "could cover more ground on the plains in two weeks than he could in a month in New Mexico."[34]

Added to these woes were those occasionally inflicted upon freighters by Indians. A particularly violent period existed during and immediately following the Civil War when Indians were emboldened by the weakened military installations on the frontier. When on the warpath, the red men tended to be indiscriminate in their attacks, and wagon freight trains (especially if teamsters could be caught off guard) were among the tempting targets. Whenever an attack did come the Indians made it according to a familiar pattern. They would come during early morning hours and twilight. The Indians would dash out on ponies from the places of concealment, open fire, and while so doing, encircle the train. Their object, short of total annihilation, was to run off the livestock and in general disable the train as much as possible. At times of threatened attack, alert teamsters corralled their wagons, kept their livestock within their improvised circular fort, grabbed their guns, and opened fire on the elusive red men. Such quick, effective action by teamsters usually discouraged the Indians. As a rule, only in cases where there was failure to display determined action were heavy casualties suffered.[35]

*T*HE GRADUAL PACIFICATION of the Indians and the resultant rapid advance of settlement caused those in the freighting business to undergo many changes. As towns sprang up "like mushrooms during a night" along routes of travel, it became possible for teamsters to enjoy drinks ("dust-cutters") served at bars and meals served at roadside restaurants rather than, as formerly, partake of the wagon bottle and self-prepared camp-site meals. When this happened teamsters began to pay some attention to manners. Some actually used a comb, others even cleaned their fingernails—with their forks—and teeth were picked with the same instrument. Inns, notably those catering to the freighting trade on California's heavily traveled Sacramento-Virginia City line, became so competitive that teamsters developed discriminating tastes. It finally reached the point, wrote J. A. Filcher, that "A defect in the table bill of fare, or the quality of the free whiskey, or the quality of the free cigar, or in the efficiency of the attending hostler," or drawbacks in the attractiveness of the waitress were resented. And if one place did not suit, they moved to another. But refinements in the selection of menus apparently had little effect upon the speed with which food was devoured. Eating was done with a system. At most inns a warning bell was rung to inform customers that mealtime was approaching, and then a final gong denoted that dinner was served. When the final bell sounded, there was a rush to the tables and within fifteen minutes the room would be empty and preparations made for "second tables."[36]

Not only teamsters' manners but their language as well contributed significantly to frontier lore. Tales are extant telling of fantastic marksmanship in the whirling of twenty-foot bullwhips, landing "poppers" of buckskin on a fly lodged on a lead mule's ear, and heroic sagas of struggle in the face of terrifying weather in the great, and always unpredictable, West. There are stories, too, of how effectively teamsters could regale stubborn mules. In the Sierra Nevada, where mule teams were called upon to make extra exertions in order to pull loads over the summit, conditions were highly conducive to the enrichment of what was called "mule talk." There was, for example, "Pike," who was praised on his swearing. In all modesty he declined the compliment, saying:

"Swear?...Me swear? No, I can't blaspheme worth a cuss. You'd jest orter hear Pete Green. *He can exhort the impenitant Mule.* I've known a ten-mule team to renounce the flesh and haul thirty-one thousand through a pool of clay and under one of his outpourings."[37]

"Teamster Black" of the Yuba River country was another man well known for his ability to exhort mules. It was said that when a mule ceased to cooperate Black could, upon rising to his tiptoes, let out a string of oaths so terrifying and epithets so derisive that they "fairly turned the sky blue and gave a sulphurous odor to the atmosphere, and caused every living thing within hearing distance to shudder."[38] When this occurred the mules feit obliged to deliver the extra pull.

More inhibited than either teamster Pike or Black was a muleskinner convert, unknown by name, who vowed never again to take the Lord's name in vain. All went well with the vow until he discovered that his mule team no longer understood either the convert's language or his manner of speech. Finally, in desperation, he burst out: "I'm saying —— gee, you ——! ——! ——! ——! I'm saying if you want me to have religion, you'll have to get somebody else to drive this team.' "[39]

Not all teamster stories concern mules, for many of them allude to a freighter's love of the bottle, his unlimited capacity for drink, and the dangers and vicissitudes of a teamster's life on the road. There is, for example, the story of Roy Bean, who with Pancha, his Mexican boy helper, forded the Pecos:

"By Dogs," said Bean, "she swum like she was a first class sea schooner. Hist the sides of them sheets there, Pancha, and let the sun dry the stuff."
"The can goods, I fear heem soaked," interjected Pancha, "and the bacon—heem ver wet, too."
"How's the whiskey?" asked Bean.
"Oh, the wheesky, she's fine. No water got at all to heem."
"Hell!" retorted Bean, "there's nothing to worry about thin, Pancha. Nary a thing."[40]

Contributing significantly to the ultimate demise of overland wagon freighting in the West was the advent of railroads. As railroad construction advanced, wagon-freighting lines were correspondingly restricted. When the railroad reached Denver a local newspaper declared: "Good-bye oxteam and bull-whackers! Welcome locomotive!"[41] The transition from wagons to freight trains was, however, more gradual than this newspaper would imply. Railroads needed feeder line service and until rail companies constructed a network of subsidiary lines, and, too, until the coming of motor trucks, wagon freighters continued to perform important feeder line service for the trunk line railroads within the trans-Mississippi West.[42]

The end to wagon freighting finally came early in the present century. With its passing was left a record of service to frontier development. For more than a half century big lumbering wagons and long strings of oxen, mules, or horses had somehow kept moving a flow of precious goods between the riverboat ports, railroad terminals, and isolated military posts and mining and agricultural communities of the trans-Mississippi West. In other words, the wagon freighter was an important link between the eastern centers of trade and frontier merchants and mining concerns. He carried essential equipment and supplies to railroad construction camps; and when the rail lines came into operation he helped these railroads move agricultural and mineral commodities to market.

⊲ **4** ⊳

Stagecoaching as Frontier Enterprise

*L*ong before 1865 the rocking Concord stagecoach, drawn by six spanking, prancing steeds and carrying passengers, mail, and express, had become a well-established image of frontier transportation. Dotting lonely roadsides and accenting nearly all towns—no matter how remote and forlorn—were stage stations. The coaches bearing "U.S. Mail" insignia and the rude, unadorned staging stations and inns were, in many respects, the symbols of the frontier West. They were also, as Horace Greeley observed, the representation of "Civilization, Intelligence, Government, [and] Protection" that somehow reassured the pilgrim family of the existence of "a terrestrial Providence."[1]

Ever since its introduction on the Atlantic seaboard in the mideighteenth century, the stagecoach and attending services had moved westward with the advancing frontier of settlement. Passenger-carrying coaches first appeared in St. Louis in 1820 and shortly thereafter regular coaching services provided a means of transit and communication between several scattered settlements and towns along the west side of the Mississippi at a time when this area was about to enjoy, also, rapidly developing river steamboat services. In 1837 regular stagecoach business was established in Iowa.[2] In addition to serving Mississippi River communities the major lines of this state were to run east and west, connecting such Mississippi River towns as Dubuque and Davenport with the Missouri River ports of Sioux City and Council Bluffs. The Western Stage Company and the Frink and Walker Line were to be among the more prominent Iowa concerns.[3]

By midcentury stagecoach lines had even reached out from such other Missouri River towns as Independence and St. Joseph southwest to distant Santa Fe. Shorter lines within New Mexico Territory subsequently came into being and maintained connections in this highly valued link between the New Mexico capital and the states.[4] By 1865 Santa Fe was also to be connected with Denver by means of still another operation called the Southern Stage Line.[5]

Stagecoach beginnings in Texas, and elsewhere in the Southwest, followed a seemingly general pattern. A multiplicity of small operators who aspired to make a living out of the staging business usually managed to obtain contracts to carry United States mails, and with such financial backlogs offered regular service over specified lines. The first of such stagecoach lines appeared in Texas before midcentury, and with thirty-one independent lines in operation at the outbreak of the Civil War the Texas stagecoach business had by that time reached its maximum development. By then nearly all settled portions of the state were served. Again in keeping with trends elsewhere, consolidations ensued; and one company named Sawyer, Richer and Hall ultimately emerged with control of over one-half of the Texas lines.[6]

In a short time Minnesota Territory also had coach service. At first this northern region had been largely dependent upon river boats during summers and upon dog- or horse-drawn sleighs during protracted winter seasons, but in 1849 the inevitable stagecoach made its debut. Most prominent was the Minnesota Stage Company, founded in 1851 with headquarters at St. Paul. In 1867, when acquired by two steamboat operators named Russell Blakely and C. W. Carpenter, this thriving concern declared its holdings to include seven hundred horses and an adequate supply of coaches. By then it operated over a two thousand-mile network that embraced not only all settled areas within Minnesota but also penetrated into parts of Wisconsin, Dakota Territory west to Pembina on the Red River of the North, and Manitoba in Canada.[7] It is little wonder that one of St. Paul's local chroniclers wrote with pride that the Minnesota Stage Company "chalked out more new roads and built more new bridges than any other hundred or thousand men in the State." In its earlier years the company's staging services became closely linked with steamboat lines;

then, as in other areas of the West, connections were established with the railroads. With a subsequent change in name to Northwestern Express and Transportation Company this concern continued operations until the end of the century.[8]

Nowhere within the trans-Mississippi West did the stagecoach business enjoy more patronage and attention than on the Pacific slope. Not only did San Francisco become the mecca of the great transwestern services, but the Golden State as a whole was host to an intricate network of local staging lines. Contributing immeasurably in this development was the California Gold Rush. Scarcely had the first Argonauts arrived in the autumn of 1849 when a staging concern inaugurated passenger service between San Francisco and San Jose. Then during the next year one company followed another in an almost frantic effort to link the main river ports of Sacramento, Stockton, and Marysville with the accelerating number of gold-mining camps.[9]

As in other portions of the trans-Mississippi West, the trend in California was toward consolidation, if not monopoly. It began in northern California where in 1854 the veteran stagecoach operator James Birch, in association with others, formed the California Stage Company. So successful was this merger that when completed no less than five-sixths of all staging lines in this northern region had joined. The new company offered daily service over most of its lines and at fairly reasonable rates. As the population of the state increased and as roads, including turnpikes, were extended and improved—not only through taxation but by private agencies, including the California Stage Company—there came a corresponding expansion in stagecoach services. Thus by the 1860s the California Stage Company, armed with the bulk of available mail contracts, operated 28 daily stage lines covering over 1970 miles of California road. On these it used 1000 horses and 134 coaches, and employed 184 agents, drivers, and hostlers.[10]

This was not all. By 1860 the stages of the ambitious California Stage Company had found ways to surmount the rugged Siskiyou Mountain terrain separating California from Oregon and had pushed on north from Sacramento to Portland, 710 miles away. This achievement brought the daily dispatch of coaches that carried mail and passengers beween Sacramento and Portland on a seven-day schedule. Moreover, this operation linked the California Stage Company system with an equally impressive network of Pacific Northwest steamboat and local stagecoach lines extending eastward to points where they were connected with a centrally established overland stage and mail service. In short, settlement, wherever it occurred on the frontier, was invariably accompanied by the quick arrival of the ubiquitous coach.[11]

*O*DDLY ENOUGH, the stagecoach business came to the trans-Mississippi West at a time when portions of the eastern United States were undergoing a rapid transition from horse to steam power. In view of the fact that steamboats could not serve all settled parts of the West, and due also to the slowness with which the railroads penetrated the region west of the Missouri River, stagecoach enterprises emerged that were both local and transregional in character. Isolated western communities re-quired—in fact demanded—that some means be provided not only for carrying passengers locally but for transporting people, mails, and express by horse-drawn coaches between eastern railroad and steamboat connec-tions and west coast cities. Due to the high cost involved, such large-scale commitments necessitated government support in the form of mail con-tract awards, rather grudgingly granted by a lethargic and sectionally oriented Congress to private stagecoach operators.

Such transregional services began modestly in 1851 when a Post Office contract was first let for the conveyance of monthly mail service between the Missouri River and Salt Lake City, and shortly thereafter between the Mormon capital and Sacramento.[12]

With these first steps taken, Congress had set a pattern, in fact had entered upon a policy, whereby the United States government was sub-sequently to consummate a series of contracts with private entrepreneurs for the conveyance of mails, and incidentally passengers, throughout many parts of the West. Not, however, until 1857 did the Post Office Department sponsor its second, and still far from expeditious, overland mail project by awarding a contract to James E. Birch for the semimonthly mail service between San Antonio and San Diego on a thirty-day schedule. Birch used mules for pulling his coaches and the project became popularly, and satiri-cally, known as Birch's "Jackass Mail." For all the ridicule heaped on this slow-paced operation the fact remains that Birch offered regular passenger service, twice monthly, over his fifteen hundred-mile course across the Southwest desert, with military escort provided across Apache country.[13]

Scarcely had Birch's San Antonio and San Diego stages gotten into operation when Congress began to realize that the construction of a much hoped-for transcontinental railroad faced indeterminate delays. Accordingly, steps were finally taken in 1857 to establish what was to become the first truly transcontinental stagecoach service. The company that was awarded a contract to perform this service was to be officially designated as the "Overland Mail Company," but in a more familiar way it was to be known and remembered, out of deference to its president, as the "Butterfield Overland Mail."

The reasons for Congressional procrastination were largely political. Sectional interests and attitudes had been in evidence whenever proposals had been made for an adequate overland mail service. During 1856, for example, four overland mail bills had been introduced in Congress, all without enactment into law.[14] But with each delaying action came a rising voice of protest from the West. From California and New Mexico came memorials addressed to Congress pleading for roads and the means of communication necessary to protect the Far West. Also, in their speeches before Congress, California senators added their voices of protest against delay in the enactment of a suitable overland mail bill. Senator John B. Weller declared there was a moral obligation to provide for mail services. "You have refused to give me the railroad," said Weller. "You have given me a wagon road, and I say to the Senators, that creates a sort of moral obligation to give me coaches or wagons to carry the mail over that road." Senator William M. Gwin, also a California Senator, lashed out against the inadequacies of the ocean mail service then being provided by a concern called the Pacific Mail Steamship Company, calling it a "gigantic monopoly." Rather than be at the mercy of such a strangling octopus, Congress, declared Gwin, should hasten to pass an adequate overland mail act.[15]

Positive Congressional action finally came during February 1857 in the form of an amendment to the Post Office appropriations bill. In order to meet objections of a sectional nature, the proposed amendment called for a route with an eastern terminal on the Mississippi River and a western terminal at San Francisco. The measure, however, granted the Postmaster General and future mail contractors discretionary powers pertaining to the intervening course to be adopted. Such a proposal appears to have placated several senators who had formerly stood firm on the establishment of either a southern overland route or a central overland route. In any event, the final favorable vote was taken March 3, 1857. A twenty-four to ten result revealed a remarkable reversal of attitude; the ten opposition votes came from the South; those favoring a measure which in all likelihood would favor the South came from the Northern states and from the states which stood to gain directly from the proposed operations.[16]

The bill as signed by President James Buchanan authorized the Postmaster General to contract for regular, through overland mail service between the aforementioned points; stated that said service be performed "with good four-horse coaches, or spring wagons suitable for the conveyance of passengers, as well as the safety and security of the mails"; and provided that the scheduled service "shall be performed within twenty-five days for each trip."[17]

Bids were called for by Postmaster General Aaron Venable Brown, and the award went to John Butterfield and associates who included such widely known transportation magnates as William B. Dinsmore and William G. Fargo. The terms of the contract specified two eastern termini rather than one: Memphis and St. Louis. Lines from these two places were to converge at Fort Smith, Arkansas, and from there make a deep dip through Preston (Texas), El Paso, Fort Yuma, across the Imperial Valley to Los Angeles, and finally swing north through the San Joaquin Valley and Pacheco Pass to San Francisco. The total length of this so-called oxbow route was to be 2795 miles. It combined, reported Postmaster General Brown, "more advantages and fewer disadvantages than any other."[18] Further, the contract required that letter mail should be carried semiweekly each way over this route within the twenty-five days prescribed by law. Mails were to be securely stowed away in a "boot," preferably under the driver's seat, "free from wet or other injury," and should, of course, be distributed to the recipients along the route. "Good four-horse post coaches or spring wagons" should be employed and passenger and mail service was to begin, as it did, on September 16, 1858, one year after signing of the contract. For its services the Butterfield concern was to receive six hundred thousand dollars per annum.[19]

The laying out of this enormously long route under John Butterfield's direction and close supervision, doing the necessary road building, stocking and equipping the line, and working out operational details was a staggering feat. The route passed over some existing roads, but also over much natural, smooth, open desert country. Some grading was necessary, many bridges had to be built, wells dug, 141 stations either had to be built or provided for, many with accompanying corrals. Needed too were 1000 horses, 500 mules (and forage for same), 250 stagecoaches and additional freight and water wagons, food and assorted equipment, and about 800 men to operate the line.

The way-stations were designed to serve multiple purposes in that they were to operate not only as ticket offices but also as hotels or inns where passengers could, if necessary, obtain both lodging and food. Whenever the stage line passed through cities and towns, arrangements were made with existing hotels for providing these services; but in the open country stations were built by the contractors at distances ranging from ten to fifty-two miles apart. For this construction work the builders used, whenever possible, the material at hand. Therefore, some of the stations were built of stone, some of logs, and still others of adobe bricks. They varied in size from one-room shacks to others that were large enough to accommodate four to ten employees and, if necessary, about a half dozen guests.[20]

The government established postage rates at ten cents per letter, whereas package rates varied. All those sending mail over the Butterfield facilities were to be required to mark it "via overland" or "per overland mail." After a brief period of experimentation, passenger fares from St. Louis to San Francisco, or vice versa, became fixed at two hundred dollars.[21]

While many details were still unattended to on September 16, 1858—the last day of grace allowed under the terms of the contract—the company was on that day ready to begin operations. By that time rail service from St. Louis reached Tipton, Missouri, from which point westbound mails and passengers were to transfer from a train to a stagecoach for the long ride to San Francisco.

*F*EW RECORDS were left by those who traveled over the Butterfield route, but happily there is one account that describes the journey on each of the first two stages, one going west from Tipton and the other east from San Francisco. The westbound passenger was Waterman L. Ormsby, a correspondent for the New York *Herald*. He stated in his dispatches to the *Herald* that he considered the southern plains and desert the most dangerous portion of the trip, that a fare of hardtack, dried beef, raw onions, and black coffee had left much to be desired, that the jolting of the stage was at times rugged, and water in places was scarce.[22] For all its frustrations and hardships, on a near–twenty-five day journey, Ormsby reported that he arrived at San Francisco "fresh enough to undertake it again." The eastbound passenger was G.[?] Bailey, a special agent for the Post Office Department. Bailey's account consists of a brief official report to Postmaster General Brown. Even though "attended with many difficulties and embarrassments," wrote Bailey, he was happy to report that the elapsed time was twenty-four days, eighteen hours, and twenty-six minutes. It was Bailey's opinion that the line was well stocked with stations and coaches. "Thus far," he wrote, "the experiment has proved successful."[23]

Public reaction to establishment of the Butterfield Overland Mail varied. Postmaster General Brown's decision to approve the deep southern route aroused bitter feelings in some parts of the North. The Chicago *Tribune*, for example, declared the whole operation "One of the greatest swindles ever perpetrated upon the country by the slave-holders."[24] And even though California profited immeasurably by this new service, northern California, which had hoped for the adoption of a central route, expressed its resentment. "The deed is done," declared the Sacramento *Daily Union*. Expressing its skepticism the *Union* added: "Four-horse stages cannot be driven from San Francisco, across the seven deserts . . . in twenty-five days—nor in forty days—nor at all. It never has been done. It never will be done."[25]

Caustic as were some of the critics, the Butterfield Overland Mail was widely regarded as a successful frontier business venture. The Sacramento *Union* notwithstanding, the stages usually managed to cover their overland course within the allotted twenty-five days, the average time being twenty-one days and fifteen hours. Moreover, the line attracted customers; by 1860 the combined volume of mail and passenger business taxed the capacity of available facilities. Not only did this frontier transportation enterprise prove a boon to the West coast but it was as well an aid to the Middle West and East, especially the eastern manufacturers of stagecoaches.

In spite of its successes, the Butterfield Overland Mail was doomed. Northern opposition to the Oxbow route mounted as sectional controversy deepened in intensity. Without waiting for the disruption of the Union, there was introduced in the United States Senate, early in 1861, a bill which would direct the Postmaster General to take steps leading to a shift in the Overland Mail route from the deep southern to a central route that would extend from St. Joseph, Missouri, to Sacramento. By March 12 both houses of Congress had approved the measure; but even as it did so, zealous prosouthern raiding parties had begun to harrass the line by driving off company livestock, taking possession of rolling stock, and destroying bridges along the stagecoach route. Then on March 6, only two days following Lincoln's inauguration, Butterfield's Oxbow line came to a halt. The end had not come unexpectedly, and for this reason Congressional action turned out to be a mere official recognition of an accomplished fact.[26]

The shift of the Butterfield Overland Mail to the central route spelled disaster for another principal prewar stagecoaching concern operated by the well-known freighting company of Russell, Majors and Waddell. Success in the wagon-freighting business had led the imaginative and venturesome William H. Russell to commit himself and his two reluctant partners to not one but two new transportation enterprises. One of these was a stagecoach passenger and mail line; the other, the now memorable Pony Express.

The first of these was prompted by the Colorado mineral discoveries and came into being when Russell, in the nation's capital on business, encountered a fellow-freight operator, John S. Jones. During February 1859, Russell (committing his partners) joined with Jones in formally organizing the Leavenworth and Pike's Peak Express. The new concern was to provide stagecoach and express services across the 687 miles of open prairies and plains separating such Missouri River ports as Leavenworth, Atchison, and Westover from the new boom town of Denver. Scarcely had the partnership with Jones been made when in further pursuit of an ambition to establish a transwestern mail service over a central route, Russell purchased from the J. M. Hockaday Company a postal contract involving a twenty-day mail transport between St. Joseph, Missouri, and Salt Lake City.

Service was expeditiously established during the spring of 1859; but in spite of its enthusiastic welcome in the prairie and Rocky Mountain West, the venture proved financially burdensome to the already heavily committed firm of Russell, Majors and Waddell. Misgivings on the part of Majors and Waddell were fully justified, for by late October 1859, the Leavenworth and Pike's Peak Express went into bankruptcy. Thereupon the freighting firm managed to gain full control of the defunct concern and, in an effort to extricate itself financially, proceeded, with others, to organize an entirely new concern to be known as the Central Overland California and Pike's Peak Express Company. The new concern, chartered under the laws of Kansas Territory, was capitalized at a half million dollars, and William H. Russell became its first president.[27]

The name of the new company gave at least a clue to its ambition—the establishment of central mail service between the Missouri River and the Pacific coast. But if this was indeed president Russell's main objective, the steps he took to achieve it turned out to be as devious as they were spectacular.

It has been contended—and with some sound evidence to support the contention—that during the winter of 1859 Senator William Gwin of California suggested to Russell that he establish an overland pony express. Such an operation, a pony relay service between a Missouri River port and Sacramento, would prove, first of all, the practicality of a central as opposed to a southern route; and that the successful implementation of such a pony relay service would be a necessary condition for securing a lucrative stage line mail contract.

In any event, the necessary funds were raised, and the Pony Express became a reality. During the spring of 1860 a trail was laid out between St. Joseph, Missouri, and Sacramento, California (officially San Francisco).

Even to a nation accustomed to exciting adventures in the West, Russell's project was one not to be ignored. When completed the route was 1966 miles long. Broken into five divisions, the pony trail passed through such places as Forts Kearny, Laramie, and Bridger, then on through Salt Lake City, Carson City, and Placerville. One hundred and nineteen stations were established (about a score of these were "home stations"). Hired to do the job of handling 500 ponies were approximately 120 hard-riding horsemen, many station keepers, stock tenders, and roustabouts.

The Pony Express first went into operation April 3, 1860. Pony riders started from both ends of the route, going forward in relays. Each horse covered about ten miles (the average distance between stations) and each rider rode from thirty-five to seventy miles at a stint, depending upon terrain, before passing on his mail bags to another. The average elapsed time in covering the full course of the trail was about ten days.

*P*OSTAGE RATES via Pony Express ranged from two to ten dollars per ounce, but the volume of mail carried was not sufficient to meet the tremendous costs of operation. Ironically, it was speed in communication, and not really costs, that put a speedy end to the Pony Express. Even as the first pony riders galloped over their long course they saw telegraph wires being strung on poles—westward from Kansas City by the Pacific Telegraph Company and eastward from San Francisco by the California State Telegraph Company. When these two lines were joined, as they were October 24, 1861, the Pony Express was doomed. Two days later the last of 34,753 pieces of mail were delivered.[28]

Meanwhile the Central Overland California and Pike's Peak Express Company tried somewhat desperately to maintain a stagecoach mail and passenger service. Helping to stave off disaster was a share in a million dollar contract attending the transfer, in 1861, of the defunct Oxbow route, or Butterfield Overland Mail, to a central route. The terms of this new Overland Mail contract, which had been approved March 2, 1861, provided for daily mail service between St. Joseph and Sacramento requiring twenty-three to thirty-five days.

Even though the recipient of this million dollar contract was the Overland Mail—the old Oxbow company of which William B. Dinsmore was president, having succeeded John Butterfield—the deployment of funds and services was to benefit its rival. President Dinsmore retained for the Overland Mail operations between Salt Lake City and Virginia City, Nevada, but sublet to the Central Overland California and Pike's Peak Express Company the operations between the Missouri River (actually the western end of the Hannibal and St. Joseph Railroad) and the Mormon capital. And it also leased to a California staging concern known as the Pioneer Stage Company the westernmost section between Virginia City and, as it turned out, the terminal city of Sacramento.

Three months elapsed before on July 18, 1861, stagecoach service over the central overland route actually began between St. Joseph and Folsom, California, where a short railroad line connected with Sacramento.

These complicated changes at least accomplished the desires of Congress to shift overland mail services from the southern to a central route, but the remunerations involved were not sufficient to save the

C.O.C. & P.P. Exp. Co. Losses incurred by Pony Express operations, financial mismanagement, disruptions brought on by the outbreak of the Civil War, Indian depredations, and failure to secure sufficient funds all contrived to throw this Russell-inspired company into insolvency. When in December 1861 a note held by Benjamin Holladay fell due, the C.O.C. & P.P. Exp. Co., along with the firm of Russell, Majors and Waddell, was unable to meet its obligations and early the next year went into bankruptcy and ruin.[29]

Holladay was by no means a stranger to this rough and tumble scramble for stagecoach and mail lines. Long active in western transportation businesses, Holladay had become associated with Russell, Majors and Waddell and had become a creditor to this freighting firm. As the new owner of the C.O.C. & P.P. Exp. Co. the ambitious and energetic Holladay made many changes, not least of which, much to the company's advantage, was to drop the elongated name. It was first changed to "The Overland Stage Company"; then, in 1866, the combined Holladay holdings were assigned the name "Holladay Overland Mail and Express Company."[30]

These holdings had by then become enormous and far reaching. Not only was Holladay's control of the eastern Missouri River-Salt Lake City line reaffirmed by Post Office Department contracts, but extending northward from the Mormon capital Holladay managed to penetrate, and take advantage of transportation opportunities in, the new and booming inland empire. One contract provided for regular stagecoach and mail service between Salt Lake City and Virginia City (Montana), via the Corinne Road, and subsequent contracts extended similar services to such other important mining towns as Boise (Idaho), Walla Walla (Washington), and The Dalles (Oregon). Viewing the postwar Holladay empire as a whole, the assets were: a 1250-mile mainline from St. Joseph to Salt Lake City, plus a 950-mile extension from the Utah capital that ultimately reached the lower Columbia River steamboat junction at The Dalles. The import of this was tremendous. Not only were the rising populations along the Central Overland Road being offered regular daily stagecoach and mail service but the inhabitants of the growing mining camps of the inland empire were liberated from their dependence upon either seasonal Missouri River steamboats or upon turtle-paced covered wagons.[31]

Holladay had indeed traveled far—and fast. But he was not to go unchallenged. The source of this challenge was the 1864-founded D. A. Butterfield freighting firm operating out of Atchison. During March of 1865 this firm had become reconstituted as a joint-stock company with eastern capital and had expanded its services to include coaching and express. To the newly formed division was given the name "Butterfield Overland Dispatch," or "B.O.D." The initial route would be the Smoky

Hill Road lying between Atchison and Denver; the immediate objective was to outdo Holladay operations over the longer Platte River route by way of Fort Kearny; and the long-run objective of this concern was to extend services over the full distance from the Missouri to the Pacific coast. But for all its aspirations and promise, the B.O.D. was destined for a short life due to devastating Indian attacks, problems of overcapitalization, and strangling competition from the Holladay Overland Mail and Express Company.[32] When insolvency threatened, as it did in March 1866, Ben Holladay was ready to act. "Now," the wily Holladay is reported to have said, "I am going to take the bull by the horns." He arranged for a meeting with B.O.D. officials in New York, and over "a fine lunch, with wines and cigars" he made his antagonists an acceptable offer.[33]

With this important deal consummated, the Holladay stage line holdings reached their greatest height. For their day, they constituted a vast transportation empire over which Holladay ruled briefly as the undisputed "stagecoach king," or as his enemies preferred to call him, "The Napoleon of the West." Within this far-flung realm he now operated these route-miles: Topeka to Denver via Smoky Hill, 585; Atchison or St. Joseph to Denver via the Platte River route, 650; Omaha to Kearny, 150; Denver to Salt Lake City, 600; Salt Lake City to the inland empire, with branches to Montana, Idaho, and Oregon towns, 970; miscellaneous local lines, 190; a grand total of 3145 miles.[34] Stations were located roughly at ten-mile intervals and therefore would have exceeded three hundred in number. As with the Southern Overland Mail Line, hundreds of men were employed; livestock and vehicles likewise numbered in the hundreds. Between 1862 and 1868 Holladay had held nine United States government mail contracts that netted him $1,905,513.[35] Records on receipts from passenger and express services were unfortunately lost in the San Francisco fire of 1906, so a full accounting of the volume of business is unavailable. Some measure of the marketable value of Holladay's stagecoach business may, however, be derived from events to be related.

Beyond Holladay's effective control were the so-called western divisions of the Central Overland Mail, the route between Salt Lake City and Folsom (or Sacramento). But there, too, the war years brought important changes. A forwarding firm known as Wells, Fargo and Company gradually gained control—first of the Pioneer Stage Company and then of the parent Overland Mail.

Why and how these developments came about may be explained in part by the phenomenal rise of Wells, Fargo and Company. Wells, Fargo had been incorporated in New York state in 1852, but it had been formed chiefly to take advantage of opportunities in California—conveying gold dust, mails, and other valuables between the mining frontier and the eastern seaboard. The company prospered from the outset. During 1855 it weathered the financial storm in California that caused the failure of Adams and Company Express, a strong competitor in that state. Thereafter Wells, Fargo and Company dominated the entire express business on the west coast. By 1860 there existed 147 Wells, Fargo and Company offices within California. Inasmuch as most of the gold dust and express parcels being forwarded by the company were conveyed in stagecoaches, Wells, Fargo and Company gradually extended its financial interest and control over staging operations connecting Sacramento with the silver mines in Nevada, especially Virginia City. Furthermore, inasmuch as William G. Fargo had been associated with John Butterfield and others in the Overland Mail venture, it came as no great surprise that the firm of Wells, Fargo and Company in time gained control of the entire western end of the Central Overland operations between the Mormon capital and Folsom (or, by including the short-line railroad, to Sacramento). Nor did Wells, Fargo and Company rest on its oars. By 1866 this aggressive firm not only maintained fifty-three stagecoach stations between Folsom and its Salt Lake City junction but it had also established connections with numerous independent stagecoach lines serving the entire Pacific slope.[36]

Such was the over-all operational situation in 1866 when two powerful outfits—the Holladay Overland Mail and Express Company and Wells, Fargo and Company—took measure of each other.

Holladay, who doubtless coveted a major tie with the Pacific area, had but one effective club that might be wielded to serve his ends: he could refuse to convey Wells, Fargo express over Holladay lines at tolerable rates. Reciprocally, Wells, Fargo could—and in fact did—seek a union with Holladay's competitor, the (D. A.) Butterfield Overland Dispatch. Had this merger materialized, Wells, Fargo and Company could have stocked and operated a line extending all the way from St. Joseph or Atchison to Folsom. But when, as happened in 1866, Holladay acquired the B.O.D. interests, the stagecoach king was in a position to say to his secretary: "Answer those express companies, and tell them be d——."[37]

A rapprochement to this aggravating tug-of-war came rather suddenly. For one thing, Holladay's stages had suffered severely from Indian attacks during 1864–1866; for another, Holladay had the foresight to realize that completion of the Pacific railroad would ruin his staging empire. On November 1, 1866, he therefore accepted as payment for his business a Wells, Fargo and Company bid of $1,500,000 in cash and $300,000 of Wells, Fargo and Company stock, plus a directorship in the express firm. By this master stroke Wells, Fargo and Company took over the Holladay crown, and with it came control of all major express and stagecoach lines west of the Missouri River. Twelve days following this major transaction the name Holladay Overland Mail and Express Company was dropped; adopted in its place was Wells, Fargo and Company. From the point of view of Holladay it would appear that he had bargained well; from the point of view of Wells, Fargo and Company it was believed that the express firm had gained a more advantageous position from which to transfer its specialized carrying business from stagecoaches to railroad cars when, in the not very distant future, the last spike was to be driven on the first transcontinental railroad.[38]

Revolutionary as were the changes to be brought on by the railroads, their coming into the trans-Mississippi West did not put an end to stagecoach transportation. When, for example, in 1876 a gold rush occurred in the Black Hills of South Dakota, the result was actually a mushrooming of coaching operations centering upon the town of Deadwood. At the time of discovery Deadwood's nearest railroad station to the south was Sidney, Nebraska; its nearest rail connection to the north was Bismarck, North Dakota; and a third point of contact was Yankton, South Dakota, a Missouri River steamboat landing. These places were all more than two hundred miles from Deadwood, and at the time of the gold discovery there existed no established trails or roads over which stages could operate.

Connections of a sort came shortly. Before the end of 1876 an intermittent staging service was established between Deadwood and Yankton, via Fort Pierre, South Dakota. A concern known as the Merchants' Transportation Company of Yankton captured the bulk of a bulging business that in 1883 reached a peak of five thousand passengers. Simultaneously, Northwestern Express, Stage, and Transportation Company opened a line between Deadwood and Bismarck, where connections were made with the Northern Pacific Railroad. As construction of the Northern Pacific advanced westward, additional railroad shacktowns emerged to serve as North-South stage gateways to Deadwood and other Black Hills mining camps. One place along the Northern Pacific track was Medora, where in 1883 an adventurous Frenchman, Marquis de Mores, established a 215-mile Medora and Deadwood line. The Marquis made a noble effort at offering good service, but his venture turned out to be a losing one. Contributing to a rugged and highly competitive situation was the offer by [John] Gilmer and [Monroe] Salisbury Company of comparable connections between Deadwood and the Union Pacific stations at Sidney and Cheyenne. As early as 1869 the Gilmer and Salisbury concern had purchased an Ogden to Helena stage line from Wells, Fargo and Company (formerly a part of the Holladay system). By establishing a link with the Black Hills this ambitious outfit was in position to round out a stagecoach network that specialized in serving most major mining camps in the Rocky Mountain West.[39]

One more staging operation in Dakota Territory is to be noted. When in 1873 the Northern Pacific Railroad reached Bismarck and there halted for six long depression-ridden years, it was the stagecoach that was looked upon as a potential link between the end of the track and such places on the Yellowstone River as Miles City, Fort Keogh, and points farther west. That military posts in this region, in particular, should be served had been a matter of considerable Congressional interest, and the trail first blazed in 1862 by Captain James L. Fisk between St. Paul and Fort Benton had been scrutinized as one feasible stagecoach route that could, in fact, bridge the gap between the Dakota frontier and existing west coast avenues of communication. But Indian troubles leading to the Custer Battle delayed all efforts to inaugurate the desired service until 1878 when the Postmaster General finally approved the necessary mail contract. This contract called for six weekly two-way trips between Bismarck and Miles City, and the route followed was generally the one taken by General Custer on his ill-fated expedition to the Little Big Horn. Light four- to six-horse wagons, rather than Concord coaches, were used in this service, and throughout its existence the bulk of business remained that of carrying mails rather than passengers. With resumption of Northern Pacific Railroad construction the "Fort Keogh-Bismarck line," as it has often been called, went into decline. When in 1882 the iron rails brought the locomotive to Miles City, service over this stage route ended abruptly.[40]

For all their shortcomings—and there were many—the staging businesses made possible the transference of people, letters, and express parcels to and from practically all populated points within the entire trans-Mississippi West. River steamers, of course, augmented this service, and railroads were seen to supersede both the bouncing stagecoach and the deep-throated steamboat. In regions not penetrated by either rail or steamboat, the stagecoach lines clung tenaciously to life, and in such areas they continued to perform important services even beyond 1900. They met strictly local needs that involved travel between one town and another not in any way served by other modes of commercial transportation.

◁ **5** ▷

Overland by Stage

*E*ver since Sir William Dugdale, in 1659, "set forwards toward London by Coventre coach"[1] travelers have contributed liberally to the literature on coaching. By 1865, however, the steamboat and the railroad had effectively displaced the stagecoach in many parts of the world, including the older and more settled portions of the United States. Only within the trans-Mississippi West did travelers continue to look with mixed praise and scorn upon the stagecoach or stage wagon as a necessary vehicle of transportation. A "stage," as such passenger-carrying vehicles were often called in the West, answered to many shapes and descriptions. The earliest of "stage-chariots" on the eastern seaboard were lumbering, springless wagons that bounced and jolted passengers over crude, tortuous colonial roads. The post-Civil War transportation frontier was, by contrast, blessed with the ultimate in horsedrawn rolling stock—the resplendent, egg-shaped, western Concord coach.

The Concord coach was a product of craft-conscious Yankee New England, more especially the Concord, New Hampshire, firm of Abbot, Downing and Company. It was 1813 when Lewis Downing from nearby

Lexington, Massachusetts, first set up a wheelwright shop. Later Downing was joined by journeyman J. Stephen Abbot of Salem, Massachusetts, in forming the coach-making firm that, after several name changes, became in 1865 Abbot, Downing and Company. By 1873 this firm was incorporated with a $400,000 capitalization, and the factory facilities by then had spread over a six-acre tract.

This highly reputable firm produced vehicles of many types, but the most superb was the "Concord coach." The Concord possessed numerous distinguishing features. It was made of top-quality wood, iron, brass, and ox-hide leather and was most carefully and skillfully engineered. Its hard, oval-shaped body was suspended on heavy thorough-braces, or heavy leather straps, that enabled it to roll rather than jerk or bounce, and at the same time to retain a moderately level position irrespective of the position of the wheels. In short, a Concord coach looked good, and it performed remarkably well under varying travel conditions.

The Abbot, Downing and Company factory was something to behold. Horse-powered saws cut out felloes for wheels, and band saws had come into use for cutting the many needed irregularly shaped parts. The broad axe, jack-plane, and joister likewise were employed in giving proper shape to the best of thoroughly seasoned bass, elm, poplar, white ash, and white oak used in manufacture. Tires on the western Concord were from two and a half to three inches in width and were three-fourths of an inch thick, and as such gave strength to the wheels. Coach bodies were made with inside front, rear, and center drop seats to accommodate nine passengers. Outside on top there was, of course, the driver's seat with places for two passengers; and, at least for short runs, room could be found for a dozen more on top. There was a front boot under the driver's seat, and another leather-covered triangularly-shaped one extending from the rear. In all, fourteen sides of leather (a side represented half a cowhide) were used in the making of a single coach.

A finished Concord coach was a thing of beauty. Colors varied, depending somewhat on the buyer's choice. In the case of Holladay's Overland Stage Company, the body of the coach was English vermilion; running gear, straw; leather upholstery and curtains, russet or black. Among other color combinations were dark bottle green bodies and brown running gears. Scenic pictures decorated the door panels, and frequently the likeness of some contemporary actress was painted on either side of the footboard or driver's seat. On all mail-carrying coaches appeared in gold letters: "U.S. Mail." For ornamentation as well as use there were oil lamps on the upper sides. As a final step in manufacture the entire painted surface of the coach was given two coats of varnish. Concord coaches of the type used in the West weighed about twenty-five hundred pounds and cost about twelve to fifteen hundred dollars upon delivery. Extant records indicate that between 1858 and 1900 approximately six hundred coaches were produced by Abbot, Downing, and it may be presumed that the largest share of these found service on Far West roads. One single rail shipment to Wells, Fargo and Company (destination Omaha) consisted of thirty Concord coaches, requiring fifteen flatcars to transport.[2]

Popular and versatile though it was, the Concord coach was not used to the exclusion of other types of vehicles. John Butterfield employed a number of more lumbering, rectangularly shaped "Troy" coaches, which like the Concord could accommodate passengers on top as well as inside. Also of eastern manufacture, the Troy coach was made by Eaton, Gilbert and Company at Troy, New York. The "Celerity" wagon was also familiar to travelers over many of the western staging routes. Designed for swiftness, it was manufactured both by Abbot, Downing and Company and by James Goold at Albany, New York. The Celerity was lighter in weight than the Concord; it seated nine passengers inside, but none on its rounded top. The Celerity wagon was not as comfortable as the Concord for daytime travel, but its unupholstered seats could be adjusted for sleeping. Still another type of wagon widely used in the West was the "mud," or "stage," wagon. It too, had thorough-brace construction. Due to its comparative lightness, narrow wheels, and maneuverability it was regarded with favor for fast driving and on extremely muddy, and also mountainous, roads.[3] To these best-known wagon types may be added the appropriately named broad-wheeled "Jerky," or springless wagon, and a variety of other spring and springless passenger-carrying vehicles made by wagon-makers in many parts of the land. Many of the coaches, wrote one observant traveler, were mere imitations of the "Concord wagon," but "never equaled" it.[4]

Regardless of make, no coach was entirely suitable for winter travel in regions where the snowfall was often extremely heavy. In such places and times, as, for example, Minnesota in midwinter, runners either replaced wheels on standard coaches or sleighs were used as conveyances.

Judging from reports by long- and hard-suffering travelers, none was a match for the popular, durable, dependable, colorful, and graceful Concord coach. "If there is a prettier street picture of animation than a red Concord coach, with six spirited horses in bright harness, and a good reinsman on the box," wrote an enthusiast, "we have not seen it."[5]

Most United States mail contracts specified the use of four- or six-horse coaches, and this number of animals—horses or mules—was used in most staging services in the West. If horses were shunned by wagon teamsters, they were usually favored by stagecoach operators. Horses, many of them wild mustangs broken to drive, lent speed and dash to overland staging.[6]

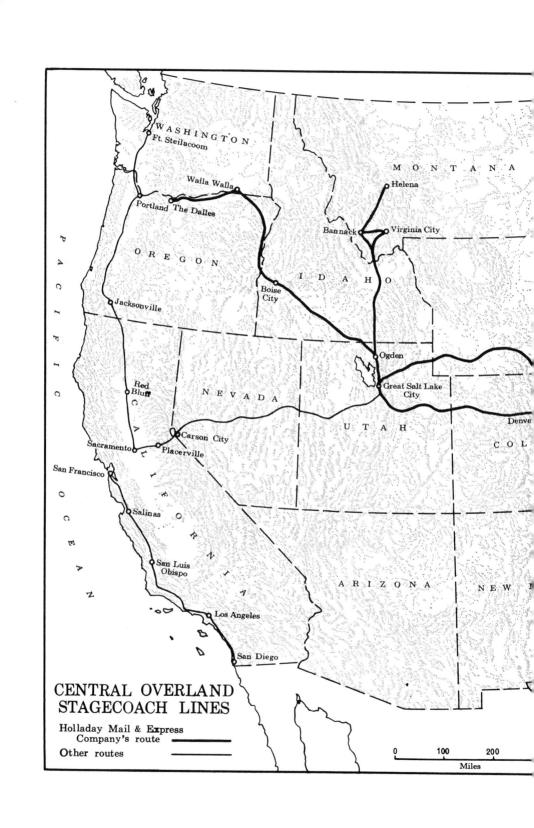

CENTRAL OVERLAND
STAGECOACH LINES

Holladay Mail & Express
   Company's route ━━━━━━━

Other routes ━━━━━━━

0   100   200

Miles

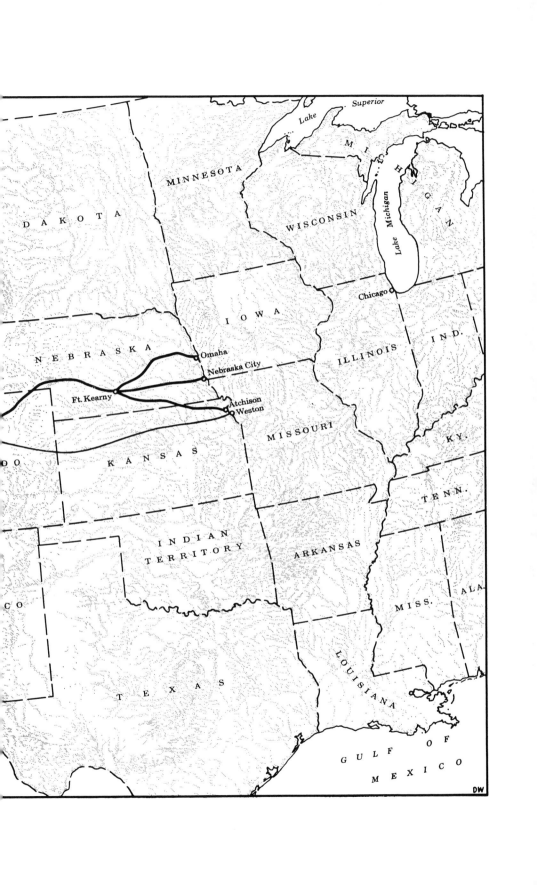

Western stage teams wore specially-made harnesses, different from those used on draft animals. The stage team harness was the essence of simplicity. The main unit consisted of belly and back bands, hames, neck-yoke straps, reins, and tugs or traces. Collars and bridles completed the outfit. The neck yoke slipped easily onto the "gooseneck" end of the tongue, and T-shaped links at the ends of tugs were made to be fastened readily into rings on the whiffle trees. When as was his duty the stock tender hitched the teams to the coach, the left tug of the left wheel horse remained unjoined until the driver had taken his seat on the box and given the appropriate signal. With the fastening of this tug the teams sensed that all was in readiness and off they would gallop.[7]

*S*IZE DETERMINED not only the number but the types of jobs provided by a given staging concern. All outfits, of course, had to have drivers, and most employed stock tenders as well. Large concerns such as Butterfield and Holladay employed in addition superintendents, station keepers, blacksmiths, roustabouts, "shotgun messengers" (or guards), and conductors.

Driving required the greatest amount of skill and acumen within the staging business. The handling of six spirited mustangs hitched to a coach was an art not to be compared with the ordinary driving of a team of horses pulling a privately owned buggy or wagon. It was a skill that called for control over steeds. It needed split-second coordination of the three pairs of reins held and manipulated by the fingers of the left hand while leaving the right hand free for controlling slack and for wielding the whip normally housed in a right-side socket. In making turns, for example, the movement of the lead team had to be coordinated with the swing (middle) team, and then in turn with the wheelers hitched to the tongue. Without proper coordination teams often tangled and injury and confusion ensued. Overturning of coaches was always within the reckoning of both coach builders and drivers, and upsets did occasionally occur. In order to minimize damage from upsets, hitching was so arranged that only one pin was used in attaching coach and team. This important pin fastened the doubletrees (to which the horses were hitched) to the coach. The pin was held in place by its weight only, so in the event of upset it would presumably fall out by force of gravity and thus disengage the team from the coach.[8]

All who have left records of travel experiences agree that most western stage drivers possessed positive and distinctive personality traits. Characterization of this group came, of course, from passengers, and individual portrayals varied somewhat according to the experiences and personal reactions of individuals. Some drivers were labeled daredevils and madmen, others jovial and friendly "whips" or "jehus." The drivers were a product of the frontier. Their individual backgrounds varied in that some were farmers who had turned coachmen; others, as one driver recalled, were just plain fighters, gamblers, and drinkers. There is general concurrence that drivers were self-confident men when in the box and with hold upon the reins. In this position, wrote one traveling English merchant, the stage driver "is inferior to no one in the Republic. Even the President, were he on board, must submit to his higher authority."[9]

Customarily, the driver allowed his most distinguished passengers on a given run to share the box, and to indulge in good-humored conversation. Such privileged travelers have credited most drivers not only with great skill at managing their teams, but with considerable intelligence as well. "In short," wrote J. M. Hutchings, "he is a living road-encyclopedia."[10] Most whips shared with teamsters an assiduous devotion to the "quid" and an uncommon ability to emit profanity;[11] and although generally credited with sobriety while on duty, exceptions are noted. James A. Garfield remarked about one Montana whip, "Steve," that his "genius as a driver is exhibited in the ratio of his intoxication"; he was "brilliant as a driver."[12] When one Englishman was departing from Denver over perilous mountain roads, he asked his driver who had eyed the whisky barrel if he would like a drink. "Waal, guess I will"; whereupon he "took hold of the barrel, uncorked it, and for twenty seconds there was some 'star-gazing' through the wooden keg."

"Wall, that's rale good!"

It was not long before the driver, slightly perturbed, inquired, "'Why, what's gone with the whisky? Why ain't there none thar?' Then in answer to his own question, added, "Waal, guess it's leaked down my throat."

> "Down your throat! Why, man, you don't mean to say you've drank the whole of that keg of whisky?"
>
> "Why not? thar warn't much whisky nither. . . . what's one keg of whisky amongst one stage-driver?"[13]

Stage drivers were, by and large, a fairly mobile class of men, who worked at their trade in a number of different areas. For this reason drivers came to know one another quite well and to indulge in exchanges of experiences, which in the form of good yarns were passed on to one another and to the traveling public. The trouble with stage drivers, according to the widely traveled John W. Boddam-Whetham, was that they repeated one another's stories and jokes. But for all their faults this Englishman concluded: "The stage-drivers doubtless are as a rule, very intelligent, and may be relied on; but some of them have really such excessive regard for the truth that they use it with penurious frugality." It was the opinion of yet another British traveler that the Western stage-driver was a man of iron nerve, recklessness, and daring. But these were qualities needed for a good driver. "The way to go down those [California] mountains is to rush it."[14] For all the strong pro and con feeling with regard to stagecoach drivers, it must be borne in mind that it was good business interest on the part of frontier stage proprietors to employ capable, dependable, experienced, and careful men. "A prudent, level-headed driver," as one driver saw it, "does not fail to realize that in his hands are held the lives of a load of passengers, and, usually, he is as anxious to please all. . . ."[15]

Each man in a staging organization had essential roles to play. On Central Overland stages, a "conductor" was employed to look after the mails, passengers, and baggage, and as Mark Twain phrased it, serve as "Captain of the craft." On Far Western stages—and especially in areas subject to holdups—"shotgun messengers," so-called, served as special guards. When on duty the shotgun messenger usually occupied a seat beside the driver, where he held his loaded shotgun in readiness. The duties of most personnel were by and large what their titles indicated. A stock tender did what the term implies, but it was also his duty to hitch and unhitch teams at stations either in preparation for or in termination of runs.[16]

The routes, ranging as they did from a score to several hundred miles in length, were operated according to patterns dictated by practical and physical circumstances. A suitable run for horse or mule teams on any given day was ten to thirteen miles, and at appropriate intervals "swing stations" were established where teams could be changed.[17] "Home stations," on the other hand, were situated from forty to fifty miles apart; that is, every fourth station was a home station. It was at these home stations that a driver began and finished his day's run. For the coaches and for many passengers, there was no turning in until final destinations had been reached. Cross-country runs were conducted on an around-the-clock schedule. This was necessary in order to maintain a called-for average speed of 9.29 miles per hour, and in the case of the Central Overland, to achieve its 2226-mile run from the Missouri River to Sacramento within twenty days.[18]

One must not, of course, think that stagecoach runs were completely uninterrupted. It was necessary for stages to halt at all stations in order to take on and discharge passengers, make team changes, and deliver and collect mail and express. Moreover, meals were served at appropriately designated stations and time was allowed passengers for hurried intake of food.

Home stations were more elaborate establishments and two to three times larger than swing stations. Usually the home stations were of plain construction, but they were also sufficiently commodious and well equipped to meet passenger and postal requirements. Such places normally contained lodging and eating facilities, a ticket and postal office, store, barn with stable, and, of course, staging equipment and livestock. Some home stations were located within towns, even within cities, and when this was the case the offices were housed in hotels, the horses and vehicles in livery stations. At Atchison the well-established Tremont House and Planters' House served as central staging depots. The Crescent and Orleans hotels in Sacramento and the Merchants' Hotel in St. Paul played comparable roles. Streets fronting such places were the scenes of bustling activity. During early morning hours several coaches could be seen standing in readiness to take on passengers and depart for sundry destinations.

Most stage stations, however, were necessarily located along bleak country roadsides. Such places were simple frame, sod, log, adobe, or stone structures. If local building materials were not available, lumber was usually hauled to designated sites for construction purposes. Along the Overland Stage Company's Central route there were 153 stations spaced on an average of twelve and a half miles apart. Most of these, especially those in the Platte River Valley, were of similar construction. They were square, one-storied structures with walls built of hewn cedar logs; roofs were sod. Most of the home stations contained three rooms, but some were limited to one room divided by muslin draperies into a kitchen, dining room, and sleeping quarters.[19] Many of the stations were ranch houses, the occupants of which served in the double capacity of agents and ranchers. In addition there were places answering the purposes of stations that were mere caves, or what Bayard Taylor called "half-subterranean lodgings" in embankments cut out to accommodate the station agent and his horses or mules.[20]

In areas subject to Indian attacks it was not uncommon for stations and stables, regardless of size or type, to be enclosed by stone walls or barricades of some type. Portholes for rifle fire were added to make such places as defensible as possible.

Another type of improvised fortress was known as the prairie monitor, namely, a dugout located in close proximity to a stage station and connected by an underground passage. A monitor roof was at ground level and consisted of heavy timbers covered with dirt. Guns and ammunition were stored in such subsurface arsenals, and slits were provided to make effective crossfire possible. Needless to say, monitors provided a welcome point of defense to make a stand when and if stage stations were overwhelmed and set ablaze by marauding Indians.[21]

Stations in general, according to Alexander K. McClure, a correspondent for the New York *Tribune* who in 1867 traveled over three thousand miles of western mountain roads, were devoid of cleanliness; those in the mountains excelled in dirt. At most such places a single room often served as ticket office, kitchen, dining room, bed chamber, and carpenter shop.[22] "Of all the filthy, repulsive stations on the route," wrote this newspaperman, those in the Rocky Mountains, and in particular at Pleasant Valley, Montana, took the prize. At this place McClure found himself ankle-deep in mud, accommodations wretched, and the "square meals" consisting of a "miserable apology for coffee, no butter or milk, stale eggs and bacon, and bread almost as gritty as the mountain boulders." Even where ranch houses served as stage stations the degree of cleanliness depended entirely upon the industry and disposition of the occupants. In one such home station McClure reported that his couch was made up on the earthen floor in a kitchen corner opposite from where the proprietor, his wife, and children slept. McClure's bed consisted of ticking filled with "musty hay." He could only speculate as to the color of the ticking when clean. During the night he struggled constantly with bedbugs. " 'They *do* be aw-ful,' " admitted his landlady whose bare feet had not been washed for months.[23] Bayard Taylor's excursions in the Rockies brought similar reactions to stage station appointments, and especially the food. To Taylor a Rocky Mountain "square meal" was something that consisted of "strong black coffee, strips of pork fat fried to a sandy crispness, and half-baked, soggy, indigestible biscuits.... For these," said Taylor, "I paid the square price of one dollar."[24]

*A*CCOUNTS of Southwest desert travel indicate an obvious shift from gray, shadowy filth to sun-baked dirt and dust. The remark, "I carried most of my grub with me," is a not uncommon type of entry in travel journals pertaining to this area.[25] The reason for this is understandable. One traveler asserted that the biscuits provided at stage stations in the Southwest were hard enough to serve as "round shot" and that the tortillas were probably made of a mixture of blue flint and New Mexican corn. One traveler of the purple sage, creosote, and mesquite reported that stagecoach travelers who made stopovers at Southwest towns were not infrequently treated to some spectacular night life. When James Swisher stopped over at bleak La Paz, Arizona, the "whole town seemed to be in a riot." Everybody was intoxicated. Some were fighting, some stripping for a fight, the rest taking sides. Nor was Swisher's hotel a haven of quiet and ease. There was commotion everywhere, but none quite so pronounced as when the call came that hash was ready. After dinner men took to their quids, if for no other reason than to remove the taste of their meals from their mouths. Swisher retired to a candlelighted room, separated from one neighbor by a cloth partition, from another by a sparsely boarded wall. The next morning he arose to find a drunken Texan, flat on his back in the bar, a revolver in each hand, shooting at everything in sight. He was, said Swisher, "Monarch of everything he surveyed." In the opinion of the blasé landlord, La Paz had indeed become tame. When he first came to this town, it was, he admitted, a fairly rough place.[26] La Paz had no monopoly on night life. Even "one-horse towns" such as Leesburg, New Mexico, did their best to encourage hilarity. Leesburg's one sign over the front door read: "Live and let live."[27]

Accommodations and meals were by comparison much better along parts of the main-traveled central overland routes, and this in spite of the yarn that a customer said to the innkeeper, "I don't care for roast beef," and received the curt reply: "Help yourself to the mustard." Certainly comfortable hotels graced the Missouri River ports and western terminal towns. Fort Kearny was regarded as the best eating place on the Overland Stage Company route,[28] while along the full length of this line, Samuel Bowles assured his readers, "Our meals at the stage stations continued very good...." The staple foods along this route were bacon, eggs, hot biscuits, green tea, and coffee. Dried peaches and apples and pies were also constantly on the menus. And added occasionally were beef and antelope, canned fruits, and vegetables.[29] Moreover, many of those who cooked and served the meals along this route were, in the opinion of Richardson, "comely and lady-like, adapting themselves with grace and heroism to the rude labors of cooking meals for passengers, and the horrible, ever-present peril of capture."[30]

Viewed in retrospect this elaborate, and in some areas superseded, transportation system had one redeeming feature: it worked. In the absence of steamboats and railroads, stagecoaches succeeded remarkably well in moving people, post, and express from one place to another. It cannot be said, however, that passengers were conveyed in great comfort. Those setting forth on overland journeys, say from Atchison to points west, were awakened from their morning slumbers and given a hasty breakfast. The luggage, usually limited in weight to twenty-five pounds, and consisting mainly of blankets and greenbacks, was stowed into the rear "boot" or "shoe" or on top. When the guest of honor had boarded the box and nine passengers had scrambled into fifteen-inch spaces inside the coach (often among the mailbags) and where front and middle occupants had to interlock knees, they were said to have been "accommodated."[31] The time for an eight o'clock departure had come. From his lofty position "on deck" the driver would call "all aboard" and signal the tender to hook on the final tug. Then off would roll the coach behind four or six prancing horses through the rough city streets leading to the open country road that followed the bank of the Little Blue.

The ensuing trip could not be said to be pleasant, wrote Barnes in 1865, but it was interesting. "The conditions of one man's running stages to make money, while another seeks to ride in them for pleasure, are not in harmony to produce comfort. Coaches will be overloaded, it will rain, the dust will drive, baggage will be left to the storm, passengers will get sick, a gentleman of gallantry will hold the baby, children will cry, passengers will get angry, the drivers will swear, the sensitive will shrink, rations will give out, potatoes become worth a dollar each, and not to be had at that, the water brackish, the whiskey abominable, and the dirt almost unendurable."[32]

In addition there was the problem of sleep. Stage riding induced drowsiness, and as Taylor observed there were aboard "no *corners* to receive one's head."[33] The first night was always the most uncomfortable. After a period of song and reminiscent chatter, wrote another, there would come the remarks "bedtime" and "what a misnomer!" Various devices and positions were contrived in an effort to obtain a longitudinal position: the top, if there was a rail guard; the boot, if not packed with baggage and mail; lengthwise on a seat, if not shared with others. But if the stage carried its full complement of passengers, there was nothing else to do but doze in sitting position, let the head roll, allow oneself to be pummeled, pounded, and bruised, and await the morning cramps.[34] So prolonged and great was the fatigue endured by passengers on long rides that some approached a point of insanity. At times drivers compelled such persons to stop over for sleep and rest at way stations, but some passengers were known to have wandered off in aimless fashion and, when this occurred in the desert, at considerable peril.[35]

Such were the routine inconveniences of stage travel. To these were added the somehow expected but nevertheless unscheduled incidents and accidents of the road that ranged from mere inconveniences and aggravations to tragic mishaps and attacks from Indians and holdup men. Even the relatively smooth, gently rising roads of the Plains posed irritations and dangers to stagecoach travelers. Among these were the long and seemingly endless number of emigrant and freighting caravans for which the lighter and faster moving stagecoaches yielded rights-of-way and made driving along dusty, bumpy side roads a necessary inconvenience.

Not least of the miseries were induced by weather. Semitropical electrical storms, so familiar to the Great Plains area, accompanied by heavy rains often played havoc with travelers and at times even capsized stages moving over ungraded and ungraveled roads. Samuel Bowles described such a storm with appropriate awesomeness when he wrote: "First came huge, rolling, ponderous masses of cloud in the west, massing up and separating into sections in a more majestic and threatening style than our party had ever before seen in the heavens." Thereafter came tornadic winds to which the coach turned its back but not without being stripped of all loose baggage. Then came the finale, a terrific downpour of hail "as large and heavy as bullets" and "swift" rain that made the horses quail in pain and passengers shudder in fear of losing their lives.[36] Rains in Kansas and Nebraska did not need to be either torrential or tornadic to impede vehicular traffic. Once rain had fallen upon the deep rich rockless soil, wheels would begin first to slip and then to sink hub-deep into muddy ruts. When this happened passengers were unceremoniously invited by the driver to get off and either help pry the wheels loose by means of a pole or apply their pushing power directly to the rear end of the coach. On such occasions a standard Kansas canard that stagecoach fares were "ten cents a mile and a [fence]rail" seemed anything but funny.

Plains travel was nothing compared with the terrors of mountain staging. Mountain roads were at best narrow, circuitous ledges cut on what were generally high, undulating embankments. From their seats within the coaches passengers could gaze out over high precipices and realize that one misstep by a team could send the complete outfit— horses, coaches, passengers, and baggage—crashing into an abyss below. But in spite of all this, mountain drivers seemed little bothered by these conjuries of mind and proceeded merrily around curves and down hills at breakneck speeds. Hills, wrote an English traveler, are "descended at a full gallop, and ascended at a smart trot."[37] Drivers sought to gain time on downgrades, and in doing so passengers were tossed about uncontrollably against the interior confines of the coach. The saving grace of traveling under such conditions was that in time passengers became accustomed to most of the viscissitudes and dangers of the road. Even fast mountain driving became "so novel a sensation, so exciting . . . ," wrote Boddam-Whetham, "that you cannot help cheering on the horses in spite of a very probable upset on the brow of an almost perpendicular rock several hundred feet in height." Even the surefooted horses seemed to have enjoyed it, added this dedicated traveler.[38]

*N*OWHERE IN THE WEST did stagecoach travel seem more impeded than over the coastal roads of the Pacific Northwest where rainfall during winter seasons was heavy. There passengers appear to have become involved in repeated acts of extricating coaches from "mire," as travelers liked to call mud, and in removing fallen trees from across routes of travel. There were mountain stretches along the California-Oregon road where even in the late 1880s the rate of travel was not more than two miles per hour.[39] In the rainsoaked Willamette Valley, Oregon, corduroy roads were widely used, and while the slab or board surfaces kept coaches from sinking into mire, they did, on the other hand, induce excessive bumpiness.

Driving across the hot desert country of the Southwest appears to have assumed a more leisurely pace following the transfer of Butterfield operations to the central route. When J. Ross Browne toured Arizona in 1864 he reported that a twenty-five mile run was considered a fair day's ride, and that double this distance would have set a record. The quality of service in that region appears to have varied greatly among individual operators.[40] Some lines advertised the latest in Concord coaches; others used the poorest quality equipment. Hardly typical, however, was a contraption described by a lady passenger traveling through southern Utah. The vehicle on which she rode was a rickety two-seated open wagon. From his seat the driver controlled his team not only by reins but he restrained a kick-prone gray horse by means of a long rope tied to a foreleg and extending to the driver's hand. Whenever the steed showed a disposition to strike out from behind, a lusty simultaneous yank at the rope would throw the recalcitrant animal off-balance and thereby circumvent the intended kick.[41]

At no time in the trans-Mississippi West was stagecoach travel more trying and difficult than during cold, winter months. Even in the relatively sunny Southwest there were times when roads were sheets of ice. One traveler recorded the terror of descending Raton Pass during winter. He related that the front and rear wheels had to be tied together in order to prevent "jack-knifing." Once when the driver stepped off his box to check on roads, he slipped and fell with his feet landing in the air. When the ruffled driver was asked if he could make it down the slippery grade, he retorted, "I *kin* eat biled crow, but I don't hanker arter it."[42]

Wherever temperatures were at zero degrees Fahrenheit or below, and where snow abounded, the chief problem for staging concerns and for travelers was how to cope with penetrating cold and sudden storms. In cold weather drivers were, of course, appropriately dressed in woolens and buckskin underclothing, and they usually wore fur caps that covered the ears, and fur-lined overshoes. But hands were necessarily exposed. When gloves were worn, they were often of silk that enabled the wearer to manipulate his fingers between which the reins were held. For all their care, drivers often suffered frozen feet and hands, and in some cases amputations became necessary.[43]

Blizzards were the demons of all staging outfits, and normally caused drivers to become blinded by snow. Horses, similarly afflicted, would in such situations refuse to budge. When this happened there was no alternative but to try sitting out the storm. But in violent ones, as for example the so-called "great blizzard of 1873" in the northern Great Plains, many stranded stagecoaches and travelers succumbed to the lashing furies of the relentless storm.

One gathers that in general stagecoach travel was more pleasant in retrospect than in actual experience. And yet it offered some delights. There were things of interest to be viewed along the way, and sometimes conversation was lively, amusing, and even scintillating. Jokes were told, news was exchanged not only aboard but at station stops, and there was gaming in abundance.[44] Best of all the stages rolled on, and served well as an essential mode of transportation until finally replaced by the railroad and motor car. The shift from stage to locomotive was not, however, made without tribute to the coach that had given way to a "palace car"—to the "bright stages" that "will soon be dusty, the shining harness rusty, the handsome prancing four-in-hands descending to the position of farmhorses or drafthorses. The overland boys will be scattered."[45] In 1930 the Dodge City *Globe* reported that its city's last coaches were being sold (presumably as items of curiosity) to pay storage bills.[46]

Steamboats on a Vanishing Frontier

*T*he river steamboat performed an inestimable service to the development of the trans-Mississippi West and it contributed immeasurably toward ameliorating the hardships of frontier travel. The Civil War years roughly date the peak of western river steamboat navigation.[1] One could then have viewed in retrospect what had been a remarkable development in water transportation in the West. It was Robert Fulton, the most successful steamboat inventor, who with his associates in 1809 founded the Mississippi Steamboat Company and first secured exclusive navigational rights on the Mississippi River. In 1811 this concern sent what was to be the first steam-powered vessel from Pittsburgh to New Orleans. For two years this trouble-plagued craft chugged in and out of New Orleans and then sank. Whatever skepticism may then have existed, it was not long before the steamboat proved its worth as a public carrier by outstripping such traditional western river craft as flatboats, keelboats, arks, mackinaws, pirogues, and one-way sailboats.[2]

Throughout this period of drastic transition New Orleans retained her triumphant leadership in Mississippi River commerce. With each passing year river and nearby coastal steamboat landings rose from zero in 1810 to 3566 a half century later.[3] And due very largely to its favored geographical location near the confluence of the Missouri and Mississippi rivers, with more than ten thousand miles of navigable streams then at its disposal, St. Louis also emerged as the metropolis and river gateway through which the bulk of western domestic trade and traffic was to pass.[4] So great in fact had this St. Louis commerce become by the eve of the Civil War that its 3149 steamboat arrivals placed it a close second to New Orleans; and in the transportation of steamboat passengers (exceeding one million by 1855) St. Louis had, in fact, far outdistanced its downstream rival.[5] Out of St. Louis there then operated sixty packets and thirty to forty tramp vessels, and it is significant to note that more of these vessels operated between St. Louis and the upper Mississippi and Missouri river points than between this city and New Orleans and other lower Mississippi River ports.

These were the so-called palmy days of packet trade, which the Civil War brought to an end. The war imposed barriers upon Mississippi River shipping. With the outbreak of hostilities steamboats were placed in the service of either Union or Confederate forces, and great losses due to military action occurred.[6] Disrupting as the war was, those most concerned with the river trade were nevertheless mindful, in 1866, of the huge potential of the steamboating business on the Mississippi River and its tributaries. Steamboats then afloat on this river system had an estimated value of sixty million dollars.[7] To be sure, the peak in the passenger service had been passed, but as it turned out steamboating in an ever-changing form continued to play an important role, especially in the western trade.

A postwar upswing did not go unnoticed, even in demoralized New Orleans. There, during and after 1866, a reawakening occurred along the levee, marked by the emergence of new lines equipped with new low-pressure steamers and by a revival of the New Orleans upriver trade, principally with St. Louis. By the end of the 1860s there were six lines offering regular scheduled packet services between New Orleans and St. Louis, along with an indefinite number of unscheduled steamboats plying those turgid waters. The peak postwar year was 1880, when New Orleans registered 2521 landings.[8]

Many of these landings were by steamboats not, however, from Mississippi River ports but from scores of towns scattered along the 986 navigable miles of the Red River of the South and 984 miles of the Arkansas.[9] Long the principal highways to the interior, both these important western tributaries became hosts to steamboats almost as early as did the Mississippi.

*T*HE FIRST STEAMBOAT entered the Red River of the South in 1814. Commercial developments, however, awaited necessary clearing operations that were made during the 1830s by the War Department under the direction of Colonel Henry N. Shreve. By the time of the Civil War, steamboating on the Red had become fully developed. Shreveport, named for the Colonel, had by then become a bustling port and at least thirty landings existed along a nearly five hundred-mile stretch of river above the town. The boats served plantations in the area, but the principal business was supplying military posts. Steamboat navigation on the Red revived after the war, but for a short period only. The advent of railroads in the Red River Valley brought, by 1872, an end to the steamboat in that area.[10]

The beginnings of similar services on the Arkansas River followed those on the Red. The *Robert Thompson*, an early steamer on the Arkansas, reached Fort Smith in 1822, and for a while this military outpost was regarded as the headwaters of Arkansas navigation. But it was not long before a steamboat zigzagged 240 miles further on an upstream course to Fort Gibson within Indian Territory. As in the case of the Red, military supplies constituted the bulk of the cargoes on the Arkansas, and much of this freight moved directly from New Orleans to these interior landings. Steamboat navigation on the Arkansas also continued after the Civil War—in fact, for several years—but a general decline set in in 1868. During the 1870s experiments were undertaken with flatboat tugging, and in this connection Arkansas City, Kansas built in 1878 its first steamboat. Named the *Cherokee*, it saw service towing cargoes into the Indian country. Railroad construction in Kansas during the postwar years ended steamboating here too.[11]

In many respects steamboating on the upper Mississippi and its upper western tributaries constitutes a separate and somewhat distinct history. Ever since 1823 when a sternwheeler, the 109-ton *Virginia*, churned its way in twenty days upstream from St. Louis over the Rock Island rapids and on up to Fort Snelling below St. Anthony Falls at the confluence of the Mississippi and Minnesota rivers, the upper Mississippi and tributaries had been the scene of growing steamer operations. These were looked upon with marked favor in this frontier area, for until the coming of railroads, steamboats provided the main and often only avenues for bringing settlers to the area and for maintaining communication between Minnesota's pioneering communities and the outside world. St. Paul emerged as the headwaters entrepôt. By 1844 steamboats began operating in and out of St. Paul on regular seasonal schedules, and during the period between 1850 and 1862 the number of steamer arrivals and departures climbed from about one hundred to one thousand.[12] These vessels operated at first under various banners and over a variety of routes. From St. Paul steamers connected with various landings along the Minnesota River (especially Mankato) and mainly with such Mississippi River ports as LaCrosse, Dubuque, Galena, and St. Louis. Cutthroat competition had resulted in mergers, the most important of which led in 1866 to the formidable Northwestern Union Packet Line. However, steamboating in that area remained highly competitive until 1873 when Captain W. F. Davidson, a riverman, gained control of virtually the whole business and formed the Keokuk Northern Packet Company.[13]

St. Paul, in addition to reaping the commercial benefits attending the upper Mississippi River trade, was able to exploit an emerging steamboat business on the neighboring Red River of the North. St. Paul's enterprising merchants were quick to grasp a close relationship between the lucrative Red River fur, or "cart," trade and steamboat development. In an effort aimed at dominating, even monopolizing, the Red River fur and other trade, St. Paul's Chamber of Commerce is credited with having actually financed in 1859 the first steamboat operation on the Red. This was done in the belief that such steamboat service—a service that would be international (American-Canadian) in character—would augment the long-established overland trade between the Red River Valley and St. Paul. Until superseded by railroads, this combined river and overland transport system worked successfully. For a decade or more after the Civil War steamboats on the Minnesota River carried goods and people to and from the Red River Valley via St. Paul.[14]

As the number of steamers on the Minnesota River increased, the trend there, as elsewhere, was toward consolidation. With this as an object there was consummated during the winter of 1873–1874 the Red River Transportation Company slated to operate no less than five steamers and twenty barges. But before this decade ended, the railroad had not only come but had conquered less efficient and infinitely more slowmoving steamboats, carts, wagons, and stagecoaches in the Red River Valley of the north.[15] In 1883 a steamboat operator there wrote his cousin: "Times out here have been very hard and it is almost impossible to make collections and to meet even running expenses.... our business is not what it promised to be."[16]

Hard pressed though they were, operators in this northern area held on tenaciously in the face of competition from the railroads. Much of the north-south oriented traffic remained in their hands. "Instead of hindering," as one historian has observed, "the railroads up to 1870 actually augmented steamboating, transporting carloads of immigrants to the various ports along the Mississippi to be carried upstream."[17] When in the 1880s St. Paul and St. Louis were connected by rail, this situation changed. Even as late as 1888, by which time railroads crisscrossed Minnesota, St. Paul's river business records reveal that 1,918,396 tons of freight and 1,438,616 passengers were waterborne.[18] Most of the passengers transported were local and, much as St. Paul's *Pioneer and Democrat* had predicted as early as 1864, most "through passenger trade" had by the late 1880s fallen into the hands of the railroads.[19]

One lone survivor among big-time riverboat operators was the Diamond Jo Line. It had struggled desperately to hold its freight carrying and towing business. To do so it launched and operated some of the most palatial passenger boats ever seen on the Mississippi River; it ingeniously sponsored upriver outings or excursion trips to St. Anthony Falls and urged its patrons to "Avoid the Discomforts of a rail trip" by traveling Diamond Jo. But unhappily these valiant efforts brought by 1890 only red ink returns. By 1911 the Diamond Jo ceased to exist.[20]

*T*HE LONGEST and by far the most important of the western segments of the Mississippi River system was the Missouri. By following the bends this river measured roughly 3100 miles from Fort Benton (Montana), navigational headwaters, to its mouth, located about 23 miles above downtown St. Louis. Steamboating on the "big muddy" began in 1819, four years before the *Virginia* reached St. Paul, but it was not until 1860 that the first steamboat traveled upstream from St. Louis to Fort Benton.[21] From this beginning until the end of the century steamboats on the Missouri encountered many navigational difficulties. Its lower reaches are sandy; its upper, rocky. It is, on the whole, a turbulent, perilous river. The rocky portions are swiftflowing, narrow, and contain rapids. The lower segment is shifting; it has many islands, sandbars, snags, and sawyers. The entire river is subjected to alternating floods and low waters. For these and other disconcerting attributes, among them a constantly changing bed, the Missouri had earned for herself the opprobrious appellation of "harlot."[22] As one old river man commented, "She's a bad actor, that old river: you can't tell what tricks she'll play. Arn't never been controlled yet and never will."[23]

Steamboat operations on the Missouri advanced somewhat in direct relation to developments in the Missouri River Valley and the northern Rocky Mountains: settlement within the state of Missouri, upper Missouri fur trade, military commitments, mining in the Rockies, the Civil War, and postwar settlement on the Great Plains. During the initial stages regular service was confined to the lower, sandy portions of the river, between the mouth and such places as Independence and Fort

Leavenworth. Then with the founding, in the mid-1840s, of Council Bluffs by the Mormons, steamboating passed the mouth of the Platte.

The need for service above Council Bluffs was prompted by both the American Fur Company, which had established Fort Union as a major supply post near the mouth of the Yellowstone River, and by the United States Army, whose activities in the upper Missouri Valley were constantly increasing. During the spring of 1831 the steamboat *Yellowstone*, built expressly for the American Fur Company, left St. Louis for Fort Union but managed only to reach Fort Tecumseh near present Pierre, South Dakota. The very next year the *Yellowstone* paddled on to its goal, and thereafter steamboating between St. Louis and Fort Union became routine.[24]

The heyday of Missouri River steamboating spanned the years 1845–1870, and it was midpoint in this era, 1860, before the American Fur Company's small sternwheeler *Chippewa* managed somehow to propel its way to Fort Benton.[25] By this time the lower Missouri was literally bustling with the constant comings and goings of fifty-nine or sixty regular sidewheelers and two score "transients," which during the year 1859 made more than three hundred calls on Fort Leavenworth alone. So active was this business that the sight of five steamboats making simultaneous landings at ports between St. Louis and St. Joseph was not at all uncommon.[26]

Construction by the War Department of several military installations along the Missouri above Fort Randall (South Dakota) and military engagements with rebellious Sioux augmented traffic during the war period as did also the mining boom in Montana and Idaho. Profits up to sixty-five thousand dollars are known to have been made in one such Fort Benton trip. St. Louis traders, intent upon using their river access to Fort Benton, entered into vigorous competition with west coast traders for a share in these distant inland markets.

Consequently, Fort Benton mushroomed from a tiny shack town into a thriving boat-to-wagon transfer point. Operations on the Missouri were on a more irregular basis than on most other streams, depending as they did not only on the weather but on the depth of water. As a rule boats would depart from St. Louis with breaking of the ice in late February or early March and would arrive at Fort Benton between May and July. Navigation on the upper waters ended about mid-September, when stopped by low water, although under extremely favorable circumstances steamboats might operate until mid-December. Following the Civil War, steamer arrivals at Fort Benton from St. Louis bounded upward, and continued on a high level throughout the decade of the 1860s. Departures for the year 1865 established a record up to that time,[27] and the over-all high point came in 1867 when forty-three light draft steamers (some "double-trippers") disgorged on crude levees of this Montana town ten thousand passengers, eight thousand tons of mining equipment, and seven thousand additional tons of foodstuffs and other goods. It was estimated that five-sixths of all of Montana's mining equipment was carried by steamboats up the Missouri. Passenger fares between St. Louis and Fort Benton ranged from one hundred and fifty to two hundred dollars, one way. Freight rates were fixed by the pound at about twelve cents.[28] From Fort Benton freighters transported the goods overland to designated places. During the year 1866 an estimated twenty-five hundred men, three thousand teams, twenty thousand oxen and mules, and six hundred wagons were engaged in this gigantic operation. Fort Benton managed to retain its role as entrepôt, but not without challenge from such other aspiring upper Missouri places as Ophir at the mouth of the Marias River and Musselshell at the mouth of a stream bearing this name.[29]

Even before the apex of steamboating was reached, St. Louis had forebodings of days to come. In 1865 the St. Louis *Dispatch* admonished the city's merchants that they were "sleeping in fancied security, trusting to its geographical position." St. Louis should, said this newspaper, turn not necessarily away from steamboats, but think seriously about augmenting railroad construction.[30] The truth and wisdom of these words became apparent when east-west oriented railroads centering on Chicago were built and did, in fact, threaten the steamboat trade of the Missouri. Instrumental in breaking the steamboat monopoly was Chicago's Northwestern Transportation Company, owned and operated by the Chicago and Northwestern Railroad. By 1868 goods consigned for Montana were sent over this line from Chicago directly to Sioux City, Iowa, where they were then transferred by steamers, and within three years thereafter most government shipments bypassed St. Louis and went directly by rail to Sioux City for transshipment upstream by river boat. By this time, too, there had come about a marked shift in freight, from Montana-bound mining equipment to military supplies being consigned to up-river army posts.[31]

Changes did not end here. Completion of the Union Pacific Railroad to Ogden, Utah, in 1869 made possible low-cost wagon routes from Ogden, or Corinne, to Montana. Then, three years later, a second west-bound railroad, the Northern Pacific, reached the banks of the Missouri from St. Paul, and the following year this railroad established the river port of Bismarck (North Dakota). Still another rail line, the Dakota and Northwestern, laid out the river port of Yankton (South Dakota). Completion, in 1887, to Helena, Montana, of yet another Pacific-bound rail-road—the Great Northern—all but delivered the knock-out blow to St. Louis' once-lucrative upper Missouri River trade.[32] The shift of the center of upper Missouri River trade from St. Louis to such places as Sioux City, Yankton, and Bismarck meant, among other things, that new companies, new personalities, and even new steamboats would become almost exclusively identified with trade on the "old muddy" above Council Bluffs. Not only did the Northwestern Transportation Company assume prominence during the 1870s but so too did the Kountz Line, the Peck Line, the Fort Benton Transportation Company, and, most important of all, the Missouri River Transportation Company, which was managed by Yankton's capable and enterprising Sanford B. Coulson.

New ports and new management could not, however, withstand the adverse trends in Missouri River shipping. The 1880s witnessed further diminution of the trade. By then additional railroads both reached and followed the Missouri; the mining boom in Montana had become a thing of the past, with a resultant leveling off of Fort Benton trade; and peace with the red men lessened government shipping requirements. By 1885 both Sioux City and Yankton had joined St. Louis in the denouement of this upper-river trade, leaving only Bismarck—far upstream—to carry on a trickling local trade with Fort Benton in grain, groceries, lumber, and hardware. In a small way this trade lasted into the present century. However, for all intents and purposes this exciting era of upper Missouri River steamboating was over when in 1890 the last commercial river steamboat from St. Louis arrived at the all but deserted Fort Benton levee.[33]

Everywhere along the Mississippi and its western tributaries, where steamboating came into direct competition with railroads, victory went to the rails. Nevertheless, steamboats in this area continued to serve where needed as feeders to the railroads and in an increasing manner as necessary adjuncts to a growing barge traffic. For these and other reasons federal government agencies never entirely deserted their interest in or support of river navigation. As late as 1890 there was navigation of one kind or another on forty-five rivers of the Mississippi River system for a grand total of 16,090 miles. Not only does this figure represent a huge increase over that for navigable mileage in 1865 but through federal aid it was slated for a further increase in the future. Even though railroads had won their competitive battle with steamboats, the Mississippi River system would remain as "a balance-wheel which is destined to regulate the railway freight movements of the great interior of the nation."[34]

By "interior" was meant not only the Mississippi but its western tributaries. Not unlike the ubiquitous stagecoach, the river steamer—restricted though it was to navigable streams and lakes—moved ever westward with the advancing American frontier. The bayous of Texas and Louisiana and the rivers of the Lone-Star State shared as well in the steamboating bonanza. Steamboat navigation on the Rio Grande, Trinity, Sabine, Brazos, and other Texas rivers totaled twenty-five hundred miles, all with direct outlets to the Gulf where goods could be transshipped to world markets. Some packets confined their scheduled runs to major river ports, but others maintained regular transit between river landings, coastal ports and bayous, and New Orleans.[35]

The Pacific coast was no exception. Scarcely had gold been discovered in California when the steamer *California* carried the first immigrant Argonauts to San Francisco. And hardly was the Gold Rush under way when the steamer *Pioneer* began taking passengers up the Sacramento River to jumping-off places for the diggings. Soon both the Sacramento and San Joaquin rivers and their respective ports of Sacramento and Stockton became the scenes of intense riverboat activity. The pattern of development there was the now familiar one: fast growth; cutthroat competition; consolidation (in this case by the California Steam Navigation Company); an ensuing period of stabilized operations; and then ultimate decline and extinction because of railroad competition.[36] Before and during the era of consolidation regular steamboat services within California were extended beyond the Sacramento-San Joaquin river system to include San Francisco Bay, the coastal ports, and even the erratic Colorado River.

Steamboat navigation on the lower Colorado followed upon the heels of an 1850 army exploratory mission to determine the feasibility of developing steamboat services between Fort Yuma and the river mouth. Before the 1850s passed, steamboating over this approximately one-hundred-and-fifty-mile stretch of river had assumed a regular schedule, and there had even been some experimental steamboat navigation above the fort.

Initiated as a means of supplying the military at Yuma, other opportunities for trade subsequently developed. Mormons in Utah Territory, in their efforts to import needed supplies, saw in this riverboat trade an opportunity to connect a relatively inexpensive water freighting route with wagon freighting lines from west coast ports. Mineral developments in southern Arizona also served as a stimulant as did the hauling of army supplies and such produce as wool, hides, and pelts, farm machinery, household commodities, newsprint, and general dry goods. So by 1865 an initial period of development emerged into a decade of active steamboating during which one concern, the Colorado Steam Navigation Company, triumphed over its competitors and established active trading between San Francisco and Yuma by offering twelve-day boat service between these two points. During this period annual shipments ranging roughly from one hundred forty thousand to five hundred thou-

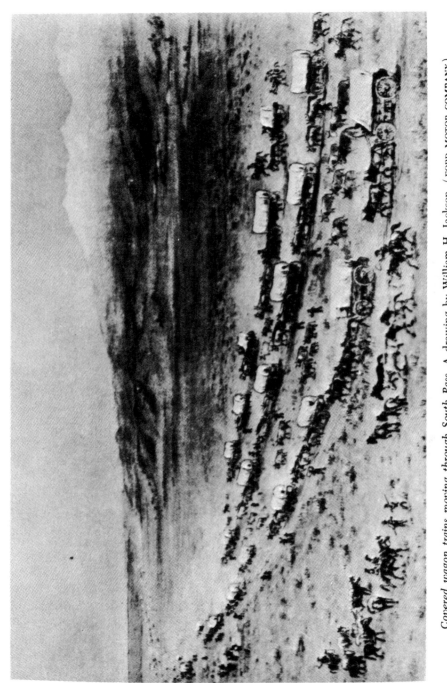

Covered wagon trains moving through South Pass. A drawing by William H. Jackson. (FORD MOTOR COMPANY)

Pembina carts and bois brûlé *drivers in St. Paul.* (MINNESOTA HISTORICAL SOCIETY, ST. PAUL)

(Opposite) *Mountain wagon road in the Pacific Coast area.* (FORD MOTOR COMPANY)

Wagon freighting on the Plains. A drawing by B. Kroupa in B. Kroupa, *An Artist's Tour* (London, 1890). (HENRY E. HUNTINGTON LIBRARY, SAN MARINO)

A Concord stagecoach. (WELLS FARGO BANK HISTORY ROOM, SAN FRANCISCO)

RED COACH LINE.

ALLEN & CHASE, PROPRIETORS.

OFFICE NEXT DOOR BELOW THE AMERICAN HOUSE.

Stages leave St. Paul Daily for Anoka, Monticello, St. Cloud, Sauk Rapids, Little Falls, Fort Ripley, and Crow Wing.

STAGES FOR ST. ANTHONY AND MINNEAPOLIS ARE AT THE LEVEE, AT ALL TIMES, ON THE ARRIVAL OF BOATS.

Stagecoach advertisement in St. Paul City Directory, 1859. (MINNESOTA HISTORICAL SOCIETY, ST. PAUL)

The stagecoach between Salt Lake City and Ophir City. An artist's drawing, from *The Graphic,* London, March 28, 1874. (UNIVERSITY LIBRARY CAMBRIDGE, ENGLAND)

(Left) *St. Paul during the steamboat era.* (MINNESOTA HISTORICAL SOCIETY, ST. PAUL)

(Below) *The St. Louis levee during the steamboat era.* (MISSOURI HISTORICAL SOCIETY, ST. LOUIS)

Fargo, Dakota Territory, head of steamboat navigation on Red River of the north. (HARPER'S WEEKLY, AUGUST 27, 1881)

Steamboat General Meade (1875–1888). Built for the Missouri River trade. (MISSOURI HISTORICAL SOCIETY, ST. LOUIS)

The first temporary Missouri River railroad bridge connecting Omaha and Council Bluffs, 1867. A pencil drawing. (FREE PUBLIC LIBRARY, COUNCIL BLUFFS, IOWA)

Union Pacific Railroad construction train, 1868. (UNION PACIFIC RAILROAD COMPANY)

Construction camp on the Union Pacific Railroad. (ASSOCIATION OF AMERICAN RAILROADS, WASHINGTON, D.C.)

Central Pacific Railroad construction camp, Utah Territory, 1869. (SOUTHERN PACIFIC RAILROAD COMPANY)

Railroad construction operations on the Montana Plain, 1889. (MINNESOTA HISTORICAL SOCIETY, ST. PAUL)

sand pounds reached the upriver terminal. The life span of Colorado River steamboating was in keeping with the pattern elsewhere. It began slowly, had a few years of prosperity, and then, with the arrival of the railroads, came to an abrupt end. In 1877 a rail line built westward from San Francisco, namely the Southern Pacific, reached Yuma, and this event marked the end of what had come to be known as "Arizona's fleet."[37]

Nowhere in the Pacific coast area did steamboating assume the lasting importance that it did in the Pacific Northwest, which, before the coming of railroads, was dependent upon rivers, lakes, and coastal waters as avenues of trade, travel, and general communication. The small (109-ton) Hudson's Bay Company *Beaver* was the region's first steamer. It was brought from England to the Company's Columbia district in 1836, and for many years it maneuvered about the lower Columbia River, Puget Sound, and other local waters.[38] The *Beaver* served well the needs of the "Honourable Company," and it was not until the fur traders gave way to American settlers that steamboating emerged as a full-fledged enterprise in the old Oregon country. Beginning in 1850 and continuing throughout the remainder of the century, locally built and imported steamboats served the growing enterprises in the Willamette Valley-Puget Sound trough, and, importantly, the mining camps within the so-called inland empire. Portages were effected at the Willamette River Falls at Oregon City, and at the Cascades, The Dalles, and Celilo Falls on the Columbia River. Moreover, combination steamer, wagon freighting, pack train, and stagecoach services were established that effectively linked the Columbia River watershed with that of the Missouri.[39]

In this area, also, emerged eventually the problems of overexpansion. The devastating competition attending this situation led to inevitable mergers among which the Oregon Steam Navigation Company, founded in 1860, emerged supreme. The principal figures in this combination, including Simeon G. Reed, John C. Ainsworth, and R. R. Thompson, had all pioneered in the steamboat business of the region; henceforth, acting in concert, they were eventually able to catapult the Oregon Steam Navigation Company into an unrivaled monopoly capitalized in 1868 at five million dollars. When in 1879 Henry Villard purchased this giant steamboat combine as a highly desirable western feeder system to his Northern Pacific Railroad, it was at this dollar figure that the transfer in ownership was consummated. And it was with these new acquisitions that Villard formed the Oregon Railroad and Navigation Company which, as he had hoped, emerged as a profitable rail-ocean and river steamer adjunct to the Northern Pacific following completion of this second transcontinental rail line to the Pacific in 1883.[40]

*T*HESE THEN were the major areas and most significant features of steamboat transportation within the trans-Mississippi West. There were additional streams and lake areas, too numerous to mention, where also the deep-throated whistling of paddlewheelers was a familiar sound. The rise of the steamboat business may be correlated with the advance of settlement and, consequently, public demand. However, steamboat business within any given area shows a pattern of cycles within cycles wherein the volume of passenger business (long distance and local) and freight business (carrying and barge) are differentiated. In the central and lower Mississippi River area the height of steamboat transportation had been attained before the outbreak of the Civil War, and it was in the late 1870s or early 1880s before the peak of steamboating was reached on the Pacific coast. In all major areas, however, the ultimate fate of the steamboat business was affected, if indeed not sealed, by the extension of railroads into the Far West. During the first two decades following the Civil War steamboat tonnage dropped roughly one-third.[41]

In the last analysis the general public sought greater speed and lower rates; competitive success depended to a large measure on these two major factors. The extent to which the river traffic could hold out against the inroads of rails depended to a great extent upon government support of river improvement projects and administrative organization and general efficiency of steamboat businesses. It also depended on how well it could cope with the directional flow of freight and people. During the postwar years the increased demand for east-west transit could, of course, be met more readily by man-made rails than by steamboats obliged to follow natural water routes.[42]

Doomed as steamboats were in most areas in the West, the Tenth Census (1880) *Report on Steam Navigation* nevertheless reveals how tenaciously this mode of transportation on the trans-Mississippi West frontier fought against extinction. At this late date there still operated on the lower Mississippi River system (exclusive of ocean vessels but including all navigable tributaries) 315 steamers totalling 48,303 tons, valued at approximately three million dollars. The ships employed 5665 men, carried an annual passenger load of 212,417 persons (exclusive of ferry passengers) and 1,276,972 tons of river freight (exclusive of upper river traffic).[43] The *Report* gives comparable figures for the upper Mississippi system and other areas as well. Figures for the upper Mississippi include not only the Missouri but such eastern tributaries as the Wisconsin, Iowa, and Illinois rivers. In this area 366 steamers were in operation in 1880, measuring 83,918 tons, and valued at more than three million dollars. Persons employed numbered 7824. The passenger load there was 341,371 (not counting ferry passengers) and the freight movement (counting barges) amounted to 3,500,035 tons for this year of 1880.

And finally, out on the Pacific coast during this year there were 319 steamers in operation: 178 in California, 89 in Oregon, and 52 in Washington Territory; they measured 97,004 tons and were valued at $6,477,500. These west coast inland steamers carried 300,752 nonferrying passengers, plus 838,019 tons of inland steamer freight.[44]

By the end of the century steamboat passenger services had all but ended, but steamboat freighting and barge traffic continued. Rivalry between the rail lines and the steamboats for the freighting trade was, of course, carried on in deadliest competitive fashion. As the battle raged on, the steamboats lost out relatively, but in actual freight tons carried they first lost and then after 1885 regained and even surpassed lost business on some streams. The fact that the steamboats failed to gain in the new and ever-rising transportation markets posed a serious threat to the once-thriving ports of New Orleans, St. Louis, and St. Paul; and only to the extent that these cities developed their rail facilities were they saved from complete economic debacles.[45] In spite of the rise of the barge towing (or pushing) business, the transportation sceptre had by the 1880s passed irrevocably from those who ran the boats to those who controlled the rails.

The passing of the river steamboat at this time did nothing that belittled the role this vessel had played in the everyday economic and social lives of frontier peoples. During its heyday the business of steamboating had assumed patterns in the trans-Mississippi West that in some respects were uniform, and in other ways variegated. First of all, the steamboat generally carried both freight and passengers. Steamboats designed essentially as freighters usually had accommodations of a sort for a few passengers, and, conversely, the most palatial floating palaces took freight aboard. Each of these types of river craft, so long pleasant and familiar objects on western waters, had its unique features, but architecturally all steamboats had much in common.

At first little distinction could be made between ocean-going and river-type craft. But gradually river boats were engineered and fashioned to meet the special weight, draft, over-all shape, and power requirements of river commerce. The trend was toward increasingly flat hulls and toward greater lengths in relation to widths. This situation pertained especially to the upper Missouri River operations where the water was often shallow. Capacities ranged roughly from one hundred to five hundred tons, and sizes varied correspondingly. Lengths normally ranged from 132 to 216 feet; widths from 24.3 to 36.2 feet. Long after river passenger service had passed its peak, however, some river steamboats tended to grow in size. Reputedly the largest on the Mississippi, if indeed not in the world, was the *Great Republic*. Her burden was 2600 tons, her cabin, 275 feet long, and she provided sleeping berths for 200 passengers.

While many river steamboats had low, sitting-duck profiles, the general appearance of a fully developed western river steamer was one of a top-heavy, grossly stacked ship, seemingly devoid of a hull. As one writer aptly phrased it: steamboats appeared to sit on the water and glide over it rather than cleave through the water as did ocean-going steamers.[46]

Much of the boiler equipment, machinery, fuel, and freight was placed at the near-water level, or open main deck. The passenger-carrying cabin deck (technically called the boiler deck even though no boilers were ever placed there) comprised the second level. The texas on the hurricane deck towered above. Guards, namely extensions of the main deck providing extra buoyancy, protruded from the hull line to where they were flush with the outer edges of sidewheeling paddles.[47] On extra-large boats a pilot house, or wheelhouse, surmounted the hurricane deck, and huge, double, smoke-belching stacks completed the multistoried structure.[48] Most river steamers were sidewheelers, although those used in the shallow upper reaches of many rivers, especially the upper Missouri, were mainly of the sternwheeler variety. Said one scrutinizing river traveler, Julian Ralph:

> These river boats—and I include all the packets that come upon the Mississippi from its tributaries—are more like the work of carpenters and house builders. It is as if their model had been slowly developed from that of a house-boat, or barge with a roof over it. . . .

Ralph, who had an artist's eye for detail, was not impressed with the quality of steamboat construction; basically it was flimsy. Too often sheathing was used where solid timbers were called for; doors and windows were, he said, "hung on without frames around them—all loose and thin." The cost of such a boat ranged from about seventy to one hundred thousand dollars.[49]

Within this basic framework existed a wide range of differences. A westbound passenger departing from New Orleans, or some other lower Mississippi river port, would in all probability have begun his journey aboard a luxury boat and ended it on a simply constructed sternwheeler where scant attention would have been given to the comfort and amusement of passengers. Even though the days of "floating palaces" on the Mississippi were passing by 1865, such boats nevertheless continued in service for a decade or more following the Civil War. To many observers they represented a sort of decadent splendor that was exemplified by an abundant display of gingerbread ornamentation. Cabins usually extended through the full length of the main deck with staterooms on either side. Here mirrors were used to accentuate the effect of great length and breadth. Highly skilled artisans produced ornamental lathe, jigsaw, and carved woodwork used in interior finishing. Belgian weavers contributed a profusely floral design to the Wilton carpeting placed on cabin and stateroom floors. Painters generously applied gilt in the adornment of pillars, arches, cornices, and bars. Oil paintings, figured tapestries, and mirrors were hung in profusion upon interior walls. And from crystal chandeliers oil-burning lights cast a soft glow on the faces of relaxed patrons of the palace steamboats.

Service aboard these magnificent vessels was of the best. Comfortable chairs were available in the forepart of the cabin for gentlemen; aft were sofas and "Yankee rocking chairs" for ladies.[50] Drinks were available at bars at all hours and a sumptuous fare, including entrées with French names, was served in the dining saloon. Generally, the between-meal indulgences varied with individual tastes. Some of the men resumed drinking at the bar, some gambled or did both; those who overcame their social inhibitions danced with the ladies and indulged in affairs of the heart and flesh.[51]

Even though the facilities aboard palace steamers were, as Mark Twain said, "finer than anything ashore," not all found it entrancing. "Take it all-together," wrote an Australian luxury-class passenger, "the journey from St. Louis to the mouth of the Mississippi is one of singularly little interest."[52] In any event the so-called golden age of steamboating passed with the Civil War. Following the war, services of this kind continued, but to a decreasing degree. When in the late 1880s Charles Beadle visited New Orleans he observed that fancy multitiered river steamers were still in existence, but, he added, they "will not much longer be seen, as the railways are running them off." The largest boats, he said, "have not moved a wheel for at least two years."[53]

Such plush cabin class accommodations as had graced Mississippi River passenger service were usually not available either on the western tributaries or on the west coast, nor were they within the reach anywhere of the great mass of the traveling public either on or west of the Mississippi River. Not only westbound emigrants but many established western settlers as well were obliged to travel second class or as deck passengers, and, accordingly, in simpler style. In fact, conditions of travel, excluding cabin class, were often lamentable. Deck passengers in particular were obliged to find accommodations where best they could on or about the freight, or, as was sometimes the case, with livestock. Then, as the emphasis on passenger service gave way to freight carrying, a deterioration of palace boat service gradually set in. In any event, not all river steamboats offered sumptuous and exotic accommodations and fare, and on many river craft passengers were obliged to endure innumerable inconveniences and to accept plain food, simply served. The English traveler George T. Borrett wrote about his travels aboard a small steamer that there was no evidence of cooking aboard, but "You may stake your fortune, that where there are Americans, there will always be plenty to eat."[54]

On the smaller river craft passenger accommodations were often uncomfortable and inadequate. As the Californian J. Ross Browne reported, movement was often accompanied by a "convulsive vibration all over the boat." and by "strong smells of grease, whisky and machinery." But even at its worst the traveling public in the trans-Mississippi West preferred the steamboat to the stagecoach as a mode of travel. They even preferred sleeping on benches and grain sacks on the main deck and eating a simple but plentiful fare to suffering bruised heads, swollen legs, and general starvation aboard the coach "jumbling across the prairies."[55]

*I*N CHOOSING a mode of travel, those electing the steamboat could scarcely have been unaware of the many frustrations and potential dangers aboard this craft: possible boiler explosions and fires, collisions with other boats and snags, ice, groundings on bars, fog, storms, and general panic brought on by any one or a combination of these causes. Here the actual records tell a story of loss of lives and severe injuries counted in the hundreds.[56] Not all accidents, however, were the fault either of nature or of steamboat operators. Many casualties were caused by fights aboard ship, by persons being pushed overboard, and by suicides.

The chronicle of losses on the lower Mississippi during the winter of 1865–1866 is illustrative.[57] During two days, December 16, 1865, and January 12, 1866, a total of eleven ships were crushed by ice. Later in January a steamboat operating out of Memphis exploded, killing 130; during February an explosion and sinking occurred at New Orleans, four boats burned on the St. Louis levee, and another on the Red River. An explosion sank a steamboat near Buck Island killing twelve persons, and ice sank another on the Platte during March. In April five additional vessels burned on the St. Louis levee.[58] Comparable catastrophes occurred in west coast steamboating. Reports on ships' losses due especially to explosions and fires constitute many tragic pages in the marine history of this area. And much as the Far West wished to view its inland steamers with pride, the press of the area could scarcely resist referring to paddlewheelers as "floating coffins."[59]

"There is no doubt in my mind," wrote a St. Louis newspaper correspondent, "that the terrible loss of life upon the lower [Mississippi] river the past ten years is the main cause of passenger travel leaving the river and taking to the railroads."[60] The *Alta California* speculated, "What an immense fleet would astonish the observer, [could] all the steamers that have been burned or sunk ... arise fresh and lifelike as once they were." Seldom if ever, added this newspaper, was a steamer saved if once on fire.[61]

Some of the ordinary, routine annoyances attending steamboat operations, especially upriver navigation, are clearly revealed in captains' logs. The log of a round trip by the steamer *Lillie Martin* between St. Louis and Fort Benton in 1865 serves as illustration. The 210-ton *Lillie Martin*, a sternwheeler, set out from St. Louis April 6, 1865. She left in a heavy wind, taking nine days to reach St. Joseph, "where we learned of the assination [sic] of President Lincoln and Secretary Seward." There then followed several days' delay while cleaning out the boilers (a recurring job on the "big muddy"). When above Nebraska City, the *Lillie Martin* tied up for the installation of a new rudder while passengers and crew cut cordwood. On May 18 the cargo was lightened to permit progress over shallows, a process that called for further unloading at deeper water and a return for the cargo left behind. Due to fear of Indians when traveling through wooded areas, the steamer tied up at night. Other entries indicate stops because the machinery was out of order; to unload cargo at Fort Union; to hold funeral services for a dead passenger; and still another due to running onto a bar. Running aground, a very common occurrence on a meandering shallow stream, was handled in several ways. One was to wait patiently for rising water to lift the boat; another was to jostle the vessel in the hopes that such action would loosen the prow from the sands; and a common remedy was "sparring," or the use of long poles to pry the boat loose from its unintended mooring. For all its many interruptions the little *Lillie Martin* reached its destination and returned to St. Louis July 23.[62]

Many other riverboats encountered snags, or sawyers (fallen trees rooted to the bank), in their upstream journeys. What could happen if a steamboat hit a snag is recounted by a ship's officer to his wife. "I was down on Deck collecting from Deck Passengers," wrote William M. Tompkins in describing the wreck of the *Florence* on the upper Missouri. "I felt a slight jar, but had no idea that we had struck a snag." Then came the command from deck hands for all to come forward, whereupon came panic, the like of which, wrote Tompkins,

I never witnessed in my life. Men left their wives, Mothers their children and in fact everyone seemed perfectly crazy. I ran back when we were sinking and found three little children all alone, not another person being with them. I snatched up the two smallest & started on the run, but the other little one rather beat me running on.[63]

Most feared of riverboat disasters were those caused by explosions and fire. They were due largely to inadequate engineering and to negligent riverboat captains who did not observe the safeguards at their disposal. But both the captain and his passengers appear to have nonchalantly accepted the general philosophy expressed by one ship's clerk "...if she blows up, we'll all go to where we belong, together. Them that sleeps over the boilers'll get thar first—that's all."[64] Newspapers of the river cities appear likewise to have treated such disasters with casualness. When the *City of Memphis* exploded with such force that the entire forward part of the ship was hurled in splinters into the water in early June 1866, the New Orleans *Daily Picayune* reported briefly that the river was "absolutely blackened with forms of the dead and the struggling."[65] It is not uncommon to find a steamboat explosion noted in briefest terms, such as the report that the *Corona* exploded killing the captain, officers, several members of the crew, plus "Eight rousters." Only one body was recovered. The cause of the explosion was unknown.[66]

During April 1875 the ship *John Kyle* caught on fire in New Orleans. She was cut loose from her moorings and like a floating torch drifted into a second ship, the *Bodmann,* which in turn caught on fire. When the *Bodmann's* hausers were cut, she drifted in flames into the *Pittsburgh,* setting this ship ablaze. Passengers jumped overboard, and, reported the New Orleans *Daily Picayune,* "The surface of the river was dotted with human beings, some swimming, some grasping at planks, appalling screams and cries rending the air."[67]

Collisions involving two steamboats were also frequent, and these accidents were usually followed by recriminations. For example, the skipper of the *Colonel Chapin* blamed the collision on the skipper of the *Kentucky,* and was quoted as saying: "If I had the power, I would hang the captain and pilot [of the *Kentucky*] to the first tree I could find."[68] A compilation of riverboat accidents of all kinds for the period 1865–1910 lists approximately twenty-five hundred mishaps, many of which were multiple accidents on a given vessel.[69]

Even though accidents, and especially explosions, occurred most frequently during speedy departures rather than during full-speed travel on course, steamboat racing serves to illustrate the river captains' propensity for recklessness—recklessness often aided and abetted by passengers and crew. Wherever there were fleet steamboats—whether on the Mississippi, Missouri, Sacramento, or Columbia rivers—captains took pride in being able to streak past rivals at close quarters and then dart across the bows of lagging ships.

Speed, however, was not all important in western river steamboat transportation, for no boat could compete with the speed of the railroads. As a rule steamboats chugged along leisurely, called at towns large and small and at plantations and landings seemingly without connection with populated areas; and when night came, they tied up ashore.[70] Sometimes they pulled into landings to take on and discharge passengers and cargo; at other times they pulled ashore chiefly to take on wood for fuel. River towns and steamboats were largely dependent upon each other. A change in course that left a river town without a levee indeed left such a place high and dry.

Steamboats often lent a gay, social touch to otherwise isolated river communities. A riverboat, anchored for the night and with a band aboard, often provided meals, dancing, and as one wrote, some "all night" gaiety for townspeople. Reciprocally, the town's saloons and billiard parlors lured the weary roustabouts and others who worked the boats. Even their distinctive bullfroggish whistles offered welcome sounds to river people. It must not, however, be construed that steamboats were hosts to general ribaldry and licentiousness. Most captains ran well-ordered ships, many of them reserved Sundays for religious observance aboard, and some even refused to travel on the Sabbath. In these and many other ways steamboating was not just a form of transportation; it contributed to a way of life not only for the men who worked on the boat but for those ashore with whom western river steamboats came into contact.[71]

For all its services, river steamboating had its limitations as well as its assets. It marked a tremendous advance over wagon freighting and coaching where the existence of water made steamboat operations possible. Each mile of river was conquered only by heroic efforts. High bluffs and thickly forested areas made serviceable landings inefficient if not prohibitive in places where much needed; waterfalls, rapids, swiftness of current, unnavigable stretches of rivers and tributaries, and manmade bridges placed handicaps and obstructions in the way of this form of transportation.[72] Despite these obstacles, steamboats became important adjuncts to the Rocky Mountain fur trade and to mining frontiers within the trans-Mississippi West. Steamboats also made possible the movement of supplies and agricultural produce in many areas on the frontier. While facilitating the exploitation of the trans-Mississippi West, they accelerated the frontier process.

◁ **7** ▷

Railroads Blanket the West

*I*n 1865 there were 35,085 miles of railroads within the United States; of this figure only 3272 miles lay west of the Mississippi River. Only one line, the Union Pacific-Central Pacific, was in the process of spanning the great unsettled West between Omaha and Sacramento. Any discerning person who at the close of the Civil War may have examined data on railroad construction trends could not, however, have escaped certain simple, clear-cut facts: for three decades railroad building had been an accelerating process; rail networks had been moving relentlessly westward; and, therefore, the trans-Mississippi West faced an inevitable postwar railroad boom. Moreover, Americans were fully aware that large-scale railroad building, such as was in prospect for the West, tended to speed up the frontier process.

American railroad history had, indeed, been spectacular. Adults in 1865 could readily have recalled a quick succession of events that followed Englishman George Stephenson's successful development of an operational locomotive—the "Rocket": construction in 1828 and after of the westward-oriented Baltimore and Ohio Railroad; the emergence of giant trunkline systems; and the linking by rail during the 1850s of the Atlantic Ocean and the Mississippi River. Accompanying these tangible demonstrations of man's ingenuity and industry had been heard the demanding calls for the construction of a railroad to the Pacific.[1]

When in 1857 celebrations commemorated the completion of the Baltimore and Ohio Railroad to St. Louis, Mayor Thomas Swann of Baltimore expressed a feeling of national accomplishment by saying to the celebrants: "Look at the great enterprises . . . the New York and Erie, the Central Pennsylvania, and the Baltimore and Ohio Railroads. What country on the face of the earth can boast of such enterprises . . . ?" And then, expressing as much confidence in the future as he had pride in the past, the mayor asked his jubilant listeners if this were going to satisfy the restless spirit of the American people. "No, no." The westward projection of the railroads had then merely reached St. Louis, a junction, as it were, on their "giant march" that could be halted only "by the distant shores of the Pacific."[2] Spurred on by a succession of railroad conventions, by other forms of private and governmental promotions, and by an incessant public clamor for more and still more railroads, builders were in fact striving to reach that goal. Not only had the Congress by 1864 made definite provision for the construction of Pacific railroads but the then existing mileage west of the Mississippi River[3] provided the material evidence that railroads in this region could operate successfully.

*I*T WAS 1854 before the first eastern railroad line reached the Mississippi River, but the slowness with which this objective was attained in no manner thwarted railroad promotions and construction west of that giant waterway. St. Louis, ever eager to forestall Chicago's threatening commercial hegemony over the West, had been a prime mover in initiating railroad construction within Missouri. The first line undertaken was the Pacific Railroad, later to become the Missouri Pacific. Begun in 1851, the line achieved its river-to-river goal in 1865 when, 283 miles distant from St. Louis, it reached the important Missouri River ports of Independence and Kansas City. A rival, the Hannibal and St. Joseph Railroad (later to become a part of the Chicago, Burlington and Quincy Railroad) had meanwhile, in 1859, become the first Missouri railroad to make the 209-mile westward crossing of the state.[4] Numerous other lines of varying lengths combined to give Missouri a prime, pivotal position in trans-Mississippi railroad mileage in the closing year of the Civil War.[5]

Iowa's prewar railroad beginnings differed but slightly from those of Missouri either in magnitude or aim. Earliest proposals for Iowa go back to the 1830s, but due to lack of adequate leadership and capital it was midcentury before the Davenport and Iowa City Railroad Company, the state's first, was actually organized; and in 1856, under a different label, service on this line began. By then Iowa was in the grips of a veritable railroad fever. The cities of Burlington, Davenport, Lyons, and Dubuque were designated starting points for what resembled a four-entry river-to-river race westward across the state. By 1865 six separate railroads had each built between seventy-five to 221 miles of track; four others, less than this mileage.[6] The Panic of 1857 and the Civil War had slowed the progress of these roads and it was not until the postwar period, when there occurred a rush to establish connections with the westward-building Union Pacific Railroad at Omaha, that this formidable program was fully realized. One of the commanding figures in these early developments was John I. Blair, whose lines were designated "Blair Roads." Peter A. Dey and Grenville M. Dodge, both destined for prominent roles in constructing the Union Pacific Railroad, enhanced their skill with the transit on Iowa soil during this early period.[7]

Ranking third among the states of the trans-Mississippi West in prewar railroad mileage was Texas. In 1852 (sixteen years after issuance of the first charter by the Lone Star Republic) construction of the state's first railroad, the Buffalo Bayou, Brazos and Colorado Railroad (or "Harrisburg Railroad") was commenced. Harrisburg was the starting point from which this line headed toward Richmond on the Brazos River, with Alleytown on the state's navigable Colorado River as its ultimate goal. Twenty miles of track were the product of the first year's construction efforts, and late in 1853, regular service (second of its kind west of the Mississippi) began.[8] By 1865 this line had not only reached its objective but there had been constructed a citizen-financed tap to Houston. A later and separate enterprise known as the Houston Tap and Brazoria connected Houston with Wharton in the prospering lower Colorado River Valley.

Throughout this nascent period Texas promoters were ever eager to connect their cluster of thriving, but still isolated, frontier municipalities with New Orleans, where the sentiment was reciprocated. At the Crescent City the New Orleans, Opelousas and Western Railroad aspired to tap the Texas Gulf, and in the Lone Star State the Texas and New Orleans Railroad (again with Houston as a starting point) began building eastward, seeking consummation of this highly desirable union. By the time of secession, the Texas road had reached Beaumont on the lower Neches River, the New Orleans line had come to Berwick's Bay, and the intervening distance, still very much a rugged frontier area, was being covered by stagecoach. The fall of New Orleans brought further construction to a halt, and not until 1881 (and then only after much political maneuvering and reorganization) was the gap filled and through passenger traffic offered between Houston and New Orleans.

Texas had no dearth of typically frontier railroad projects, and before war brought them all to a standstill, a total of eleven companies had laid portions of track. The Galveston, Houston and Henderson Railroad had by 1865 built seventy-two miles between the cities mentioned, the San Antonio and Mexican Gulf connected Victoria with Matagorda Bay, and the Houston and Texas Central connected Houston (the emerging railroad center) with Hempstead on the upper Brazos.[9]

Louisiana's ventures in railroading go back to 1830, to the very beginnings of American railroads, and in 1833 there was organized a concern that became the west side Red River Railroad. But not until 1851 was a serious effort made to build a western line, the above-mentioned New Orleans, Opelousas and Great Western Railroad, with Texas as its immediate—and San Diego as its stated—goal. In 1857 this westbound road—eighty miles of it—reached Berwick's Bay, where it was stranded, still aiming for Houston, when war broke out. When in 1873 G. W. R. Bayley published his substantial history of Louisiana railroading in the New Orleans *Daily Picayune*, he concluded what Louisiana had been saying for four decades: "We need a trunk line of railway to Texas. . . ."[10]

Not only Louisiana but also Arkansas shared in the early railroad excitement within the Gulf-Delta area. By 1865, however, Arkansas had produced but thirty-eight miles of one line—Memphis and Little Rock—then connecting Marshall, Arkansas, with Shreveport.[11]

Far to the north the pioneers of Minnesota Territory had felt their isolation most keenly during the 1850s; they had, therefore, sought railroads that would connect them with the main arteries to the south and that would help to entice settlers in their frontier areas. First attempts at railroad building in Minnesota Territory proved abortive, and although Congress provided for land grants and for the location of routes, Minnesota's 213 miles of rail extant in 1865 had all been built during the last three years of the Civil War.[12]

In Kansas Territory the first chartered railroad (1855) was the Leavenworth, Pawnee and Western. Of the five lines chartered during this period the L.P. & W. was the only one that began construction before the war's end.[13] Territorial Nebraska's first venture into railroading was the direct outcome of federal legislation and the organization of what was to become the first transcontinental railroad. The 122 miles of track laid within its borders by 1865 had been west from the capital of Omaha. A far western counterpart of this transcontinental project accounts for most of California's 214 miles.

Founded in 1852, the Sacramento Valley Railroad (Sacramento to Folsom) was to be California's first. This line, like other small mushrooming railroads in California, was destined for eventual absorption into the Central Pacific, or into what was eventually to become the Southern Pacific Company. Oregon's meager nineteen miles of railroad in 1865, the first being wooden portage tramways at the Columbia Cascades, were but a sign that even in this distant northwest corner of the nation locomotive fires were being kindled.[14]

*A*S MATTERS STOOD in 1865, railroads had already become well rooted on settled portions of trans-Mississippi soil, and most of them were designed for extensions westward. They owed their origin to factors familiar to the nation as a whole. Both the Panic of 1857 and the Civil War had disrupted earlier efforts at construction. The end of hostilities, however, brought not only a resumption but a veritable boom in railroad building in the West. The most distinctive and ambitious of the postwar projects were to be the realization of plans earlier conceived: to connect major eastern trunk lines with major western railroads either in operation or under construction; to seek and obtain water outlets; and to push with all haste the building of new railroad lines to the Pacific.[15]

Those who were able to capitalize upon the opportunities for railroad construction in the trans-Mississippi West could profit immeasurably by the judicial and legislative pathways that, by 1865, had been cut for them. Chief Justice Isaac F. Redfield of Vermont greatly clarified the legal status of railroads in his able work entitled *The Laws of Railways*, published in 1867. Justice Redfield made clear the range of permissible or legal contractual arrangements; he pointed out the ordinary powers of a railroad company not otherwise restricted by its charter or the laws of territory or state (and these were considerable); he spelled out the meaning of "prerogative franchises." Moreover, of utmost importance to builders, Justice Redfield made clear the meaning, rights, limitations, and obligations pertaining to *eminent domain*, a feature recognized in Roman law and one legally and widely exercised in the United States.[16]

It was one thing to possess favorable legal guide lines; it was another to find actual ways and means to finance the construction of such ambitious railroad projects as those proposed for the trans-Mississippi West during the *post-bellum* years. Much depended not only on what capital could be raised but on who would pay the bills. In this category, too, precedent had been established by 1865. Before the end of the Civil War most conceivable fund-raising schemes had been tried. They fell into two major, but not mutually exclusive, classifications. One of these was to secure government aid in all its forms—federal, state, county, township, and city; the other was to secure private investment capital from the sale of securities at home and abroad.

The legal patterns followed in the West were not unlike those established in the East. Both federal and state governments granted charters and enacted enabling legislation, but it was usually to the states, if such existed in the areas concerned, that promoters first applied for the rights to build railroads. State governments were also solicited for financial aid in the form of land and money grants, state-secured bonds that could in turn be sold or exchanged for other bonds that could be floated, usually at discounts on the public market, and for the authorization to sell preferred and common stocks and issue stock certificates to would-be investors.[17]

As a rule, local governments had no public lands to offer, save perhaps plots for yard and station sites, but some of these subordinate units were nevertheless authorized under state law to make financial commitments to railroad companies. Such aid was often prompted by pressures on the part of railroad promoters who held out the kiss-of-death prospect of bypassing aspiring municipalities reluctant to contribute their "proper" share in aiding railroad projects. In some states there existed rather stringent financial restrictions pertaining to such procedures, but local units of government were usually allowed considerable latitude in assuming financial obligations with regard to railroad projects. In Iowa, for example, counties were extravagant in their issuance of seven to ten percent twenty-year bonds, the return from which was used for railroad construction. To vote "no" in such bond issues was to vote "no confidence" in the future of one's locality. It was common practice in Iowa for a county of relatively modest population to vote bond issues totaling as much as $200,000. Then strange things often happened. In Cedar County where $50,000 in bonds had been voted in support of the Lyons Iowa Central Railroad a judge issued a goodly portion of these bonds in advance of any construction of the road. The result was disastrous; the railroad was not built and the promoter, with bond money in hand, vanished.[18] In Iowa and elsewhere there was a delayed shock associated with state and local aid in the form of bond issues. Due dates inevitably arrived, and even if railroads failed in their obligations, the local citizenry had little chance to escape payments of their obligations. Attempts at evasion were generally viewed with staunch disapprobation by the courts.

*S*TATE AND LOCAL aid to railroads came to an abrupt and painful intermission induced by the financial Panic of 1857. States that either forbade financial aid to private corporations or that imposed stringent debt limitations were fortunately spared some of the embarrassments involving default. The tragedies incurred by the panic were to have a salutary effect in the future upon most states; once burned, local lawmakers became increasingly reluctant in matters pertaining to state and local aid to railroads during the post-Civil War era.

The story of western railroad development was, however, not confined to state and local communities. Even as early as 1820, before the advent of locomotive-driven railroads, a Baltimore engineer and the designer of the Washington Monument, Robert Mills, advocated the construction of a railroad between the Missouri and Columbia rivers. Such a road, Mills predicted, would make possible a coast to coast crossing of the continent in sixty days. As a result of expanded trade with China during the mid-1840s, agitation for a Pacific railroad moved immediately from the dream stage into the realm of practical and earnest planning. One imaginative individual seeking to tie a Pacific railroad project to trans-Pacific traffic was Asa Whitney, a New York merchant. Whitney made firsthand investigations of market prospects in China and concluded that a transcontinental railroad would provide enormous economies in the conduct of oriental trade. The Whitney plan called for the construction of a railroad from the Great Lakes to the mouth of the Columbia—a proposed gateway to the Orient—and he proceeded to memorialize Congress with a view toward realizing this goal.

First looked upon as immature, it was not long before Whitney's scheme had followers, each with his own special plan and route for extending rails to the Pacific. George Wilkes was one such proponent, John Johnson and Isaac I. Stevens still others. Perhaps the most avowed advocate of the Pacific railroad idea was the powerfully influential Senator Thomas Hart Benton of Missouri. Early in 1849 Senator Benton, who heretofore had favored the interests of river transportation above those of railroads, actually introduced into the Senate a Pacific railroad bill calling for the construction of a rail line to run from St. Louis to San Francisco. Senator Benton favored the sale of public lands as a means of financing the project.[19]

The war with Mexico, the subsequent Mexican Cession, development of a mineral empire, and the accelerated flow of migrants westward into frontier areas increased the need and desire for not one but possibly two or three Pacific railroads. It might even be said that during the 1850s the frontier population clamored for such railroads, and rarely did a congressman from the West make a speech without at least a passing reference to the desirability of wedding the oceans with ribbons of iron or steel. A series of railroad conventions were held during the decade; newspapers championed the mounting crusade; memorialists submitted pleas to Congress; and then finally, in 1862, Congress passed and President Abraham Lincoln signed a measure designed to accomplish this major national objective.

Such gigantic undertakings as this legislation envisaged called for a large measure of federal aid. Whatever hesitancy had emerged on state and local levels about public support of railroads did not prevail in Congress. Beginning with a federal grant of public land in 1850 to the Illinois Central Railroad, Congress not only embarked upon but continued to pursue a policy of doling out public lands and loans to railroad companies.

If at midcentury congressmen showed relatively few scruples about making public land grants to railroads, for reasons of selfish sectional interests they were hesitant about agreeing upon the exact location of a Pacific railroad. Nevertheless, during March 1853, Congress passed a Pacific Railroad Survey Act. This called for the impossible by instructing the Secretary of War to conduct, within a ten-month period, an extensive survey of the trans-Mississippi West in an effort to find practical railroad routes. The surveys were undertaken by the United States Corps of Topographical Engineers who diligently, if not confidently, conducted their searches over belts lying between the forty-seventh and forty-ninth parallels, the thirty-eighth and thirty-ninth, along the thirty-fifth, and over the extreme southern routes. Important as were the findings, the survey failed to settle the question of which was the best route; it also failed to help a sectionally split Congress decide which of several practical routes it was willing to endorse for Pacific railroad construction. It remained for later surveys undertaken by individual construction companies to determine the precise routes railroad lines were to follow.[20]

This dilemma over where to locate a Pacific railroad was resolved by the withdrawal of southern states from the Union. Measures dated July 1, 1862, and July 2, 1864 (the second act amendatory to the first), provided for the incorporation, under federal laws, of the Union Pacific Railroad empowered to construct a Pacific-bound railroad between the Missouri River (the exact point designated by President Abraham Lincoln as Council Bluffs, Iowa) and the base of the Rocky Mountains. The same acts authorized the Central Pacific Railroad Company of California, incorporated under the laws of that state, to construct the western portion of a Pacific railroad from Sacramento, California, eastward to connect with the Union Pacific. Still another act dated July 4, 1864 provided for the construction of a second railroad connecting Duluth on Lake Superior with Puget Sound and to be known as the Northern Pacific Railroad.

By these acts the federal government provided generously for the railroad companies concerned, not only with respect to land but also in direct financial aid. In the case of the Union Pacific-Central Pacific, a two hundred-foot right-of-way and ten alternate sections of government domain on each side of the right-of-way were granted to the builders for each mile of line constructed. The act provided as well for a government subsidy equal to $16,000 per mile of road constructed over the relatively smooth plains country; double this amount through the irregular and undulating region between the Rocky and Sierra Nevada mountains and in the western foothills of the Sierras; and then a whopping $48,000 for each mile built through the Rockies and through the Sierras.

To be sure, this subsidy was not an outright gift; rather it was given to the companies as a second mortgage loan. Payment to the companies was to be made following completion of stretches of road and given or paid in the form of United States interest-bearing bonds that could be sold and were redeemable by the United States Treasury after thirty years. Moreover, the government asked for some special privileges in use of the railroads to be built, and demanded "fair and reasonable rates." The companies concerned were not to be allowed to keep all receipts from government hauling; payments for services rendered to the federal government were to be applied on bond and interest payments. The railroad was to be of uniform, four feet eight and one-half inch, gauge and was to meet other prescribed specifications. Finally, Congress reserved the right to modify, even repeal, these acts. This legislation represented the best bargain that the prospective railroad builders could obtain from Congress. There were some drawbacks, but these acts enabled the builders, in addition to tapping other sources, to obtain more than ample funds for the construction of a Pacific railroad. With money in hand the builders set men and road-building equipment into motion and in 1869 completed what with eastern connections became the first railroad line to cross the United States.[21]

Plans for the second transcontinental railroad, the Northern Pacific, were also approved by Congress. The company was authorized to build an east-west rail line between Lake Superior and Puget Sound, with a branch line down the Columbia River to Portland, Oregon. It too was to receive a generous land grant, but no cash subsidy was awarded. The federal land grant was, however, double that of the central line, namely, a four hundred foot right-of-way and alternate sections within forty miles on each side of the track. In 1869 a joint resolution of both houses of Congress authorized a bond issue secured by the company's physical assets.[22] The initial construction efforts of this railroad were disappoint-

ingly meager. Not until 1869 when placed under the control of Philadelphia's distinguished banking firm, Jay Cooke and Company, did track-
laying move ahead at a formidable pace. By the time Bismarck in Dakota
Territory was reached in 1873, Cooke's banking house failed and an
ensuing financial panic brought construction to a temporary halt. It
remained for Henry Villard, a newcomer in New York's moneyed circles,
not only to gain control of the Northern Pacific Company but to push
construction to completion in 1883.

A NOTABLE exception to government-nurtured railroads in the
West, of which there were several, was the Great Northern. Headed by
the shrewd and indomitable James J. Hill, this line pushed west from
St. Paul along an extreme northerly course to reach Puget Sound a decade
behind its Northern Pacific rival. Before the tide of track-laying had
run its course, the Pacific Northwest was also to be served by the Oregon Short Line—Union Pacific's extension from Granger, Wyoming, to
Portland, Oregon; by the Southern Pacific through a northern extension
of its California system; and, finally in 1909, by the Chicago, Milwaukee,
St. Paul and Pacific Railroad, or Milwaukee Line.

Important in the successful operation of these lines was access—
directly or indirectly—to Chicago. For this reason these Pacific railroads either sought connections with or actual control of one or another of such vital Chicago-oriented systems as the Milwaukee, the
Rock Island, and, of course, the Chicago and North Western.[23]

Meanwhile the Southwest was not being overlooked, either by railroad promoters and builders or by a munificent federal government.
Under an 1866 act, Congress bestowed land grants upon the federally
chartered Atlantic and Pacific Railroad, which was to construct a rail
line westward from the Missouri and Arkansas rivers (actually Springfield, Missouri). The route was to pass through Albuquerque, reach the
Colorado River, and there establish a junction with the Southern Pacific
system.[24]

The Southern Pacific Railroad Company had been incorporated in
1865 under the laws of California by the builders of the Central Pacific
Company. It had been formed to combine and provide unity to a number of southwestern railroads either purchased or constructed by the
Central Pacific. Under terms of the Railroad Act of 1866, Congress
bestowed generous land offers on the Southern Pacific on the condition
that this concern would extend its railroad from the San Francisco Bay
area to Los Angeles and thence east for the contemplated junction with
the Atlantic and Pacific at Needles on the Colorado River.[25]

For a time it appeared that this two-pronged approach toward establishing a truly southwest railroad system was about to be realized, but before the critical junction could be established the Southern Pacific Company changed its mind. Rather than tie in with the Atlantic and Pacific line, thereby opening its west coast empire to competitors, the Southern Pacific Company (thanks largely to more generous concessions in the land grant acts) decided on a drastic new course. It chose instead to make its own and separate crossing of the Colorado at Yuma, build track eastward across Arizona and New Mexico, and acquire the vital Galveston, Harrisburg and San Antonio Railroad leading to the highly prized objective—New Orleans. On January 12, 1883 this gigantic project was completed, thereby bringing San Francisco and New Orleans into direct rail communication with each other. Los Angeles was, of course, linked with this system, and the trains servicing New Orleans and the City of the Angels were to travel over what the company decided to call its "Sunset Route."[26]

To many Americans of that day, the Southwest seemed well- if not overstocked with cactus-enshrouded rail lines. But no such views were entertained by the Atchison, Topeka and Santa Fe Railroad Company. This concern had been incorporated and chartered in 1859 with Cyrus K. Holliday as its first president. After a slow start it had, by the end of 1872, pushed from Topeka to the western boundary of Kansas and had closed its eastern gap separating Topeka from the vital Missouri River port of Atchison. Having thus met its initially prescribed goal it was with renewed courage that in his 1872 annual report the company's president was moved to write that "at no great distant day" the Atchison, Topeka and Santa Fe would also reach the Pacific.

This was a prophecy realized gradually during the late 1870s and early 1880s. This railroad achieved significant goals. It surmounted Raton Pass and pushed on to Albuquerque. It obtained an embattled lease of the newly constructed north-south–oriented narrow gauge Denver and Rio Grande Western Railroad[27] within the Rocky Mountains, carrying with it access to both Denver and Salt Lake City. And, finally, after long and bitter opposition from the Southern Pacific Railroad, the A.T. & S.F. reached Los Angeles in 1887.[28]

Railroad construction on such a breath-taking scale was not accomplished without many financial vicissitudes and changes in management and controls. By all odds the leading figure in the financial manipulations of central plains and southwestern railroads was Jay Gould. Many railroad lines, long and short, fell under his control, among them the Kansas Pacific, the Union Pacific, and a conglomerate rail network in the Southwest, the Missouri Pacific. Out of the Missouri Pacific Gould molded the Wabash, which anchored in St. Louis. Linked together, these varied holdings gave Gould vital rail line holdings from Nebraska south to the Gulf.[29]

By the 1890s this great, in one sense magnificent, race to cross and crisscross the West with glistening rails of steel (not to mention telegraph lines) began to taper off. In 1890 Congress, by passing a land forfeiture act, brought to an abrupt end a twenty-one year period of conspicuous generosity on the part of the federal government toward railroads. The great boom subsided and hard times set in. As a consequence many persons both in and out of political circles not only asked how and why this act was passed but what would be its ultimate meaning to the West and to the nation as a whole.

One important element in this and other speculation about western railroads concerned the enormous acreages of public lands granted to railroad construction companies. During the period beginning with the Illinois Central grant in 1850 and ending with the Texas and Pacific award in 1871, Congress had directly granted over one hundred thirty million acres of land (not counting forfeitures) to western railroads; it had advanced sixty-four million dollars of government bonds; and it had transferred additional acres of land to states, some of which also ultimately was acquired by railroads. In all, seventy-nine railroads received either federal or state land grants, or both. In addition, the return on the sale of stock certificates and of the railroad lands and monies raised from other forms of private investment, mortgage loans, and credit had made this great construction feat not only financially feasible but personally remunerative to some builders. Great fortunes had in fact been acquired by the building, and not the operating, of railroads.

The era had begun in 1865 with 3272 miles of railroad west of the Mississippi River; it had attained a mileage of 72,473 by 1890.[30] Five railroad lines by 1893 connected the Pacific with the major networks of the East. At that time the railroad map of the prairie lands looked like a tangled fisherman's net; that of the Great Plains, Rocky Mountain, and Pacific coastal regions then revealed a generally east-west orientation with the exception of one continuous line of rails stretching from Los Angeles to the Canadian border.

*T*HE FULL IMPACT of this mighty track-laying operation was at once immeasurably great and profound. The heavy burden of bonded indebtedness incurred in the railroad construction programs added greatly to the financial stringencies of an already hard-pressed agricultural West. Farmers who had looked upon railroads as their highway to economic salvation became, due mainly to high freight schedules, disillusioned and thoroughly disgruntled. Likewise, western townspeople discovered that the coming of railroads did not always fulfill their dreams of achieving metropolitan stature. Many frontier towns had been unceremoniously bypassed by the railroads and for this reason often died of economic stagnation. Communities directly served by the railroads, and that grew as a result, discovered that benefits were at least partly offset by stock losses incurred by individual citizen investors and in meeting, through heavy taxation, railroad bond obligations.

In general, all major segments of western society—merchants, farmers, and laborers—came to feel abused by the railroads. Through the press, from the pulpit, political, even academic, rostrums, and in many other ways these grievances were vehemently expressed. The railroad companies were accused of condoning dishonest practices; they were charged with capitalization and bonded indebtedness in excess of actual cost of construction. They were blamed for exacting excessive rates, practicing favoritisms and discriminations, and for operating as monopolies indifferent to public interests.[31]

Somehow the railroads weathered the storms of protest. Viewed in retrospect, it is apparent that, for good or ill, it was chiefly railroad companies that promoted the West, facilitated the migration of great numbers of settlers from home and abroad, and were the first to penetrate and spearhead settlement in the plains country. In short the railroad, more than any other single agency, brought to a rapid end the frontier of the trans-Mississippi West. It was this process that ex-Governor Alva Adams had in mind when he addressed a trans-Mississippi West Congress at Omaha in 1891: "They talk of the frontier. Where is the western frontier? It has been driven westward until to-day it is lost upon the broad bosom of the Pacific."[32]

◁ 8 ▷

Laying the Track

*T*o professional railroad men and engineers in the year 1865 there was nothing new or bewildering about building railroads. The 35,085 miles of line constructed in the United States by the end of the Civil War had provided experience in engineering and operating techniques. Even the prospect of building railroads fantastic distances across Indian-infested western plains and over towering mountain ranges was accepted with considerable equanimity once the matter of who would pay the piper had been agreed upon. "Where a mule can go, I can make a locomotive go," supposedly boasted one railroad engineer.[1] Thus it was with confidence and self-assurance that general contractors, surveyors, engineers, and workmen entered upon their tasks of building 69,201 miles of railroad in the trans-Mississippi West during the quarter century following the war. This achievement—a distinctly American one—remains unsurpassed. The Poors (H. V. and H. W.), in their *Manual of the Railroads*, observed retrospectively in 1900 that "the construction of railroads in this country in the past seems to have proceeded in great waves" that had become "the absorbing passion of our people."[2] The wave after the Civil War was certainly the largest and probably, too, the most exciting.

The most important aspect of this intensive engineering and muscle-flexing activity was the laying of track. Not only did this operation assume formidable proportions west of the Mississippi River, but there, more than elsewhere, construction work became an integral part of frontier life.

In the vanguard of all railroad construction operations were the surveyors. In many respects they were the unsung heroes of this great western drama. They usually worked in small parties, and, although technically under military guard in acutely dangerous areas, their work was hazardous. The formal survey of the Union Pacific Railroad was begun under the direction of Peter A. Dey in 1863 and concluded by General Grenville M. Dodge, who replaced Dey after a three-year period. From Dodge one learns how this difficult task was accomplished:

> Each of our surveying parties consisted of a chief, who was an experienced engineer, two assistants, also civil engineers, rodmen, flagmen, and chainmen, generally graduated civil engineers but without personal experience in the field, besides axmen, teamsters, and herders.

In each party there were about twenty-two men, all armed.

Normally about ten soldiers to each survey unit were required to cope with Indian threats and attacks. Every mile, recalled the general, had to be run within "range of the musket." In spite of these precautions, Indians succeeded at times in killing, scalping, and wounding members of the surveying parties. They succeeded as well in running off with livestock, literally by the hundreds. The work, nevertheless, moved rapidly forward. Men toiled from dawn to dusk. Chiefs reconnoitered ahead of the main party staking out the course, designating cuts, grades, and stream and river crossings.

In a sense, the surveyors' work was never-ending. Even after completion of main lines, the railroad companies remained constantly on the lookout for lower and better grades and for new and more feasible routes. During the late 1880s *Scientific American* wrote about these railroad surveyors as persons who were still exploring, living in tents, and working the year round in the field. Two teamsters and a cook who doubled as hunters provided these skilled workers with the necessities of life.[3]

In the case of the Union Pacific Railroad, the route followed contained some surprises. Ground was broken at Omaha. The route followed the Mormon Trail on the north of the Platte River, for reason of cost bypassed disgruntled Denver and Salt Lake City, and ultimately reached Promontory northwest of Ogden, Utah Territory, 1034 miles from its starting point. Recalled Dodge in later life,

> When you look back to the beginning at the Missouri River, with no railway communication from the East, and 500 miles of the country in advance without timber, fuel, or any material whatever from which to build or maintain a road, except the sand for the bare roadbed itself, with everything to be transported, and that by teams or at best by steamboats, for hundreds and thousands of miles; everything to be created, with labor scarce and high, you . . . ask, Under such circumstances could we have done more or better?[4]

In any event, it was on December 2, 1863, at the small but gloriously ambitious town of Omaha, that ground for the Union Pacific was officially broken. The occasion was marked by a brief ceremony held on the town's levee. There was a "solemn and impressive" prayer. The governor and the mayor turned the first spadeful of dirt amidst the roar of artillery fire and "shouts of the assembled multitude."[5]

*T*HE CONSTRUCTION WORK was done by contractors and subcontractors. Great portions of the grading and all the track laying were supervised by General John Casement and his brother Dan. War-hardened veterans and youthful immigrants (many of them Irish) made up the main work force, which at the peak of operations totaled about ten thousand men. About as many draft animals as men were used and, in addition, supply trains and countless numbers of wagons, scrapers, picks, and shovels. Grading was carried as far as a hundred miles in advance of the track laying and, as Dodge correctly noted, most supplies for this phase of operations had to be hauled by wagon freight from Missouri River ports. There were exceptions. The Mormons contracted with both the Union Pacific and Central Pacific to construct roads, and there were places en route where native timber was sawed into ties.[6]

The surveying and grading of the Central Pacific route from Sacramento eastward presented many similar, but also some different, problems from those of its eastern counterpart. Theodore D. Judah, the company's first chief engineer, and the one who located this route, explained his objective thus: he was looking, he said, for "nearly a direct line to Washoe, with maximum grades of one hundred feet per mile." By proceeding from Sacramento along the divide between the Bear and North Fork of the American rivers via Dutch Flat, eastward through Summit Valley, up the Truckee River, and then over Donner Pass Judah found the route he wanted. This route was used by the Central Pacific Company and was extended across the broad, bleak Nevada and Utah deserts to form a junction at Promontory with the Union Pacific Railroad.

The Central Pacific broke ground on the Sacramento City levee January 8, 1863. Eight hundred miles to the east lay the junction; 7042 feet above sea level stood the formidable Donner summit. The tremendous task of surveying and building this railroad was turned over to Charles Crocker and Company (a concern owned by the Central Pacific's "Big Four"), and Charles Crocker, superintendent of construction, personally directed the work.[7]

The Central Pacific Railroad Company showed remarkable resourcefulness in meeting its varied and weighty construction problems. Every pound of steel and rolling stock had to be shipped by sea to San Francisco and forward by riverboat to Sacramento. The Civil War added to the normal perils of sea voyages. About ten months were involved in shipping from the eastern industrial and commercial ports to where these goods were needed along the banks of the American River.[8] But the goods were ultimately, although at high premium, procured. Ties and pilings came from the California forests.

The company likewise solved its critical labor problem by employing about ten thousand Chinese coolie workers, obtained from the San Francisco Bay area and directly from China. Known as "Crocker's pets" these queued sons of the Orient were paid $26–$35 per month in wages (without board), and they used dugouts, tents, and shacks for lodging. They were regarded by construction superintendents as a sober lot, due mainly to the absence of saloons in the Chinese camps. "Don't ask me how we kept them out," said engineer J. H. Strobridge. "It has always been a mystery to me." Chinese coolies did not, however, preclude the use of white workers who, certainly in the work of surveying and grading, contributed significantly to the main labor force. Early in 1865 there appears, for example, the newspaper report that "Between four and five hundred white laborers, and fifty Chinamen, are now employed in grading the track of the Pacific Railroad."[9] But as the actual construction work progressed and in time reached its peak, the willing and hardworking Chinese became the ones upon whom Charles Crocker chiefly relied. Before the end of 1865 the Chinese workers numbered seven thousand; the white workers, twenty-five hundred.[10]

Tunneling proved the most difficult and costly task in preparing the Central Pacific roadbed. For example, in order to obtain the desired grade on the seven thousand-foot ascent over the last hundred-mile stretch to the Sierra summit, no less than ten tunnels of varying lengths had to be blasted and chiseled through solid granite mountain ridges and the debris hauled to gulches and depressions where fill was required. It took thirteen months alone to cut the 1650-foot summit tunnel, and as one company official reminisced, "it would have taken much longer but for the fact that a Scotch scientist, [James] Howden came to camp to make nitroglycerine, the first made in America."[11] When at last the Central Pacific roadbed had been completed, more than five hundred miles of its length exceeded five thousand feet in elevation, of which two hundred miles were above sixty-five hundred feet. This situation alone posed still another serious engineering problem—how to cope with snow through this high-altitude area. The answer was snowsheds, and in time no less than thirty-nine miles of snowsheds were built with forty million board feet of lumber.[12]

The experiences of surveying and preparing the first Pacific railroad beds were matched by other western lines. When in 1870 the Northern Pacific construction program got under way, surveyors were likewise supplied with rifles, and military guards were utilized. This company also employed large numbers of Chinese, especially in the construction of the western segment of its line. Chinese workers likewise contributed significantly toward the building of both the Southern Pacific and the Atchison, Topeka and Santa Fe. One Santa Fe employee recalled at a later date how "pigtailed" Chinese worked "side by side with border ruffians and broken men from Europe." To these workers were added wartime bushwhackers, "state-prison graduates," and desperadoes. Many Mexicans were employed, especially on the Southwest railroads. Nor were all Indians at war with the railroads. Many red men, and their squaws as well, were employed as section hands. They worked "with nonchalance and ease," wrote an observer, but as a rule the squaws outdid their mates in wielding crowbars and sledge hammers. White employees were thought to have been the most restless of all worker groups and tended to drift, hobo style, from one railroad construction project to another.[13]

By far the most complicated and formidable phase of railroad construction was the actual laying of track. Even though suitable methods of track laying had been developed in the East and were utilized to a large extent in the West, the construction operations on the Pacific railroad undertakings took on a highly distinctive character. For one thing, many of the western projects assumed gigantic proportions; and in spite of their size, they were basically frontier enterprises. Construction work was carried forward across immense unsettled areas; many of the workers, such as the Mormons, came from frontier settlements; and the rough life in construction camps, and constant conflicts with the Indians, probably left little doubt in the minds of all workers that they were participating in a frontier enterprise.

In the case of the Union Pacific two years of construction operations were carried on before rail connections were finally established between Omaha and the East. Until then, as noted by a New York *Evening Post* reporter, "every stick of timber, every spike and rail" had to be brought to Omaha under "extreme handicap and at costs above foundry prices,"[14] But in time these supply problems were greatly ameliorated. Not only did eastern rail lines, by November 1867, establish direct connections with the Union Pacific but this company exploited all possible natural resources along its route. The few available cottonwood trees in the Platte Valley and cedar trees in the mountains were cut and by a scorching, or "burnetizing," process were made suitable for use as ties. These softwood ties were not very durable, but by interspersing every fourth one with imported oak or chestnut ties, the company managed to meet government requirements. Rock quarried and crushed in the mountainous portion of the route was likewise used in construction operations.

Track laying by the Union Pacific Railroad Company was to be done methodically. By the time the 1864–1865 shipping season closed there were on hand at Omaha enough rails to lay eighty miles of track; also four locomotives, thirty platform cars, and several freight and passenger cars; a quantity of coal, bars of iron, and, of course, foodstuffs. By the winter of 1865 Omaha was transformed and, states a local chronicler, the Union Pacific had already "produced a transportation revolution in the Platte Valley."[15]

*I*NITIALLY the track-laying force consisted of about one hundred teams and a thousand men, but this number was, as indicated, increased tenfold before this giant enterprise was finished. The men were a hardy lot. They were divided into units strung out along a hundred-mile stretch of prepared roadbed. The chief of each unit was almost invariably an ex-army officer of the Union service. The men were well armed and the unit officer took special pains to organize and even drill his men in preparation for surprise Indian attacks. But their main function was to lay track.

Ties, rails, and other needed equipment were hauled into position by wagon teamsters, usually using the rail grade for a road. At first these supplies were taken off the Omaha waterfront, later from the end of a completed section of railroad to which point the material had been hauled by locomotive-pulled flatcars. Those who set the ties into position and laid and spiked the rails worked with impressive precision. Once the roadbed was scraped smooth and leveled off, gangs distributed and set the ties and plates; then another gang seized and transferred a given number of rails from the flatcars to horsedrawn wagons. When at a desired area, twelve men, working in unison with a command, would grab a rail from the wagon, carry it to location, and with the shouts of "halt!" and "down" proceed to place it where needed. Thereupon gangs of spike drivers and bolters completed a step in the process. Then at the further command "On with another!" the operation was repeated—four rails to the minute, three strokes to the spike, ten spikes to the rail, four hundred rails to the mile—eighteen hundred miles to San Francisco. Follow-up crews leveled and ballasted the track with dirt or gravel, and as these finishing touches were completed another portion of the track was ready for use.[16] At first a good day's work produced one mile of track, but at the height of the construction period, 1868–1869, it was not unusual for the Union Pacific workers to lay six to seven miles of track in one day.

The work of a construction crew was also hard and rough. The men worked long hours, at times from dawn to dusk, and not without danger to life and limb. And this was for $2.50–$4 daily wages. Indian attacks were recurrent, and casualties were suffered on both sides even though the company possessed an ample arsenal for repelling most redskin sorties. In 1868 General John S. Casement reassuringly wrote his wife from the "End of the Track": "The Indians are on the Rampage Killing and Stealing all along the line. we dont apprehend any danger from them[.] Our gang is so large."[17]

There was something magnificent, and something sordid, too, about this whole construction operation. Nearly all who witnessed it seemed moved and impressed by this synchronized, onward-moving spectacle. An "Anvil Chorus," wrote one reporter, is

> playing across the Plains . . . —21,000,000 strokes and this American marvel will be done. . . . Sherman, with his victorious legions, sweeping from Atlanta to Savannah, was a spectacle less glorious than this army of men, marching on foot from Omaha to Sacramento.[18]

By and large, construction workers lived in portable villages or camps. Most of these were at or near the ends of the tracks and usually consisted of a string of boxcars equipped with bunks in, on top, and underneath where workmen slept. To these were added eating cars, tents, and portable shacks, in which such high priority wants as food, clothing, liquor, women, and gambling were satisfied. Company officials made an effort to provide substantial, though not elegant, fare. Buffalo meat was a staple article of food, as were also bacon, hard-tack, beans, and coffee. Food was served systematically but not always with regard for sanitation. One stationary dining tent consisted of long tables and benches. Tin plates were securely nailed to the tables. After one group of men had eaten and departed an attendant with a pail of water and a mop "swabbed out" each plate in rapid succession and thus prepared the tables for the next round of eaters. " 'If we don't nail 'em down they'll pile one plate on another and take up too much room. This way we kin crowd em in,' " said the man with the mop.[19]

*C*HARACTERISTIC of many frontier mining camps and to a degree cowtowns, men worked hard, ate fast, and, especially on Saturday nights and Sundays, drank and brawled with avidity. "The usual saloon and depravity were in every camp," recalled one laborer on the Kansas Pacific Railroad, "and never failed to take a toll of human life. . . . The gun was in evidence everywhere and was freely used."[20] Corinne, Utah Territory, the last "hell on wheels" on the Union Pacific, had nineteen saloons, several dance halls, and, according to one count, no less than eighty *nymphs du pavé*, who in the West were better known as "soiled doves." When murder and general lawlessness went out of bounds (considerable latitude was allowed), vigilance committees were formed, suspects were rounded up, given a "jury" trial, and hanged.[21] When as happened with great rapidity railroad construction moved forward into new areas, end-of-track towns shifted correspondingly to advanced locations.

In the 1880s Ripley Hitchcock, a free-lance correspondent, visited some of the most rugged, if indeed not toughest, frontier railroad construction camps. These were part of the Denver and Rio Grande operations through the Gunnison Canyon and valleys on the Salt Lake City extension. The men, wrote Hitchcock, had been shipped into the area in gangs. Many of them were professional tramps who had been solicited through employment agency advertisements. Hitchcock first came to Kezar, Colorado, which he described as "a group of board shanties with canvas roofs, a wretched huddle of groggeries and boarding tents." But then Kezar had already been left to languish while new "terminal cities" had in turn taken its place. Hitchcock described how in Black Canyon materials and about four hundred men had been lowered by ropes down steep canyon walls and in this state of suspension were literally carving out a roadbed. When six o'clock came, men scrambled onto cars to be hauled to their "hotel on wheels." Even before the cars came to a halt, these famished and "begrimed" workers, men of many nationalities, dashed wildly to their food tables. Toilet, wrote Hitchcock, was a trifling matter; they could wash in the morning. Not until their lusty appetites had been satisfied did the men relax by smoking their pipes, playing cards, and perhaps patching their tattered clothes. Then to their bunks to end a day of what was "a hard cheerless life."[22]

The climax of each Pacific railroad construction project was, of course, the much awaited driving of the last, and at times golden, spike. In fact, the entire nation anticipated the ceremonies that were to observe the completion of the Union Pacific-Central Pacific Railroad in 1869. In this particular case the general public had long been noting the progress each company had been making toward joining the two lines. These operations had been viewed, and rightly so, as a race. As stated by the Sacramento *Bee* early in 1869,

> The contest is between two great Corporations as to which shall construct and forever own most of this national highway. . . . They are coming together now on the home stretch and each is using the whip and spur to hasten forward everything connected with construction.

Once, toward the end, the Central Pacific Railroad Company won a ten-thousand-dollar wager with its rival by laying 10.6 miles of track from sunup to sunset with a one hour halt for lunch, and, by accomplishing this feat, set an all-time world record in track laying.[23]

Finally May 10, 1869 was designated as the day the two lines would join at Promontory Summit, a place located in a waterless natural bowl fifty-six miles west of Ogden, Utah. From Promontory back east to Omaha then lay 1085 miles of Union Pacific mainline track; west to Sacramento there were 690 miles of Central Pacific mainline track, a grand total mileage of 1775. No less than three different dates for the completion ceremony had been set due to uncertainties about the arrival time of Union Pacific officials. But when May 10 was finally decided upon, arrangements were made on short notice. A feature of the preparations was a Western Union Telegraph Company nation-wide telegraphic hookup for announcing the news that the last spike had been driven.[24] When the appointed day arrived, the spectators on hand numbered between five and six hundred persons. Among the officials and notables present were Leland Stanford, Thomas C. Durant, Grenville M. Dodge, and Sidney D. Dillon. Present also were the chief engineers, and conspicuous in this assemblage of hardened promoters, construction engineers, workers, soldiers, newspapermen, and hangers on, was the Reverend Dr. John Todd, correspondent for the Boston *Congregationalist* and New York *Evangelist*. Most of the workers, the men who had brought the track to the junction point, had already been dismissed or shifted to other jobs. Those who remained were to lay the ties and rails preparatory to driving a "last spike" by company officials. Only one of five United States infantry companies, presumably assigned to take part in the ceremony, has been identified as having been on hand. The number of women reported present ranges from one to twenty, but a photograph shows two persons definitely identified as women. Over twenty newspapers were represented there, each by one or more reporters.

In making arrangements for this ceremony workers brought the tracks of the respective companies to within two rail lengths of each other, the closing of the gap to be part of the ceremony. Materials for this last section were placed in readiness on May 10, and at eleven o'clock that morning Chinese workers leveled the last few feet of roadbed and completed all work except placing and spiking the last tie. By then trains from the two lines were approaching, and the Central Pacific's wood-burning "Jupiter" No. 60 and the Union Pacific's coal-burning No. 119 moved into position at each side of the gap. The spectators now gathered closely around this focal point—so close in fact that not all, including re-porters, who have given their firsthand impression of the event, could see what was going on. Certain facts appear well corroborated. Two gold spikes from California, one combination gold and silver spike from Ari-zona, and one Nevada silver spike were accepted for driving into a last ceremonial polished laurel tie by Stanford and Durant. Other ceremonial spikes are referred to as having been on hand but they were not used in the ceremony. Two silver mallets were ready for the principals to use in tapping the spikes into prepared holes. Coiled around Stanford's mallet was one of the two telegraph wires used in the nation-wide hookup; the other wire was attached to an iron spike.

When all was in readiness, Stanford took a position on the north side of the track, Durant on the south side. At the appropriate time the Rev-erend Todd opened the ceremonies with a two-minute prayer. At the conclusion of this invocation, the telegraph operator sent this message on the nation-wide hookup: "We have got done praying. The spike is about to be presented." At 12:45 p.m. Durant and Stanford each received ceremonial spikes and each in the order given tapped them into prepared holes in the laurel tie with their mallets. (Some say the spikes slid into the holes without being tapped.) This act having been performed, these spikes were removed and an ordinary tie was substituted for the laurel one, and at 12:47 Stanford and Durant drove the wired iron spike into position with the wired sledge. Both men missed their blows, but some-how a connection of the telegraphic wires was established and a three-dot message "Done" was received by a delighted nation. There were cheers and picture-taking as the two engines touched noses, and on the last laid rail champagne effervesced.[25]

Many other interesting and verified details have been preserved for posterity; many, too, are shrouded in myth. It is known that Stanford spoke briefly about the future lowering of rates. The ever-imaginative General Dodge was reminded on this occasion of Columbus. "This is the way to India," Dodge is reported to have said.[26] Durant's palace car was, wrote one correspondent, "the scene of mirth and good humor in which the two Casements vied with each other in fun making. Champagne was quaffed, which even the telling future may never reveal."[27]

*W*HAT HAD BEEN the occasion for a relatively mild, formal ceremony at Promontory Summit was to be the signal for spontaneous celebrations in many cities throughout the nation. Sacramento, Omaha, Chicago, New York City, and San Francisco were noted as among the places that gave expression to rejoicing. San Francisco had expected the completion date on May 8, and this being Saturday proceeded to celebrate in "magnificent style" as originally scheduled. There were parades, bonfires, rocket firing, and speeches, and an unplanned event was a runaway team down Jackson Street that collided with a carriage, throwing the occupants to the ground. In New York City a special service marking the occasion was held at Trinity Church; in Omaha there were speeches acclaiming the great feat as "one of the gifts of Providence to this side of the continent"; in Philadelphia bell ringing was widespread;[28] and at Virginia City, Nevada, the celebrants looked back upon their observance as more long-lasting than those of bigger places—it began on the 8th and was still going on by the 11th.

In Chicago, where vested interest in the Pacific railroad was intense, the celebration was "spontaneous and general." The *Tribune* reported that a procession seven miles in length passed a given point over a two-hour period. Fifty thousand people lined the route of march on Michigan and Wabash avenues, and the event could be compared only with the occasions that marked the completion of the Erie Canal and the laying of the Atlantic cable. It brought home to every mind, said this newspaper, that " 'Peace hath victories no less renowned than war.' "[29] But what to the *Tribune* seemed most important was: "In short, the completion of the Pacific Railroad will soon be seen to add fifty per cent to the value of all property in Chicago, and largely to the worth of every farm in Illinois."[30] Such pronouncements were as venom to St. Louis, arch-competitor of the city by the lake. St. Louis also had its celebration and in the words of its press:

> Let everybody listen to the fire bells today, and hear the last spike of the Pacific railroad driven home.... Soberly considered, this transcontinental highway is the most marvelous work of human hand....[31]

Construction of the Union Pacific and Central Pacific railroads was generally regarded as a major engineering feat. The construction methods of succeeding lines, accordingly, differ more as to time and place than in ways of building rail lines to the Pacific. Completion of the first Pacific railroad does not stand alone as an event stirring general public interest. Many other celebrations were held in the trans-Mississippi West throughout the post-Civil War railroad building era. Vitally interested cities believed that direct connections with a Pacific rail line would greatly affect their destiny; they felt that such a link would transform their obscure communities into places of tremendous growth and prosperity.

Such, for example, was the feeling that prevailed in St. Paul and Minneapolis when in September 1883, the Northern Pacific Railroad likewise reached the Pacific. The twin cities viewed the completion of this railroad as the most meaningful event of all in their histories. A celebration held at St. Paul on September 3, 1883, featuring a hundred thousand flags, 725 decorated wagons, and forty-three hundred participants, including Northern Pacific's president Henry Villard, President Chester A. Arthur, Carl Schurz, and Generals Ulysses S. Grant and Philip H. Sheridan, offered the best advertisement possible. As St. Paul's *Pioneer Press* viewed it:

> With the completion of the Northern Pacific, the Northwest welcomes the dawning of the day of longing and of vision. . . . The Northern Pacific fastens its magic girdle about a smiling continent, and the struggle of years is ended and the guerdon won.[32]

And as one of St. Paul's local historians observed, it all paid off magnificently. Immediately thereafter an "ever memorable" boom began and within four years St. Paul's population had doubled and the city's material wealth had increased "many fold."[33]

In the case of St. Paul, celebrations were held in advance of the actual finish day in order to take full advantage of the presence of the notables and officials scheduled to participate at the gold spike ceremonies to be held September 8. This place was to be Gold Creek (scene of the first discovery of gold in Montana) in Hell Gate Valley near the summit of the Rocky Mountains. As at Promontory, the gold spike was a symbol; the real one was a rusty iron spike presented by Indians as a token of white man's supremacy. The ceremony there was attended by a large group of hitherto unfriendly Indians whose cries of "Grant! Grant! Grant!" (the only name with which they were familiar) were somewhat disconcerting to the main speaker Villard. When the ceremonies were finished the official party moved on toward Puget Sound, while the Indians carried on in holiday spirit; they held a powwow, had dog soup, and did some horse racing.[34] Other places along the route joined in celebrating, and, like St. Paul, looked upon the completion of the Northern Pacific as a good omen.

Thus as each major line was completed the people directly concerned rejoiced. The building of these western railroads had been in a very real sense frontier enterprises; they were, by and large, gigantic thrusts into and across the heretofore unsettled domain. But the completion of these railroads was viewed, and rightly so, as an abrupt shift from archaic modes of transportation and travel to methods that were new and up-to-date. Within this context it may be said the completion of these huge enterprises hastened immeasurably the end of the trans-Mississippi West frontier.

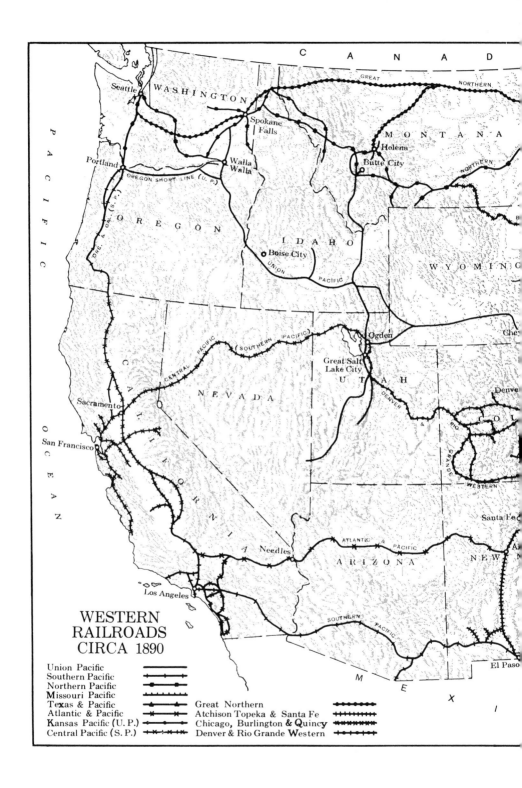

WESTERN
RAILROADS
CIRCA 1890

Union Pacific	
Southern Pacific	
Northern Pacific	
Missouri Pacific	
Texas & Pacific	Great Northern
Atlantic & Pacific	Atchison Topeka & Santa Fe
Kansas Pacific (U. P.)	Chicago, Burlington & Quincy
Central Pacific (S. P.)	Denver & Rio Grande Western

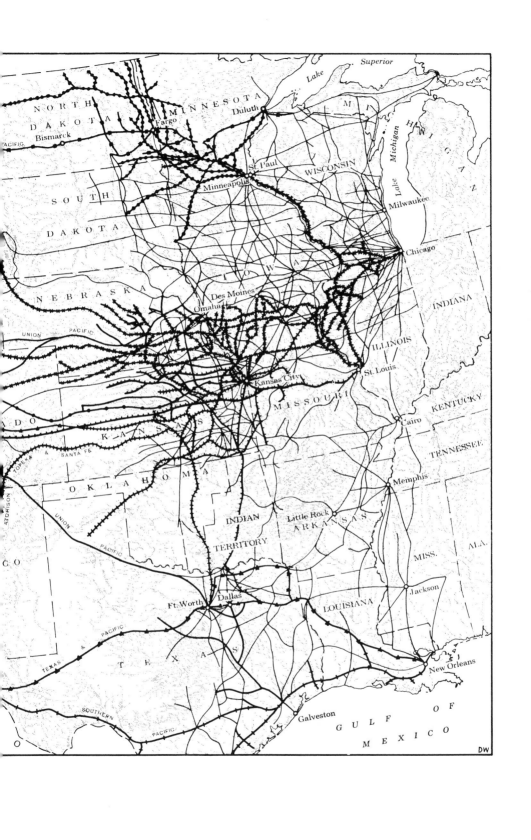

Travel by Rail

*C*louds of billowy smoke belching from locomotives streaking across the countryside were no new sight to most westerners in 1869. Many people then living west of the Mississippi River had come from the East, where by midcentury railroads were commonplace, and still others native to the West had been witnesses to railroad beginnings within their own states. Nevertheless, completion of the first Pacific railroad stirred the whole nation, in fact the entire western world, as people suddenly realized that the great breadth of the American continent could be crossed in one week's time.

It was therefore not surprising that travelers, especially Americans and Britishers, took full advantage of their opportunity to view, albeit from a passenger car window, portions of what was then generally regarded as the last American frontier. Most such tourists set out for the Far West via Chicago. There they usually paused to view, and to wonder at, the marvels of this burgeoning and ambitious gateway through which, as one remarked, "the wealth of the West must flow."[1] "What a traveler values most in this strange city," wrote one Englishman, "are good hotels, fine buildings, well stocked shops, and well-kept streets.... Compared with the bustle of Chicago, the bustle of New York seems stagnation."[2]

From Chicago the traveler moved on to his next objective, Omaha, but not without inconveniences. When service was first begun over completed segments of the Union Pacific, none of the rail lines had as yet reached this Missouri River terminus.[3] Such lines as had actually been built across Iowa were described by correspondent Alexander McClure as having been "flung down on the prairie" while the track bed was frozen. Spring thaws played havoc with the tracks. Like "Dutchman's milk," added McClure, they either were strewn in all directions over the undulating landscape, had sunk to "Hell's bottom," or were "still frolicking with the frogs." When at last Council Bluffs was reached, passengers were confronted with crossing the yet unbridged Missouri River. They were obliged to remain overnight on the Council Bluffs side, and not until late morning on the following day did stagecoaches arrive to convey weary sufferers to a ferry located some distance downstream.[4] Finally Omaha was reached, and there travelers often remained to rest and refresh themselves before finally boarding the Pacific Railroad they "had come to see and to ride over."[5]

Those who delayed their travel on the Pacific railroad until completion not only of this line but of the Council Bluffs-Omaha bridge on March 18, 1872, found travel conditions between Chicago and Omaha immeasurably improved. Even so, most tourists appear to have made Omaha a stopover point. It was a place to see. It was, wrote one traveler, a city with a "weird, disorderly look."[6] Its wide, alternately muddy and dusty streets, board sidewalks along which stood frame hotels and shanties, scattered business establishments, and army barracks, together with a bustling river-front activity, lent a distinctly frontier atmosphere. But long after Omaha had produced a façade of municipal modernity it was the city's inhabitants that gave Pacific-bound travelers their first real feeling of having arrived in the frontier West. There one was aware of the relative paucity of females, a large number of men on horseback, Pawnee Indians, and cogitating "loafers" smoking cobpipes who threatened passers-by with their expectorations.[7]

*T*OURISTS, regardless of route followed, represented many backgrounds and many walks of life. A group of westbound passengers not infrequently consisted of a mixture of Europeans and Americans, some wealthy travelers, immigrants, adventurers, and seasoned westerners. Aboard one train was, wrote an observer, a blonde eastern lady in her "dainty travelling habit," members of traveling theatrical companies, soldiers, and Indian delegations that may well have been returning to their villages from a trip to the national capital.[8]

Train service west over the Pacific railroad varied, as always, with one's ability to pay. Except for the running gear, all passenger cars were made largely of wood. The latest in sleeping car, or stateroom, accommodations awaited affluent travelers, and for the less well-to-do there were coaches and immigrant cars. In 1869 the coach fare from Omaha to San Francisco was $33.20, with extra charges for overweight luggage.[9]

George M. Pullman's sleeping cars, the rich man's "yachts on wheels," were relatively new to post-Civil War travelers. They had been introduced in the Middle West in 1865 and they were still considered experimental when through overland service began four years later.[10] These cars were skillfully ornamented inside and out. The interiors were finished in polished wood and harmonious colors and were well lighted. Each car offered private or semiprivate toilet and sleeping accommodations for about thirty passengers. Sleeping arrangements, or beds, were so constructed that they could be readily converted into comfortable seats for daytime travel. Some accommodations in these cars were more commodious and elegant than others. Viewed from a woman's angle, Susan Coolidge wrote for *Scribner's Monthly* about her drawing room. Her quarters contained four windows, six ventilators, a long sofa, two armchairs with movable backs, mirrors, and storage space. Between two drawing rooms was a dressing closet with toilet facilities. When bedtime came, wrote this lady, the porter entered and "in some mysterious way" converted the sofa and the armchairs into room beds. He gave the occupants a batch of clean towels and was on his way.[11]

Inasmuch as the Central Pacific Railroad Company regarded Pullman rates as "extortionate," the west coast concern chose to purchase sleepers manufactured by a firm called the Jackson and Sharp Company. The sleepers made by this firm contained white metallic interiors and for this reason were known as "silver palace cars." They contained single private sitting rooms, each equipped with a spittoon.[12] In fact, observed a London *Times* correspondent, "Each coach is a complete hotel—'a home on wheels.' "[13] In beautifully appointed dining cars, palace car passengers were treated to a "truly meritorious" cuisine that one guest thought comparable only to Delmonico's "of world-wide fame." Those who only weeks before had endured the rigors of stagecoach travel and rough fare at staging stations were somewhat overwhelmed far out on the western plains by what the menu offered. There was sugar-cured ham with champagne sauce and *salmon de grenoville à l'espagnole;* also the choice of nine vegetables, relishes, desserts, and drinks. "Fine French Wines" were served for only fifteen cents extra.[14] During remaining waking hours palace car passengers found ample facilities and opportunities for conversation, card playing, reading "light" literature, and viewing passing scenery through the broad car windows.

While dining car service was available to all who traveled the western trains, coach passengers were obliged to accept simpler and much less luxurious accommodations than those traveling Pullman. But coaches had their advantages. Coach fare was less than Pullman, and the coaches offered, as one foreign traveler observed, a certain amount of freedom of movement.[15] "If a man arrives at the station late he can hop on the train and select his seat after it starts." Coach seats, while firm, were more comfortable than those of the Concord coach. Since seats were unreserved, scrambles for places occasionally occurred. A wood- or coal-burning stove at one end of each coach provided heat in winter, and there were times when passengers found it necessary to huddle closely around such stoves in order to keep warm. The news, or "train," boy, whom Robert Louis Stevenson rightly declared "a great personage on an American train," supplied passengers with such wide-ranging items as books, newspapers, lollipops, canned beans and bacon, fruit, coffee, and cigars.[16] These services were not, however, appreciated by many travelers, some of whom resented the obtrusive manner in which wares would be thrown upon the laps of "inoffensive" passengers, then, after a brief "free" ex amination to have payment demanded.[17]

The Union Pacific-Central Pacific trains (and most other western ones as well) made short mealtime stops at appropriate stations where hungry passengers without private supplies of food could rush from their cars, elbow their way along the station platform through loafing Indians, cowboys, miners, and (especially along the Santa Fe route), Spanish-Americans, to a restaurant and hurriedly devour a meal.[18] The menus in these station restaurants, wrote one lady passenger, had a monotonous sameness about them—"beefsteak, fried eggs, fried potato [sic] at almost every meal" and "one grows weary of this sameness of diet."[19] For those who had brought along food prepared by "my dear old mother," as one phrased it, station stops also provided opportunities to supplement one's larder from assorted items offered by trainside vendors. For sleeping at night, coach passengers stretched out as well as they could in their seats and covered themselves with coats or blankets. To say that they slept in comfort would be an exaggeration, and most coach passengers arrived at the end of an unbroken journey stiff and exhausted.

Leading western railroads offered still another type of passenger accommodation, and one that was especially designed to serve the needs of the frontier West. This was the immigrant car. Devised by railroad companies to meet the basic travel requirements of immigrants at the lowest possible fares, the immigrant car was devoid of most comforts and all frills. Arrangements varied, but the interiors in all such carriers were extremely plain, boxlike, and poorly lighted and bore the same relationship to Pullman cars that steerage aboard ship bore to first class stateroom accommodations.[20] William A. Spalding, who traveled west in 1874 on a Union Pacific immigrant car, described it as of the "plainest and cheapest construction." Each car, to be sure, had toilet facilities and a coal-burning stove. Spalding said that the seats in his car were of woven fabric with underplaced springs. Straw-filled mattresses or sacks were supplied at prices ranging from $1.25 to $2.50, depending on the bargaining powers of individual passengers. And since the seats could, with the use of an additional board, be adjusted to provide bunks, the passengers found means for sleeping at night. Overcoats served as pillows. By "flexing the knees a little," wrote Spalding, "it served, and beat sitting up all hollow." [21]

Some of the immigrant cars, however, were equipped solely with backless benches. In order to sleep, passengers on such cars were obliged to place their rented straw sacks upon the floor between benches and in the aisles. One passenger recalled that in his position between benches his legs extended into the aisle and that an impatient conductor kicked and trampled over his feet as he passed through the car to collect fares.[22] An English parson, traveling first class, told of visiting an immigrant car that was attached to a regular express train. The parson seemed filled with a certain degree of compassion for the occupants—dozens of "men, women, and children lying asleep on the floor of the carriage." He then described what must have been a familiar scene on the western prairies. When the train stopped at a "bleak station" he witnessed a woman and three children leaving the train to be greeted at the platform by her "bearded, weary" husband wearing a western broad-brimmed hat and high boots. No doubt, mused the parson, this husband had preceded his family in order to provide a home, "and, for farmers, what a home it is!"[23] Robert Louis Stevenson, on a trip aboard such a car, viewed in the dim light his sleeping fellow-passengers, and felt the picture was not alluring. The sleepers "lay in uneasy attitudes ... there a man sprawling on the floor, with his face upon his arm; there another half seated with his head and shoulders on the bench." Many, he said, groaned and murmured in their sleep. The stench was intolerable. Immigrants were not accorded many, if any, courtesies. As Stevenson saw it, equality in America had not as yet extended down to the immigrant.[24]

For all their inconveniences, immigrant cars did provide all minimal passenger requirements. If properly stoked, a stove kept the car warm during cold weather and provided the means for cooking coffee. Passengers usually carried with them as much food as possible and ate their meals aboard the cars. All the immigrants appeared to Spalding to be "pretty well fortified against famine," and he listed as part of his own larder bread, a jar of butter, boiled ham and eggs, baked chicken, cake, and cookies. Fresh milk, and for that matter other foods, could be procured from local "hawkers" at some of the station stops. There were often no curtains to divide sections of the cars, and passengers lived aboard "like one big family." They often shared their food, sang together, joked, had their fights and even occasional gun play.[25]

Most lines offered daily immigrant service. The trains moved at a snail's pace; usually it took ten days to cover the distance from Missouri River points to the west coast instead of the normal five for express trains. The latter were given the right-of-way on the single tracks, so immigrant trains were constantly shunted off on sidings to allow passage of the faster moving expresses. But, as Spalding noted, "if passengers stood by patiently, they could get through "in a week or ten days." By the mid-1880s both the Atchison, Topeka and Santa Fe and Northern Pacific railroads announced a much improved immigrant car service. Not only did they provide sleeping cars (to be sure, without upholstery or bedding) without extra cost but these companies further announced that such cars would be attached to regular express trains to assure dispatch.[26]

*U*NOFFICIALLY there was a fourth class of passengers on western trains. To it belonged free-riding tramps, or hobos, or deadheads, who because of their great numbers were a matter of considerable concern to railroaders. A hobo was never at a loss to find ways and means to reinstate himself on a train, no matter how many times he may have been put off by irate conductors. There are endless stories relating encounters between conductors and hobos, and most of them favor the crafty tramp. "I thought I put you off. How did you get here?" a train official asked one. "Just step over here, sir. I don't want to give it away to all the passengers." Then in a loud stage whisper that brought a roar of laughter from all around, the tramp retorted wryly: "I walked."[27] Even on a special train that was transporting conductors on a tour of the West, the problem of the free-riding hobo was unresolved. On this occasion one had concealed himself in a narrow space behind an ice chest; another rode the "rod" under the car; several were on top. The estimated total of hobos aboard this "conductors' special" was twelve.[28] Much as passenger sentiment favored the person who could cheat or "beat" a "soulless" corporation, tramps were not always the winners. The distances between stations in the West was considerable, and not infrequently the free-riding passengers were unceremoniously escorted from trains in the midst of some lonely hot desert where the best hope of rescue was the possibility of "jumping" another train.[29]

Viewed by some railroad officials as much a nuisance as the tramp was the "pass" seeker. There are only two classes in America, wrote

Auguste Faure, a railroad clerk, those who pay railroad fares and those who ride free. But much as railroads grumbled at the multitudinous requests for free passes, company officials were not themselves blameless. The free pass served as a convenient, minor bribe to national and local politicians and otherwise prominent and influential citizens, and one that was freely granted and accepted. Politicians, added Faure, throw stones with one hand and take passes with the other; actually, he said, they did not even pay for the wind that goes into airbrakes. Even irate farmers wanted their passes, as illustrated by the story of one who used this argument on a reluctant railroad superintendent: "... if I was a drivin' long with my wagon in the country, and I had plenty of room and you was a walkin', and you should ask me to let you ride, and I refused, you would think I was a darned hog, now wouldn't you?" The farmer received his pass.[30] And perhaps it was with good reason that Bob Ford, too, received a pass by reminding the president of the Wabash Railroad who he was: the "Slayer of Jesse James."[31]

Neither immigrants nor hobos, not even the free-riding farmers, were tourists in the sense that they traveled to see the sights of the "great West," and few have left accounts of their journeys. On the other hand, visitors, mainly from the British Isles, Scandinavia, and Germany, looked upon a trip across the American continent over any one of the transwestern rail lines as a major part of a grand tour, deserving, they felt, immortalization on the printed page. Tourists who over the years traveled on the Union Pacific-Central Pacific facilities followed with minor variations the suggestions of the widely-consulted George A. Crofutt's *Great Trans-Continental Railroad Guide*, and, later, *Overland Tours*. The first of many editions of Crofutt's *Guide* appeared as early as August 1, 1869, and gave the traveling public information they could never extract from indifferent conductors: enlightenment on points of interest along the way; essential data about such favored stopover places as Denver and Salt Lake City; and as the first title page put it, "where to look for and hunt the Buffalo, Antelope, Deer, and other game."[32] Later Crofutt's tourist publications described and outlined additional tours totaling eight thousand miles of circuitous, scenic western travel by rail, steamer, stagecoach, and on horseback.[33]

*M*OST TRAVELERS viewed their first venture into the Far West with a considerable degree of wonderment, and, in the case of immigrants, with deep anxiety. "We are now on the rolling prairie," was a typical notation of travelers as their trains hurried west across the Plains.

We turn our faces westward, and feel as if we are leaving life and civilization behind us. We look around and see nothing but the boundless sea of grass, a verdant undulating ocean stretching to the far distant horizon in one vast perpetual sweep. . . . An indescribable feeling of solitude. . . .[34]

To even the casual traveler there was much that attracted his special attention, such as the "lazy, sluggish" Platte; in spring, profuse and gaily colored flowers dotting the rolling landscape; in summer, billowy tumbleweeds bouncing zigzag courses over parched buffalo grass. And on hot, sultry afternoons the sky would often become overcast by dark, menacing, even funnel-shaped, clouds that brought twisting winds and torrential downpours.

Rains, however, were by no means daily events. Protracted periods of midsummer drought were to be expected, and during such intervals the danger of devastating prairie fires was great. Such conflagrations were the dread of all who lived and traveled upon the plains, for they usually moved swiftly over wide areas, threatened and took their toll of life, and left a scorched earth in their wake. One traveler on the Union Pacific line recalled the sight of such a blaze. "For miles on every side the air is heavy with volumes of stifling smoke, and the ground reddened with hissing and rushing fire."[35]

Travelers on the plains often had views of wildlife. Most passengers got at least a fleeting sight of thinning herds of bison, packs of curious antelopes, and, inevitably, colonies of hospitable prairie dogs.[36] Intriguing, too, was the occasional sight of ragged, mounted Indians and long lines of westbound covered wagons. Interspersed were the railroad towns, all described in the travelers' guidebooks. Usually these were but tiny stations featuring water towers, shantylike saloons (and dance halls), restaurants, perhaps upstairs hotels, and a few scattered, weatherbeaten frame dwellings.

The diminutive and grotesque character of western towns bore small relationship to the travelers' interest in them. Some had gained great notoriety as rough, railroad construction camps, and Crofutt's 1869 *Guide* readily capitalized on points of special interest. Thus Julesburg rapidly gained lustre. "During the 'lively times,'" reads the *Guide,*

> Julesburg was the roughest of all rough towns along the Union Pacific line. The roughs congregated there, and a day seldom passed but what they "had a man for breakfast." Gambling and dance houses constituted a good portion of the town; and it is said that morality and honesty clasped hands and departed from the place. We have not learned whether they ever returned; and really we have our doubts whether they were ever there.[37]

Even a fleeting glance out of a car window at what had so recently been a wild western town tended to provide passengers with vicarious thrills. Thus H. Buss, in his *Wanderings in the West*, found sin and crime enthroned in every new railroad town: dance halls of the lowest order, wicked women, card players with revolvers on the tables. But to Buss (doubtless after reading the *Guide* and listening to parlor-car talk), Julesburg was the unquestioned "King of Hell," the true "Sodom of the Wild West."[38] Wrote one cleric who contemplated this place of iniquity from his train window: "Thieves, gamblers, cut-throats, prostitutes, stalked brazen-faced in broad day through the streets."

Not all was hearsay. Occasionally adventuresome and curious passengers would take advantage of train stops by making hurried tours of gambling dens. Aware that such visits had to be short, operators of gaming houses were fully prepared for fast service. One unsuspecting immigrant had to be rescued by companions within minutes after venturing into such a place. He was found well on the way toward intoxication and of being relieved of his small capital and perhaps his life. The proprietor showed his resentment to the intruders by throwing a spike at them. The spike grazed the head of one of the immigrant's companions and fastened itself in a wall.[39]

Nor was Crofutt hesitant about promoting the business interests of places along the route. Cheyenne, for example, warranted a fifteen-column account, in which its lurid "gambling hells," "dance houses," and "wild orgies" were relegated to the past. Pictured for passengers on their regularly scheduled thirty-minute stop was a community with pronounced cultural and business attributes—a city with an "excellent public school"; with churches ("while not very numerous" as yet, more were promised for the future); and in the area of industry, Cheyenne could claim "a manufactory of lager beer."[40]

Throughout the remainder of the century one of the most popular stopovers for railroad travelers in the West—a "must" according to most travel guides—was the Mormon citadel of Salt Lake City. Passengers would leave the main Pacific Railroad at Ogden, journey down Weber Canyon either by stage cr the Utah Central Railroad (depending on the time)[41] to view, invariably with mixed and intense feelings and reactions, the Saints and their desert City of Zion. Visitors would look and marvel at the Mormon Tabernacle, and under construction, the granite temple. They would listen with curiosity if not with incredulity to Mormon preachments on the temple grounds, and gaze, often askance, upon Brigham Young's "Lion House"—home of the Mormon president's many wives.

Most of the travelers who left records tended to heap calumny and shame upon these polygamous Saints, but most would probably agree with Finnish Baroness Alexandra Gripenberg's simple estimate of their economic achievement: "The Mormons have done a good piece of work in

Utah."[42] Most travelers returned to their trains unconvinced about "severely orthodox" Mormonism as a religion, but fortified in their belief that, as an English visitor said: "their frugal habits and patience in the endurance of many privations have enabled them to reclaim a region that once was barren, and to transform a desert into a garden."[43]

This always interesting break in the overland train ride was further marked by a shift at Ogden from the services of the Union Pacific to the Central Pacific, or vice versa. Westbound travelers from Ogden soon found themselves dashing across western Utah and Nevada, across alkali sinks and regions where "sage-brush is king," headed with great anticipation for the towering Sierra Nevada Mountains. Here at last, wrote Lady Duffus Hardy, "All the picturesque beauty and solemn grandeur of the wide world seems to be gathered together ... covered with all the luxuriance of summer's divinest bloom."[44] Finally they arrived at beautiful San Francisco with its many delights for tourists: the Palace Hotel with its 755 rooms and 270 baths to accommodate 1200 guests, Cliff House and views of Seal Rock and the sea lions, and joss houses and opium smoking in Chinatown. It was for most a satisfactory journey, on the whole a comfortable one for those who had traveled palace car, and a tolerable one for those who had toured by coach.[45] In some respects the statement in 1869, not of a foreign visitor but of the American booster Samuel Bowles, expressed adequately the meaning of this Pacific Railroad:

> It is ... the unrolling of a new map, a revelation of new empire, the creation of a new civilization, the revelation of the world's haunts of pleasure and world's homes of wealth.[46]

The Union Pacific-Central Pacific companies were not able to monopolize for long the rail travel across the expanses of the frontier West. As competing lines went into service they too made concerted bids for passenger traffic by offering speed combined with safety and comfort, beautiful scenery, appetizing menus, and, most important, access to places not heretofore reached by trains. The Northern Pacific and the Great Northern, for example, stressed seeing the industrious twin cities of St. Paul and Minneapolis, the beauty and agricultural richness of the northern Great Plains, and the majesty of the snowclad northern Rockies. The Santa Fe, by contrast, offered a whole new empire with herds of grazing cattle, "silent ruins" of cliff-dwelling Indians, picturesque old Santa Fe, trips to the Grand Canyon, health resort hotels, cowboys, Fred Harvey restaurants, and—"in a country that is as yet an enigma to itself"—southern California.[47] The Southern Pacific, by no means to be outdone, lured passengers on a "Sunset Route" out of languid New Orleans west over a line

free from all dangers from ice and snow, from all stoppages and delays
. . . over the fertile prairies of Texas and romantic New Mexico, . . . instead of through the bleak snow-clad mountains and barren alkali deserts
of Nevada.[48]

*M*OST RAILROAD TRANSPORTATION, deluxe or otherwise,
fast or slow, operated on regular, fairly well-kept schedules. In addition,
many low-fare excursions were sponsored by railroad lines themselves
as promotional ventures. Other excursion service was offered to meet
the special requirements of private groups. Some were motivated by
land or community development schemes; others by the prospects of
hunting buffalo and other big game. Still other excursions were arranged as special tours for employee groups and fraternal organizations. Railroad companies seemed eager to sponsor excursions as part
of their operational enterprises, and, judging from the demand for them,
this type of service was popular. Thus, for reasons best known to the
railroad officials, the Kansas state legislature accepted an invitation
proffered by the Union Pacific (Southern Division) to board a special
train at Topeka, enjoy the facilities of the road, and stop off at Lawrence
for a free dinner "unsurpassed in the culinary art," hear plans about
rail projections into western Kansas, and return to home base.[49] Nor
was the general public overlooked. In 1869 the Santa Fe Railroad Company waited only until the first single mile of track was laid and a train
had run over its length before scheduling an excursion picnic at Waka-
rusa, Kansas. Served were barbecued steers and "plenty of whiskey,"
followed by a speech by the company's first president, Cyrus K. Holliday.[50] And when, for example, the American Bankers' Association met
in convention at Kansas City in the 1880s and had completed their business, a special group of delegates made an extended tour to Pikes Peak.
For himself and his family each banker had a compartment, said to
represent "a home on wheels." The bankers too enjoyed sumptuous meals,
and as they viewed the bountiful wheat fields, they concluded that Kansas mortgages were safe.[51]

Catering especially to hunters was the Kansas Pacific Railroad.
Grizzly bear and buffalo hunting excursions were often large and elaborate. One buffalo hunting party sponsored by two English lords, accompanied by their ladies, included General George Custer, other army
notables, one hundred privates, and a sixteen-piece band. This party
was bound for Sheridan, Wyoming, and other points west. The excursion was a great success; they saw "scenes of grandeur," and killed about
forty buffalo, "mostly left on the field." It was, however, not necessary

to be one of an organized hunting party in order to shoot buffalo. Trains often pushed through large herds of these bovine creatures and passengers with guns shot point blank into the bewildered animals.[52]

Travel aboard western trains, even under the best of circumstances, was not unmitigated bliss. There was, as Helen Hunt Jackson reported, the "wear and tear" that came with human contacts—the faces that repel ("you pity, you resent, you loathe") and which brought on "vicarious suffering."[53] And seldom, even in Pullman cars, was the customer always right, especially in matters involving trainmen. The porter was a case in point. "Among our leading friends," wrote a correspondent for the *American Settler*, "there is no one who surpasses in effective malignity the sleeping-car porter."[54] One Englishman, for example, described an encounter with a Pullman porter who had twice literally stepped on his toes, which had extended out into the aisles from under the Pullman curtain. On second offense the traveler gave the porter a push. Thereupon "hard blows rained on me through the curtains." The end result was a fistic battle ended only after the Englishman drew his derringer in defense of his life. "It is a disgraceful thing," he reflected, "that people who pay for luxuries should get in return nothing but discomfort and danger."[55]

Travelers often complained of the intolerable summer heat aboard trains occasioned in part by the necessity of keeping windows closed to prevent dust from entering the coaches.[56] Moreover, the slowness of some trains incurred the mockery of passengers who had so soon forgotten the plodding of horse-drawn stages. Coaches on local trains were often attached to the end of freighters and the stops, switchings, and delays were innumerable. Wood-burning trains, for example, paused often to take on fuel piled alongside the track, and when this was done all trainmen, including the conductor, helped do the job.[57] Popular was the yarn about such a slow train in the Southwest on which a passenger inquired of the conductor for the hundredth time, "Are we soon there conductor? Remember, my wife's sick [at home] and I'm anxious."

"We'll get there on time," said the conductor stolidly.

Finally, in great exasperation the passenger exhorted, "I wish you would put on some steam. I'd like to see where my wife is buried before the tombstone is crumbled to pieces."

When hours later the bedeviled conductor discovered his impatient passenger in high spirits, playing cards, he said, "You don't seem to feel so badly about your wife's death now."

"No, time heals all wounds—assuages all griefs."[58]

Cattle, roaming idly on the unfenced, unprotected right-of-way, frequently caused delays by wandering in the paths of moving trains, especially following rains when graded tracks offered relatively dry and firm footing. Ranchers made no effort to keep their cattle off tracks; in fact, many welcomed their being killed by trains—an easy way, they felt, to "market" their beef and to secure cash in the form of compensation from railroad companies.[59] Cowcatchers attached to the front ends of locomotives were designed to remove bovine trespassers, but collisions with cows were invariably accompanied by violent jolts. "You seem familiar with such accidents," observed one traveler, "are they frequent?" "Now and then of a night," retorted the engineer, ". . . but they generally manage to git the worst on't." Artemus Ward, on the contrary, took a dim view of cowcatchers on slow-moving western trains. At best they wer at the wrong end. Ward felt that the danger was not from trains overtaking a cow but vice versa. And without a cowcatcher at the rear there was nothing " 'to hinder a cow from walkin' right in and bitin' the folks!' "[60]

Nor did train passengers always escape being terrorized. Those traveling in the West for the first time were often unnerved by a rumor perpetrated by station habitues to the effect that the train "just ahead" had been violently attacked by "Redskins." In Texas there occurred, for instance, what was called "a cowboy jollification." At a certain station a half dozen inebriated cowboys boarded a train, drew revolvers, and compelled the conductor to stop his train to take additional comrades aboard. There then followed some indiscriminate shooting, windows were shot out, lamps shot down, the car roof was riddled by bullets, the train boy was robbed of his peanuts and candies; but "so far as known" no person was shot. After a sixty-mile ride the gang left the train as unceremoniously as they had boarded it.[61]

Wrecks added to the annoyance, and in many cases to the tragedies, of railroad travel. The causes of railroad wrecks and train disasters were many, but most frequently they were induced by poor roadbed construction, single-track lines, inadequate braking and signaling systems, unguarded crossings, fire-prone wooden coaches, and, of course, human error on the part of trainmen. Trains frequently became derailed. Bridges were known to have given way to the great weight of trains, and, most tragic of all, trains frequently plunged headlong into one another. In such instances the loss of life, maiming, and assorted other injuries were counted in the scores. Employees suffered twice as many fatal accidents as did passengers, but by far the largest number of injuries occurred among the latter group. The forms of passenger accidents varied greatly, but people falling out of car windows appear to have been the cause of a very major portion of fatalities. Looked at from the point of view of passenger-miles, however, rail travel during the latter part of the century appeared to be relatively safe—one fatality to each fifty-one million miles, one injury to each twelve million miles of train travel. It was, wrote one contemporary student of the safety factor in railroads, much safer to travel by train than by stagecoach; only walking was considered safer.[62]

*T*HE YEAR 1876 marked, in many respects, a high point in speed and general efficiency in transcontinental travel, although improvements were added with each passing year. As a feature of the centennial-year celebration a train made the 3317-mile run between New York City and San Francisco in eighty-three hours and twenty-seven minutes actual time. The average speed was forty miles per hour.[63]

The volume of traffic over the western rail lines was at first moderate, but it mounted steadily through the years. Records kept by the San Francisco offices of the Central and Southern Pacific Railroad companies of arrivals and departures from and to the East illustrate the trend. During the first three years of operation, 1869–1871, the annual arrivals and departures totaled a mere 25,000. By comparison, the figures for a three-year period, 1884–1886, show an annual rate of 121,300. The net gain for the West (1869–1886) over the facilities of this system was 322,000.[64] These figures show that the American public was accepting the increasingly westward movement of the railroad. Despite accidents, delays, discomforts, and recurring personal problems, steel lines that girded the continent were hurrying the day when the frontier was to be completely conquered by the iron horse.

◁ **10** ▷

Indians, Outlaws, and Wayfarers

*T*ravelers on the American frontier invariably experienced hardships and perils. None of these—stagecoach accidents, steamboat boiler explosions, railroad collisions—was as grave as those brought on by Indian attacks. Perhaps at no time in American history were the hazards of frontier travel greater than at the close of the Civil War when Indians in the West unleashed widespread and violent attacks directed heavily, if not mainly, at the avenues of travel and communication in the Great Plains area. During November 1864, Cheyenne and Arapaho bands at Sand Creek had suffered a devastating blow from Colorado militiamen led by Colonel John M. Chivington, and these Plains Indians were thereafter thirsting for revenge. Moreover, Indian tribes throughout the trans-Mississippi West had become deeply resentful of the accelerating stream of settlers, miners, freighters, and railroad builders intruding relentlessly upon dwindling Indian hunting grounds. As the Indians became aware of weakened United States army frontier defenses incurred by the Civil War, they grew correspondingly more daring and hostile. Many avenues for aggression were open to the red men, but they chose to attack such tempting objects as poorly guarded stage-coaches and long, gray immigrant overland caravans—long the visible symbols of white trespassing.

The Indians struck hard and furiously during the winter of 1864–1865. When at that time General Grenville M. Dodge assumed command of the Missouri Department he found most western traffic crippled and most army troops fighting for survival behind scattered and exposed palisaded posts. Even as late as the summer of 1865 General Dodge wrote his commander that an estimated fifteen thousand warriors on the northern and ten thousand on the southern plains were in open hostility. "... never before have we had so extensive a war on the plains," wrote Dodge; "Never before have the Indians been allowed for eighteen months to have their own way to murder, rob, and plunder indiscriminately and successfully."[1]

*T*HE CONSEQUENCES of Indian attacks on the frontier were tragic to behold. Bodies of scalped travelers were found along road-sides. Telegraph lines were destroyed, mail deliveries were halted for weeks, and stagecoach services came to a halt.[2]

Typical of army post reports on Indian atrocities during this period was one given on February 5, 1865 by Colonel Robert R. Livingston, Commander of the First Nebraska Cavalry, with reference to the road between Denver and Julesburg. Colonel Livingston reported not only on burned stations, ranch houses, and haystacks, but told in addition of the toll taken on human life: "At Morrison's, or the American Ranch ... Indians attacked, captured, and burned the ranch.... A passing train found three Indians and seven white bodies in the ruins partly burned." At a place called Gittrell's, west of Fort Rankin, it was reported that Indians captured a twenty-two–wagon train loaded with government stores and private freight. The colonel further related that at Valley Station a westbound eleven-wagon train and two coaches with thirty passengers carrying United States mail were attacked and "Neither coaches nor train has been heard from since—telegraphic communication being interrupted."[3]

The reports multiplied with each passing week. From along the Central Overland Road came the news that twelve men and two women had been killed and scalped; only one person escaped. From the army's Utah press, the *Vedette*, came word that "The Indians have cleaned us out—ran off all the stock east of Sulphur Springs.... ten days now since we have had an eastern or Colorado mail."[4] And from scattered sources there is evidence that railroad lines, such as then existed in this troubled central area, were likewise attacked.[5]

News from the Smoky Hill Trail was equally disturbing. A superintendent for the Kansas Stage Company, Henry Tisdale, recalled that in the 1860s he had come by stage to Salina on a regular run when reports reached him of Indian trouble ahead. There were six passengers, the driver, and Tisdale aboard the coach, and they were all armed. "I had a Henry rifle and two revolvers," Tisdale recalled. Then one afternoon after their team had been unhitched and their mules had been turned out to graze, they saw about three hundred Indians coming toward them from a nearby creek. What happened at this point can best be told in Tisdale's own words:

> The Indians came to this upper crossing and stopped, apparently to hold a consultation. At the same time there was a freight-train from Fort Leavenworth coming up the [two] roads. . . . The teamsters, about twenty-two in all, had no idea there was any danger or Indian war. . . . the Indians started down the road, and upon meeting the teamsters, they hallooed, "How!" the teamsters returned the salutation. When they [the Indians] got near the last wagon they commenced firing at the teamsters, killing and wounding five. Four of the wounded came running into our camp in horrible shape, being wounded with arrows.

One of the injured was a boy wounded in sixteen places and scalped "so there wasn't any hair on his head, except a little below the ear and a little in the back of the neck." Not until then were the soldiers at a nearby fort ordered to pursue the Indians. But before coming within firing range, the captain ordered his men back to camp, meanwhile allowing the Indians to sack the train loaded with flour, sugar, blankets, and other articles. It was little solace to those concerned that the captain was later cashiered for cowardice.[6]

Also on the Smoky Hill Trail was the experience of the travelers who found themselves surrounded by about a hundred and fifty Indians and took refuge in a wallow near Downer Station. From their besieged position they witnessed a captured herder being put to an agonizing death. The herder was first staked to the ground, then, according to a witness, his tongue was cut out and "another portion of his body" was substituted in its place. As a final act of torture a fire was built over the screaming victim. Darkness fortunately made it possible for the besieged to escape. Downer Station, or what was left of it, also bore witness to other depredations. There the devastation was complete; everything—the station, a coach, and "everything that would burn" lay in charred ruins on which unshod pony prints gave mute evidence as to who had applied the torch. Finally, a few miles from Downer Station, the travelers came upon a scalped dead man, arrows still in the little that remained of this body on which wolves had been feasting during the preceding night. The chronicler of these atrocities found solace in one mitigating note, that "the air of the plains is glorious, pure, and dry. . . . There is no odor to a dead body [here], as it does not decay but simply dries up."[7]

*E*LSEWHERE IN THE WEST, and particularly in the South-west, Indian hostilities during 1864 and after played havoc with over-land transportation. From Fort Larned, Kansas, came a report by Theo-dore Conkey during June 1865 that a twenty-man escort of a mule train transporting corn had engaged one hundred Indians in the vicinity of that post. He further reported that an unescorted ox train of eleven wagons bearing stores for Fort Union faced attack. Fortunately, this train had corralled, and timely relief by an army detachment saved the day, except for one man wounded in the arm and the loss of one wagon left behind the main wagon group. Less fortunate were two army mes-sengers from Fort Zarah. The body of one was found lying near the road ". . . scalped, stripped, and otherwise mutilated"; the body of the other was "stripped, his head, feet, and hands entirely severed, and his body mutilated in a most shocking and barbarous manner."

Elsewhere the situation was the same: Indian attacks upon frontier transportation. And from all parts of the West the questions asked were: Why did not the United States Army provide military escort for plains traffic? What was the army going to do about quelling the Indian up-risings? Ben Holladay in particular sent urgent appeals to Washington for help in safeguarding his stagecoach operations and to keep the mails moving.[8]

At first Major General Pope was reluctant to assume the responsi-bilities of providing military escorts to stagecoaches and wagon trains. When Holladay appealed directly to the general, Pope replied by urging him to reestablish his main stations within military posts where shelter could be maintained. In October 1865 Pope expressed his misgivings to General U. S. Grant, asking if, after all, the United States govern-ment was expected to furnish mounted escorts for overland stages. "Such service is enormously expensive," wrote Pope, "as it kills up both horses and men at a fearful rate. . . ."[9] Nevertheless, while coping with the larger problem of general pacification of the Plains Indians the army reluctantly, took deliberate steps to protect traffic over the main central routes on the frontier.

The requirements for effective military escort were staggering. In order to make a road safe from Indian attack, it would be necessary to establish military posts at twenty-five mile intervals, each garrisoned by one hundred men. Stage stations would be located within such palisaded posts and swing stations, where twenty-five soldiers would be on permanent guard, midway between posts. Moreover, the plan called for mounted military escort of all coaches while en route. "By this means," explained Colonel Livingston, "the transit of the mails and passengers would be insured; but I feel satisfied that no assurance of safety can be given otherwise."[10]

While the army was not in a position to provide the kind of protection thus prescribed, General Dodge nevertheless offered some aid in the area most seriously affected by Indian outbreaks. First, freight and wagon trains within his department were ordered to report to the nearest army posts, where officers were instructed to arm and help organize the freight trains into companies which could then resume movement only under the command and, if necessary, escort of officers and men of the army stationed at forts, stockades, and stage stations along the Central Overland Road.[11]

The spring of 1865 found the escort system in operation in areas of greatest danger, and once established it remained in effect until peace was finally restored early in the next decade.[12] When a decision had been made, the army's orders were stern and exacting. Indians found near mail routes were to be "hunted like wolves." Ordered General P. Edward Connor, "Show no quarter to male Indians over twelve years of age. . . . Keep the mails running." In execution of orders, troops were stationed at stage stations; night guard duty was maintained; and each coach received, depending on the section, an escort of four to nine well-armed mounted men. At least two escorts would ride a hundred yards in advance, two others in the rear. In addition, scouts were ordered out under cover of darkness to investigate "infested areas" and during daylight were to travel along ravines looking for lurking marauders.[13]

The escort system may well have served as a deterrent to some Indian attacks upon stagecoaches and wagon trains, but it was not wholly effective. Some travelers even revealed a certain disdain for the soldier escorts, and one in particular indicated he was more concerned about being "skinned" by innkeepers than by savages.[14] A correspondent for the New York *Tribune* commented in 1867 that while one thousand soldiers were stationed at Fort Sedgwick (near Julesburg) to protect the route, these troops, mostly unmounted, were really unfitted for their task. ". . . beyond protecting themselves," he concluded that the men in uniform were of "no possible use in the West." He reported that both stage drivers and passengers preferred to travel without military escort. The soldiers, he said, seemed more interested in patronizing the local "whisky-mill" than in protecting travelers and the mails. The driver of his stage preferred to travel without escort, and if stages were obliged to be accompanied by the military, it was this traveler's view that the passengers, women as well as men, might be called upon to protect the troops.

In any event passengers of both sexes traveled well armed, according to the *Tribune* correspondent, and when approaching a danger spot the driver would give the warning: "Watch well for their heads, front and rear, and don't let them get the first fire." Under similar circumstances in the Montana area another driver passed out the added advice to his passengers that in case of attack by Indians, " 'never scar'; never scar'—they're lightnin' when you scar'." Even though evidences of Indian atrocities abounded, travelers hardened in their attitudes and even joked about losing their hair. Strange as it may have seemed, it was one traveler's opinion that if one stage load of passengers was murdered on one day, another would nevertheless start out on the next. "The movement west must go on."[15]

Railroads too were subject to Indian attacks. The red men had harassed construction workers[16] and remained to plague freight and passenger traffic. In later years General Dodge recalled that during the construction of the Union Pacific across the plains, Indians captured a freight train and took possession of both cargo and crew. Had it not been for Dodge's timely arrival with twenty men and what he called "a traveling arsenal," mayhem would have prevailed. Accordingly Dodge's men—most of whom were Civil War veterans—deployed, skirmished, and went forward "in as good order as we had seen the old soldiers climb the face of Kenesaw under fire."[17] Under such circumstances the Indians were compelled to disperse.

Every trip was an adventure, wrote one trainman who recorded his experience with the Kansas Pacific about 1870. Military guards accompanied the trains between Kansas City and Cheyenne, but this protection was often inadequate. He recalled one fight at a roundhouse in Brookville, Kansas, where Indian raiders surrounded the building, piled ties against it, and were about to apply the torch. Within were several trainmen and, on a turntable, a locomotive under steam. Escape was made aboard the engine which, with whistle wide open and bell ringing, went crashing through the door and debris onto the main track leading to Salina. This proved too frightening to the attackers, who fled from the scene. Reflected this narrator: "None but the most reckless would ever have made a second trip; many did not remain beyond the first day."[18] Not always were railroaders this fortunate, for the evidence indicates that the losses in terms of trainmen and passengers killed, trains wrecked, and destruction of freight were heavy for the period of the late 1860s.[19]

Most Indian troubles for the Union Pacific Railroad vanished with the completion of the line in 1869. By then travelers had even begun to reminisce about the bloody yesterdays. They were reminded of them at Union Pacific depots by Pawnee offering for sale white men's scalps —"'one much heap hair, one dollar'"—that were sold, only after considerable haggling, at half price.[20]

River steamboats were less frequently attacked by Indians than were land vehicles. Nevertheless, the danger to steamboats was real, and one authoritative writer was prompted to declare Indian hostilities one of the "most formidable perils" to Missouri River navigation during the period 1860–1876. Logs of steamboats on this river reveal a concern about Indians, and one captain confessed his preference for the open rather than wooded country sections of the river because Indians were less likely to attack in the open prairie country. Many raids took place and loss of life occurred. When steamboats moved through danger zones, it was not uncommon for crew and passengers to barricade decks and staterooms as a safety measure.[21]

Most vulnerable to attack were, of course, persons traveling either unaccompanied or in very small parties. Mutilated, unburied human remains found along the desolate western trails testified to the perils of venturing forth alone. Even after Indian uprisings had subsided, dangers persisted. Captain Willard Glazier, for example, related that he and two companions were captured by a roving band of thirteen Arapaho on the Laramie plains and that he barely escaped with his life. The three were mounted and well armed, but even so only a few minutes were required to settle the "unequal contest." A Mexican companion, who had shot an Arapaho, was promptly bound to a stake and tortured to death with heated arrows shot into his body. Glazier and his remaining companion were forced to accompany the Indians on their travels, and during the third night these two made a run to tethered ponies, mounted, and managed to dash out of range of pursuing Indians to freedom.[22] By the end of the 1870s such dangers had passed, and travelers could move across the plains without fear of Indian attack.[23]

*I*NDIANS WERE BY NO MEANS the only marauders that frontier travelers had reason to fear. Holdup men were also a constant danger to all who braved western roads and railroads. The art of waylaying and robbing travelers has a long and sordid history. Actually the first conspicuous wave of holdups within the trans-Mississippi West occurred during the 1850s as an accompaniment to the developing miners' frontier. Stagecoach robberies began, rather intermittently at first, in California along lone mountain roads leading to and from the mother lode country during and after 1851; they reached a sort of peak during the late 1870s and early 1880s, when the notorious Charles E. Bolton, alias "Black Bart," wearing a white duster and a flour sack over his head, singlehandedly held up at gunpoint twenty-seven stages. He carried with him a jute bag into which he tossed his loot. This lone highwayman then vanished quickly into the California woods and brush as mysteriously as he seemed to have emerged. Most of this desperado's robberies, according to reliable information, involved United States mails. "The only record of 'Black Bart' being shot at," according to William A. Pinkerton, the noted detective, "was on November 3, 1883." On this occasion the driver fired four shots at his assailant. Bart may or may not have been hit, but on his trail he left a telltale, blood-stained handkerchief bearing a laundry mark that led to his arrest, conviction, and six-year sentence in San Quentin Penitentiary.[24]

Black Bart had no monopoly on stage robbery in California during the period of his operations. An official Wells, Fargo and Company report covering the years 1870–1884 lists 313 stage robberies involving the concern during this fourteen-year period. Out of this number there were 206 convictions for robbery and attempted stage robbery. Eleven "road agents," as stagecoach robbers were called, were killed while resisting arrest, and seven others met their end on the gallows. Actually passengers suffered more from scare than from bullets. During the period indicated only four stagecoach passengers (and also four drivers and two guards) died from encounters with holdup men—none at all from guns carried by Black Bart.[25] The high proportion of arrests and convictions of those who robbed Wells, Fargo and Company express may in part be attributed to a standard three hundred dollar cash reward, plus 25 percent of all recovered treasure, for the person or persons providing the essential information.[26]

Some of Black Bart's holdups were performed on stages operating between California and Oregon, but the Pacific Northwest, and particularly the inland empire mining area, had its own coterie of transportation parasites. Most notorious of them all was the "Plummer Gang" (also known as the "Innocents") which during the mid-1860s concentrated its operations in Montana. In playing a dual role as sheriff of the Virginia City and Bannack districts of Montana Territory and leader of his gang, Henry Plummer occupied an enviable position among cutthroats. He was in a position to gather official data on gold shipments and unofficial knowledge about prospective stagecoach passengers and to relay this information to his cohorts, who would then do an efficient job of holding up stages at appropriate places along routes of travel. The Plummer road agents were ruthless in their tactics, and 102 of their victims were killed. Finally, vigilante organizations were formed, and through their concerted efforts thirty-two Montana road agents, including Sheriff Plummer, were unceremoniously hanged. The remainder of the gang left Montana either by edict or on their own accord.[27]

Not unlike honest prospectors who moved from one mining frontier to the next, road agents who managed to survive tended to operate in first one boom area, then another, before an aroused citizenry caught up with them. Thus holdup men known to Virginia City, Montana, in the early 1860s had been familiar faces in Virginia City, Nevada, in 1859; and many of the desperadoes who staged a reign of terror in Deadwood, Dakota, during 1878, shifted, when pressed by the vigilantes, to Leadville, Colorado, the following year.[28] In the latter case advance word reached Leadville, and citizens were warned by the local press of the imminent arrival of unwelcome guests and were able to forestall a crime wave slated for this bustling mining town during the spring of 1879.[29]

Nor was the Southwest spared. Not waiting for the war to end, two ex-Confederates, John Reynolds and Albert Brown, organized a gang of twenty-four men who robbed and pillaged along the Santa Fe Trail to amass forty thousand dollars; then, after being reduced by desertions to nine men, moved in upon Colorado in the Leadville and Fairplay area. At Fairplay, Reynolds held up the McLoughlin stage to net ten thousand dollars. Having pocketed the cash, the bandit gave renewed vent to his Confederate zeal by smashing the coach on the theory that the vehicle carried United States mails and that he wanted to do as much harm to the United States as possible. This gang, like others, was eventually rounded up and imprisoned.[30]

Still another gang, the Allisons, played havoc in the Southwest by robbing five stagecoaches at Alamosa within a period of one month and then blazing a path of looting and highway robbery that involved Chama (New Mexico) and Pagosa Springs (Colorado) before they too were apprehended and incarcerated.[31] Of all Southwest "bad men," none perhaps was more notorious than Sam Bass, who forsook his Christian upbringing in Indiana to become first a Texas cowboy and then, suddenly, a desperado. Bass served his apprenticeship in the art of stage robbery at Deadwood; also, while in the North, he executed the most lucrative (Union Pacific) train robbery of his career. Thereafter he returned to Texas where in 1878 he organized a holdup gang. Following the robbery of a Fort Worth-Weatherford stage, which produced four hundred dollars, Bass was credited with saying: "Well, this is the best haul I ever made out of a stage, and I have tapped nine of 'em so far. There's mighty poor pay in stages." So before being shot dead, Bass returned to the more lucrative fields of railroad train and bank robbery.[32]

The accounts of stagecoach robberies are multitudinous, and they reveal a general pattern. Road agents tended to select well isolated spots for the execution of their holdups, and they tried, so far as possible, to choose special treasure-bearing stages for plunder. Upon approach of such a stage, a masked bandit would emerge from his station, take a relatively protected place in front of the lead team, point a gun at and disarm the driver, order all aboard to step off the coach with hands up, and proceed to collect loot that included the treasure box and mail bags. Some robbers were reported to have been courteous, some possessed a wry humor, but most were surly and threatened to "blow heads off" if orders were not strictly obeyed. Most drivers and passengers followed instructions literally; and upon being relieved of their money, were allowed to proceed without harm or further indignities. One passenger, I. E. Solomon, related that when he and his fellow passengers were held up in Arizona in 1880 they managed to retrieve from the bandits their watches, plus eight dollars for breakfast and drinks.[33] After another holdup, this one in the Black Hills in 1877, the robbers supposedly passed drinks around to all passengers and wished the driver luck and a pleasant journey.[34]

Holding up stages persisted as a fairly thriving business into the mid-1890s, but noticeable on this post-Civil war frontier was a shifting emphasis from stage robbery to train robbery. The first railroad holdup in America occurred October 6, 1866, when the Reno gang from Seymour, Indiana, robbed a southern Indiana train. Perhaps the most notorious and adept of all train robbers were the Missourians Jesse W. and A. Franklin James and their cohorts, the Youngers (Cole, James, John, and Robert). The first armed robbery by the James gang was that of the Liberty, Missouri, bank (the first armed bank robbery in the American West) in 1866, but not until July 21, 1873 did they hold up their first railroad train, the Chicago, Rock Island and Pacific at a place fifteen miles east of Council Bluffs, Iowa. In this instance the bandits had received information that a large sum of money was to be shipped in an express car due to arrive at Adair, Iowa, at 8 p.m. Accordingly, the gang picked out a desirable curve in the track and loosened some rails before taking concealed positions along the bush-covered right-of-way. When the ill-fated train arrived at this prepared position the locomotive and seven cars crashed off the track. At this point the bandits forced their way into the express car where they sacked the money, then proceeded to hold up, search, and rob all passengers of money and jewelry. Thereupon the brigands mounted their steeds with grain sacks in hand, and shrieking out the rebel yell "yip, yip yaw," dashed off under cover of darkness. Casualties included the engineer, who was scalded to death, a fireman wounded, and injuries sustained by several passengers. The gang met at a prearranged hideout and there counted their take, which totaled three thousand dollars in cash. While not ending up empty handed, a mistake regarding train schedules caused them to miss an intended one hundred thousand dollar treasure shipment.

Early the next year, in company with the Younger brothers and others, the James gang held up the Iron Mountain Railroad at Gads Hill in their own state of Missouri and garnered two thousand dollars. Among their subsequent train robberies were the Union Pacific Railroad at Muncie, Kansas, in 1874, that netted fifty-five thousand dollars, and the Missouri Pacific Railroad at Otterville, Missouri, in 1876, that produced seventeen thousand dollars.[35]

The James gang, like the Bass gang, also robbed stages, but it was while attempting robbery of the Northfield, Minnesota, bank on September 7, 1876 that the James brothers and their cohorts received their most devastating blow. On that day citizens of Northfield met fire with fire. They shot and killed two members of the James gang and wounded Bob Younger. Within a fortnight the Youngers were captured and were subsequently imprisoned. Then in 1882 Robert (Bob) Ford, a cousin of the leaders and a member of the gang, shot and killed Jesse James for a ten thousand dollar reward. Finally, Frank James surrendered and was spared a prison sentence such as was given other survivors of the gang.[36]

The end of the James brothers gang did not, however, terminate train robberies. Other gangs known as the Daltons and the Doolins succeeded the Jameses in Missouri and the central plains area, and they were succeeded in turn by the "Wild Bunch" gang in Wyoming. In the Southwest, especially in Texas, Sam Bass continued his train and bank robberies until shot to death in 1878.

If the Renos were the first to hold up a railroad train, it was the James brothers who in time established the general holdup pattern that with refinements was as follows: work as a gang; pick a lonely spot; with a red lantern, signal the train to halt; cover the engineer and fireman and simultaneously enter train from rear; uncouple express car to be pulled forward beyond sight of the passenger coaches; hold up trainmen and passengers; collect booty; kill if necessary; and escape with loot on horseback. Only rarely did a lone bandit hold up a train. Even though with the closing years of the century there was a marked decline in train robberies, the decade of the 1890s witnessed (for the nation as a whole) 261 train robberies that resulted in the death of eighty-eight persons and the wounding of eighty-six more. Ninety percent of those killed were innocent, defenseless people. Two-thirds of those engaged in armed train banditry lost their lives while in the act of committing the crime, or were either lynched or officially executed. When addressing the annual convention of the International Association of Chiefs of Police in 1907, William A. Pinkerton made the statement: "I know of no train robbers or 'hold-ups' alive and out of the prison today.... Crime does not pay."[37]

*N*OT LEAST of the hazards of the general traveling public were the confidence, or "bunko," men and women—sharpers whose manipulations and objectives ranged from procuring to operating "skin games" at or near stations, river ports, or on public carriers. This form of vice was reflected in much of the moralistic literature of the period and in none more pointedly than the anonymously published *The Spider and the Fly* by "One Who Knows." Young girls traveling through Chicago must, reads this book, beware not of armed bandits but of "carpet bandits," of "foreign counts," and of "Southern gentlemen" of good address.[38] And to young male travelers there were warnings to eschew houses of ill fame then numerous in all major western cities. San Francisco's Barbary Coast, warned the Reverend B. E. Lloyd, was the "haunt of the low and the vile ... where lilbertinism is rampant" and where licentiousness, debauchery, pollution, loathesome disease, insanity from dissipation, ... blasphemy and death" awaited erring souls. The preacher did not, however, wish to say that San Francisco was the wickedest and most immoral city in the world; it was, he said, simply "the deepest shade among many brilliant lights."[39] Colon Smith, an English traveler, related how during his stopover in New York City en route to the West he made the acquaintance of what he thought was a respectable "beauty" but who turned out to be "an adventuress" who borrowed other peoples' money and then "decamped." Smith found Chicago "a collection of saints and sinners." While en route to Omaha he saw a purse snatcher grab an immigrant's pocketbook containing five hundred dollars, draw a gun, and make his escape; at Salt Lake City he witnessed a man shot on a public street.[40] Another English traveler remarked that even life on a Pullman had its hazards. He observed, for example, how one overly anxious male passenger in the company of a gorgeously dressed female managed to garner "every spoonful of honey" but also "got stung towards the end."[41]

Commonest of all the involvements aboard trains, riverboats, stagecoaches, and in hotels was gambling. Professional card sharks followed routes of travel. Boats especially, as a professional gambler, John Morris, reminisced, were infested with sharpers. They traveled in small groups both for effective operations and for mutual protection. Various inducements, including some initial winnings at cards, were used to involve the "gulls" (intended victims); and then at appropriate times various devices and stratagems were used to assure winnings, among them: smoke signals or finger signs by holdouts who looked at adversaries' cards; "scratching paper" (another term for marking cards); and the use of a wide assortment of mechanical aids such as card trimmers, sleeve clamps or "breastworks" for holdout cards, and tiny mirrors placed in pipes to reflect cards dealt in stud poker. Used, too, were loaded dice. But unlike Indian raids and holdups by armed bandits, travelers who lost at cards and dice were victims of their own inner urges to gamble.[42]

The passing of the frontier was not necessarily accompanied by the termination of crime, gambling, confidence games, and professional prostitution along the avenues of travel. But nevertheless, as Indian disturbances were quelled and as stagecoaches and steamboats yielded to the railroads, and in turn the rail coaches became more adequately managed and supervised, passengers throughout the trans-Mississippi West were then able—save for accidents—to move about from place to place with a feeling of ease and safety. The Wild West was being tamed by stagecoach and railroad, and the era of the frontier was drawing to a close.

United States trooper in pursuit of an Indian. An artist's drawing from *The Graphic*, London, March 28, 1874. (UNIVERSITY LIBRARY, CAMBRIDGE, ENGLAND)

Union Pacific railroad worker killed by Indians. From W. E. Webb, *Buffalo Land* (Cincinnati, 1872). (KANSAS STATE HISTORICAL SOCIETY, TOPEKA)

*Indians destroying railroad tracks near Russell, Kansas, 1869. Painting by I. Gogolin. (*KANSAS STATE HISTORICAL SOCIETY, TOPEKA*)*

Driving of the Golden Spike ceremonies, Promontory, Utah Territory, May 10, 1869. (UNION PACIFIC RAILROAD COMPANY)

An Atchison, Topeka and Santa Fe train crossing Canyon Diablo Bridge, Arizona. (ATCHISON, TOPEKA AND SANTA FE RAILROAD COMPANY)

(Left) *Central Pacific (now the Southern Pacific) line in the Sierra Nevada Mountains of Cali-fornia.* Note the piles of cut wood, used as fuel. (SOUTHERN PACIFIC RAILROAD COMPANY)

Lithograph showing Union Station in Chicago, 1890. Chicago was the rail gateway to the West. (CHICAGO HISTORICAL SOCIETY)

1866. 1866. 1866.

MONTANA & IDAHO

TRANSPORTATION LINE,

Give Through Bills of Lading to Fort Benton, Helena, Virginia City, Bannock City, Blackfoot City, Deer Lodge, and all points in the Mining Districts.

Boats of this Line will leave St. Louis on the opening of Navigation to Omaha for Fort Benton. From that point we are prepared with wagons of our own to transport goods to all parts in the territories of Montana and Idaho.

Our Boats are Built Expressly for the Trade,

Are commanded by skillful and experienced Officers, and, being very light draught, Passengers and Shippers can rely on being put through to their destination in good time.

For Freight or Passage, apply to

JOHN G. COPELIN, \
Or,   JOHN J. ROE & Co., } St. Louis.

J. Eager, 41 Broad Street, New York.

A typical steamboat transportation advertisement during the 1860s.

Cover of first railroad guide for the Union Pacific–Central Pacific Railroad, 1869, pub
lished by George A. Crofutt. (HENRY E. HUNTINGTON LIBRARY, SAN MARINO)

Palace sleeping cars at Chicago, the gateway to the West. (CHICAGO HISTORICAL SOCIETY)

The end of an era: a Northern Pacific Railroad lounge car, 1900. First electric lighted train in the Northwest. (ASSOCIATION OF AMERICAN RAILROADS, WASHINGTON, D.C.)

Departure for the West, Chicago, 1870. From Appleton's Journal (New York, 1870). (CHICAGO HISTORICAL SOCIETY)

First Union Pacific Bridge across Missouri River at Omaha, looking north from Omaha side. (UNION PACIFIC RAILROAD COMPANY)

A wooden trestle near Grangerville, Idaho, on the Northern Pacific Railroad in 1900. Such structures were subsequently replaced by steel bridges. (NORTH-ERN PACIFIC RAILROAD COMPANY)

(Left) *The Eads Bridge across the Mississippi River at St. Louis as it appears today.* (TERMINAL RAILROAD ASSOCIATION OF ST. LOUIS)

(Below) *Pershing Square, Los Angeles, in the 1880s.* (HENRY E. HUNTINGTON LIBRARY, SAN MARINO)

The coming of the automobile. (MINNESOTA HISTORICAL SOCIETY, ST. PAUL)

Good Roads and the Passing of the Transportation Frontier

A carriage ought as much as possible to stand upright in traveling," wrote a sarcastic westerner in alluding to the pitiful condition of roads during the administration of John Quincy Adams. A half century later there were at least a few progressive-minded citizens who were still decrying the poor state of their public roads and were proposing their general improvement. Roads, as the author of a prize essay asserted in 1870, are the prerequisite for advancement of civilization. "Without roads we should never have emerged from barbarism."[1] But in spite of an occasional recognition that good roads would benefit society, Americans in general, and westerners in particular, continued to endure both stagnant road-building programs and archaic systems of road management.

Even though federal agencies blazed many new roads, or trails, throughout the trans-Mississippi West (especially during the midcentury decades), these were mainly intended to serve military and transregional traffic rather than to meet local civilian needs. Civilian requirements were met primarily by county and township governments, but in a manner best described as inefficient and penurious.[2] The over-all result of such local policies was marked inactivity in road building and gross neglect in the maintenance of public thoroughfares.

Reasons for this continued public frustration may be attributed to several factors. From the viewpoint of the dominant agricultural elements, steamboats and railroads met basic transportation requirements in moving farm produce to major markets. Much as farmers may have been conscious of poor local roads, they were unwilling to pay the cost of improvements, and farmers, it must be remembered, controlled the county and township tax funds.

The end product, namely the local roads of the West during the first two *post-bellum* decades, was sad to behold. Rarely did one county cooperate with another in executing intraregional road programs, and none was disposed to intrust any roadwork to the state. Most road taxation was of a *corvée* type, calling for the payment of poll taxes in the form of personal labor on road projects. In the western states such work was directed by a county road supervisor who, in the opinion of one railroad official, "has about as little idea of how to make a good road as [does] a Sioux Indian." This system was not conspicuously successful. Only in Kansas, according to the United States Commissioner of Agriculture, had the labor poll tax system worked satisfactorily.[3] Even though men usually met the law's exactions, they did so more by presence of body than by spirit and enterprise. In general, state laws tended to protect the property of the farmers, and farmers often retained ownership of the land on which county roads were built.

Minnesota and Kansas serve as examples: there farmers retained rights to use the grass, stones, gravel, and sand within the so-called rights-of-way. Drovers had no legal right to allow their livestock to feed along roadsides, and children had no right to pick up apples that had fallen from overhanging trees.[4] The Kansas laws made it clear, however, that county road overseers were responsible for the removal of "all cockleburs, Rocky Mountain sand-burs, burdocks, sunflowers," and other weeds from the public highways. And in Kansas, too, it was unlawful for any person to plow up the highway for purposes of scouring plows.[5]

It is therefore not surprising that travelers and others interested in road improvement prior to 1890 were most uncomplimentary about western county roads. Travel and pioneer accounts indicate that only enough work had been done to make them passable. Wrote one commentator with special reference to the West:

If the road makers had gone to work with the intention of throwing obstructions into them they could have hardly succeeded better. Loose stones, from 100 lbs. downwards, lie thickly scattered over their surface. . . . How the community endure [sic] this intolerable nuisance, it is difficult to imagine.

He added that in the spring of the year "our roads are either a canal filled with mud and water, more fit for a boat than for wagons, or else are an almost impassable quagmire, in which there is imminent danger of sinking into the lower regions." Then with the coming of dry weather "unfathomable" ruts fill the roads over which wheels "go creaking and crashing, like a ship in a storm."[6]

When passing through wooded areas, timber had been simply cut close enough to the ground to allow vehicles to jolt over the stumps.[7] When, after the passage of years, the stumps had either rotted or had been removed, the result was called road improvement. It was pointed out by a prominent Missouri advocate of good highways that local prairie roads had, as a rule, been laid out along section lines. Therefore they tended to range in straight lines over hill and dale without regard either to natural obstructions or to general usefulness. During dry seasons dust was a constant irritant to travelers, while in the rainy seasons mud was often deep enough to "swamp a buzzard's shadow passing overhead."[8] But then, as one pioneer asked philosophically, "What could be done with no money? What could be accomplished when 'a dollar is as big as a cartwheel'?"[9]

Reports from elsewhere in the West were written in comparable vein. In answer to circulars submitted to state road officials by the United States Department of Agriculture during the late 1860s came remarks such as these: California—"The general character of public roads throughout the State, during wet seasons, is bad; in January and February, almost impassable"; Texas—"Our roads are not worked, the wagoner makes his own way. . . . Road laws in this magnificent State, like other laws, seldom executed." Utah Territory reported the existence of thirty-two miles of gravel road and eight miles of macadamized road. Where plank or corduroy roads were used, only one such road had been kept in repair.[10] In Iowa the best road in one county was surfaced with sawdust.

Fortunately, the poor condition of roads did not go either unnoticed or without lamentation. While recognizing that some of the major thoroughfares were good in places, travelers led the outcry against the deplorable conditions of roads in many of the new states in the West. In 1867 the widely traveled Bayard Taylor was moved to write:

If there are laws in relation to roads, they seem to be a dead letter. . . . Our National Government acts in the most niggardly manner towards its incipient States. There should be at least a million of dollars annually spent in each Territory between the Mississippi and the Pacific, on roads and bridges.[11]

But words of this nature went mostly unheeded. Not until the 1880s did the federal government, and to a very minor extent state governments, show signs of responding to mounting complaints and pressures, which by then came, oddly enough, from a new and highly vocal group —the League of American Wheelmen.

*I*N 1880 at Newport, Rhode Island, the League of American Wheelmen had come into being in response to the then new and suddenly emerging cycling craze. The cycle had an eighteenth-century heritage in the form of the velocipede, but by the 1880s this clumsy "boneshaker" had given way to the rubber-tired high-wheeled "ordinary," and the low, chain-driven, two-wheeled "safety" bicycle. At first Great Britain had been the main manufacturer and supplier of bicycles to the States, but in 1877 the American Colonel Albert A. Pope built a factory in Boston for the manufacture of what became the "Columbia" high-wheeled bicycle. Pope Manufacturing Company developed, produced, and led what by 1900 was to be an aggregation of 312 American bicycle makers representing a combined capital of roughly 30 million dollars and producing in that year alone 1,113,039 bicycles. By then there were approximately four million bicycles in use within the United States.[12]

The bicycle craze spread not only in the East but in the trans-Mississippi West; it appears to have been augmented by the gradual realization that in the bicycle Americans had found an economical touring device—one that offered a health-giving and pleasurable pastime for people of all ages. To be sure, the bicycle could be used for traveling to and from work, but, unlike early travel devices, the "wheel" provided easy access to the great outdoors, including the frontier West. Bicycle riders became, in a sense, cultists. They formed organizations, the leading one being the League of American Wheelmen. The *Wheelman*, a journal published by the league, left little unsaid concerning the values of cycling. When riding a bicycle, said the editor, "blood courses gladly through every nerve and fibre of the body."[13] Cycling, so *Outing* magazine declared, caused pallid cheeks to "assume a rosy hue," lips to become red, eyes to sparkle "with renewed vigour," and "cobwebs in the brain" to be brushed away. "In short, for the cyclist, mental exhaltation and exhilaration take the place of depression and weariness."[14]

Moreover, cycle traveling for pleasure provided participants with an incentive to form touring clubs. The League of American Wheelmen was made up of local cycle clubs and the national organization, which counted membership in the thousands, represented practically every state and territory. Not only did the league promote the best interests of bicycle riders in every way possible but its national journal, the *Wheelman*, launched a sustained campaign for road improvement. By far the greatest number of affiliated cycling clubs in this national organization were identified with the East, but by 1887 wheelmen and subscribers to the journal were also to be found within practically every state and territory west of the Mississippi River.[15]

By the mid-1890s the craze had reached its peak. At that time several cycling publications were on the market. Most newspapers as well as outdoor and health magazines had special departments given over to the subject, and even such monthly magazines as *Harper's, Scribner's,* and *Leslie's* published articles pertaining to the sporting and health-giving attributes of bicycle riding.[16]

Most helpful to the tourists who in great numbers wandered far and wide over western byways was *The Road and Hand-Book* issued by the league for the respective divisions within the nation. These regional guides contained many road maps never before published; they listed inns heretofore generally unknown, many new places of interest, rules of road etiquette, and gave much worthwhile advice to travelers. Perhaps the most significant aspect of the league's work was noted in the Preface to its *Hand-Book:* "Let this book be a continual reminder to you that the League of American Wheelmen is an organization devoted to the interest of cycling and road improvement."[17]

The need for better roads became increasingly apparent as more and more cyclists set forth to explore and presumably to enjoy the great outdoors. It became the custom for individual cycle groups to keep detailed records and to report on their trips. Some of these excursions were exciting, and almost invariably the accounts made pointed references to the primitive condition of western, or frontier roads. One of the most far-ranging cyclists, and correspondingly one of the most ardent advocates of road improvement, was the wheelmen's spokesman, Lyman Hotchkiss Bagg. In his book, *Ten Thousand Miles on a Bicycle,* Bagg related many remarkable cycling feats, one being that of Thomas Stevens who set out from San Francisco on a globe-cycling tour in April 1884.[18]

Stevens crossed the United States over a 3700-mile course in three months' time. According to one observer, he arrived in Cheyenne "brown as a nut, and mud-spattered. . . . His knickerbockers had given way to a pair of blue overalls." In making the transcontinental journey, Stevens had worn out four pairs of stockings and three pairs of canvas shoes, but "As for the bicycle itself . . . it stood the strain without break or any excessive wear." In recounting his cycle journey through the West,

Stevens highlighted some of his delightful and some not altogether idyllic experiences. He had left Oakland pier in a downpour. In places where no suitable roads existed he pushed his bicycle for miles, along bumpy railroad tracks and over trestles. He went across pastures, combatted mud, slept inside the Central Pacific snowsheds in the Sierras and in ranchers' cabins on the Nevada desert. He made his way with apparent ease over the salt flats of Utah and entered with obvious delight the "verdant region of prosperous Mormon farms, with orchards in full bloom." His trek over the Rockies involved, of course, much up-hill walking. Upon reaching the Fort Bridger area Stevens experienced his "toughest 24 h. of my entire tour." During this period of time he forded nine streams of icy water, carried his bicycle six miles over sticky clay "where trundling was quite impossible," had nothing to eat, and spent the night in an abandoned freight wagon on a "rain-soaked adobe plain."

In crossing the Great Plains, Stevens had expected easier cycling than was his lot. Heavy rains had left the Platte bottoms muddy and this condition, combined with long stretches of sand and constantly heavy winds, greatly inhibited riding. He described the Central Overland Road as "a continuous mud-hole." In spite of these obstacles Stevens reached his first major objective, Chicago, where he celebrated the Fourth of July and noted that he had traversed the distance between the Pacific and the Mississippi River in twelve weeks' time.[19]

Stevens' remarkable feat did much to stimulate the activities of cycling clubs, and local tours of varying lengths were reported throughout the trans-Mississippi West. Each local cycling club wore a distinct uniform normally consisting of pea jackets, knee breeches, stockings, ties, and caps or hats. Opinions differed on whether or not to wear cycling uniforms on Sundays. The clubs, locally and in national convention, evolved rules of the road, which were printed in their handbooks. Courtesy and gentlemanliness, for example, were indicated by "a quiet and unobtrusive manner." Wheelmen were advised to carry handkerchiefs, a toothbrush, and a change in underwear. They were warned that the condition of sheets in some country inns might well necessitate sleeping in one's underwear. Be moderate in drink, said the rules. Take water as often as desired, milk to satisfy the stomach, and if a wheelman must drink spirits, "it should be done only at the end of his day's run."[20]

*F*OR ALL THEIR CULTIST TENDENCIES, for all their eccentricities, the wheelmen—in whatever region they operated—did much not only to raise hems and lower class distinctions, as one author observed, but also to widen mental horizons. But their greatest contribution was their campaign for better roads everywhere. "It is one of the striking facts of bicycling experience," to quote their mouthpiece, "that, the moment any person becomes a wheelman, he is instantly and ardently convinced of the necessity of improved highways." A wheelman not only became a full-fledged advocate of macadamized roads but defiant in his attitude toward the man on, or behind, a horse. "The Great American Hog (*Porcus Americanus*)," wrote one ardent leader of the League of American Wheelmen in 1887, is that "unfortunate species of humanity" who in his "singular delusion suffuses the soul of a Hog" and thinks he has purchased "an exclusive right" to public highways. This ardent crusader firmly believed

> that in the course of a decade this repulsive type of animal may become
> as extinct as the dodo; and the credit of suppressing it would then, as
> a matter of history, belong in large measure to the League of American
> Wheelmen.[21]

If the League of American Wheelmen failed to remove the horse as a means of transportation, it nevertheless succeeded mightily in educating the American public to the advantages of good roads. At their annual national rallies (the first was held in Boston in 1880) the wheelmen never failed to make pronouncements on the poor condition of roads, on the dire need for remedies of this situation, and on the benefits that would accrue from road improvement. They also disseminated specific information on how to build and to maintain good roads.[22] Individual members wrote letters and articles for the press and appealed directly to public officials throughout the nation. Farm journals in particular were willing to publish, in most cases without change, articles submitted to them on the subject of good roads. League-sponsored books also made their appearance, and by far the most influential of these were Isaac Potter's *Gospel of Good Roads* (1891) and Otto Dorner's *Must the Farmer Pay for Good Roads?* (1898). Supplementing these efforts was the work of local clubs. One such organization in California adopted for its motto "We want good roads in California." "Good roads days" were designated as another means of propagandizing. In 1886 the league adopted what might well be called a blueprint for good roads in America. Six years later it achieved the pinnacle of influence when, during its Washington, D.C. rally in July 1892, the league's president, Charles L. Burdet, reached the friendly and receptive ear of President Benjamin Harrison. During his interview Burdet stressed that railroads were losing a tremendous volume of business due to poor wagon roads throughout the land.[23]

Burdet and his fellow-wheelmen argued that good roads would enable farmers to haul their produce to rail lines at minimal cost and effort, and during all seasons of the year; that in turn the railroads would benefit immeasurably not only by increased volume but by a more even flow of agricultural shipments over rail lines. "When highways are impassable," one pointed out, "freight and passenger earnings are necessarily diminished and the railroad securities lowered." To the contrary, good roads would enable the railroads to handle freight much more expeditiously. "There is no class in the community to whom the necessity of better roads is more apparent than the presidents of the great interior transportation lines." So effective were these appeals[24] that western railroads lent their moral, even tangible, support to new road projects. Among other things they transported free of charge demonstration road equipment and contributed in one way or another support of local road projects.[25]

The wheelmen's approach to farmers in behalf of good roads was double-edged; it was marked, on the one hand, by condemnation and even ridicule, and, on the other, by an appeal to reason. "With all due respect to the farmer," wrote Bill Nye in a publication entitled *Good Roads*, "I will state right here that he does not know how to make roads." Nye then argued that before Americans undertook to provide Jaeger underwear and sealskin Bibles to Africans they might do better "to put a few dollars into the relief of galled and broken down horses that have lost their breath on our miserable highways." [26] Basically, the wheelmen would have the farmer understand that the establishment of good roads could reduce travel time by half and would, of course, greatly reduce fatigue.[27] Even the *New York Times* was impressed by the untiring efforts and ingenuity of the wheelmen and remarked that it hardly seemed possible that so much could have been done for road improvement as has been accomplished by "an athletic organization." The work of the wheelmen, pointed out the *New York Times*, "has reached a stage where the National Government can no longer ignore it."[28]

The League of American Wheelmen did not long remain unaided in its crusade for good roads. In the wake of the wheelmen, there emerged the National League for Good Roads, the National Good Roads Association, and, significantly enough, numerous state and even county associations bearing assorted labels. The latter became very active in the West, where local conventions were held, leading directly to state and federal action.

*O*NE OFFICIALLY SPONSORED MEETING was convened at Sedalia, Missouri, in 1893. It was called by the Missouri Board of Agriculture and was addressed by the state's governor and by several professional leaders. In speaking to the convention George Burnett, president of the

St. Louis Board of Public Improvement, remarked that while Missouri had been busily engaged in building railroads, it had "forgotten our wagon roads." The time had now come, he declared, to provide the means for getting to and from existing railroad facilities. Local vested interests were, of course, represented and their influence was reflected in the convention's resolutions, which urged passage of "such laws as will enable the counties to secure practical application of the best methods of improving roads."[29]

In many ways the action of this convention was representative of similar meetings held in at least half of the states during the 1890s. Cities such as Chicago, Des Moines, Omaha, St. Paul, St. Louis, and Sacramento were hosts to the good roads conclaves and many of them were very well attended. The Des Moines meeting held during August 1892 was national in scope and was attended by three hundred delegates representing 88 counties and 130 cities. Subsequently, several hundred delegates present at the Sacramento meeting represented an assortment of institutions and groups that included universities and colleges, technical societies, commercial bodies, municipalities, county governments, farm organizations, humane societies, railroad officials, grocers' associations, and, of course, the ubiquitous wheelmen. The contagion of such meetings was so great that in 1900 alone no less than a dozen good-roads conventions were held in western states, and the total effect of this excitement was sufficient to induce President McKinley to say to Congress that "There is a widespread interest in the improvement of our public highways at the present time." Innocuous as this statement was, it represented the first formal notice taken of the road situation by a chief executive since railroads began sweeping across the nation.[30]

These conventions not only accepted the principle that good roads were desirable but they also recognized that reform must be accompanied by education. Those most in need of education were the ones who most of all needed improved roads—the farmers. The farmer, still operating under frontier or pseudo-frontier conditions, should be made to realize that good roads meant more civilized and modernized living and more money in his pocket. "The average California farmer," wrote one correspondent covering the Sacramento meeting, "loses one-fourth of the home value of his products through excessive cost in their primary transportation." Good roads, he added, would bring "good times" to the farmer.[31] And similarly at St. Paul, where more than four hundred delegates assembled in June 1893 to deliberate on Minnesota's road plight, emphasis was on pointing out to the farmer that good roads saved transit costs. In fact, asserted this body, farmers were losing more money hauling goods to railroads over their poor roads than they were paying in freight rates.[32]

While most of the conventions gave bountiful lip service in behalf of better roads, there were conflicts of interest between those who favored road-building programs under the direct aegis of state highway departments, and the county governments, whose restricted interests had become well entrenched.

For this and other reasons organizations such as the National League for Good Roads, founded in Chicago in 1892 by General Roy Stone, were of the opinion that hope lay not with the states but with the long-somnolent federal government. In 1893 this body held its convention at the nation's capital, enlisted the aid of interested congressmen, and—along with the League of American Wheelmen—lent its endorsement to a road program under federal auspices.[33] In keeping with this revival of interest in federal support, a resolution was introduced in the House of Representatives on January 23, 1893 instructing the Committee on Agriculture to incorporate $15,000 into the agricultural appropriation for making investigations "for a better system of roads."[34]

This move led to positive results: the establishment in 1893 of a federal Office of Road Inquiry supported initially by a $10,000 annual appropriation by Congress and the appointment by Secretary of Agriculture J. Sterling Morton of General Stone as Special Agent. The responsibilities and duties of this new office were to inquire and to advise on road matters, not to enter upon an actual construction program. But limited though its budget and powers were, the Office of Road Inquiry marked an official re-entry of federal participation in highway work. The annual reports of the office tell the story. It collected, and through its many published bulletins, disseminated, information on the condition of roads, the state of public opinion in regard to road improvement, obstacles that stood in the way, and the best means to obtain better highways throughout the nation. Hundreds of thousands of copies of official bulletins were issued and circulated.

Excellent macadamized and Telford roads had been constructed with success in the East during the postwar period. But studies of the road problems within the expansive, less populated, and less affluent West, where there was greater dependence upon the use of readily available materials, showed that these earlier models were not always appropriate for the region west of the Mississippi River. The bulletins, therefore, contained information not only on systems of road management current in the United States but also on methods of constructing different kinds of roads. At the instigation of the office, samples of such roads were built and technical information regarding their construction was made readily available. Machines for sample construction were usually furnished by manufacturers of road equipment; interested railroads transported this machinery and often materials as well; and local communities provided the necessary labor.

*A*S TIME PASSED the road inquiry staff grew in size, and appropriations increased correspondingly. Soon it evolved into an organization with four major divisions, each of which provided public lecturers, dispatched delegates to conventions of various kinds, and provided experts who directed or supervised sample road construction and who worked in close cooperation with agricultural college experiment stations that were becoming interested in better methods of road building. One such representative of the Office of Road Inquiry traveled a total of thirty-five thousand miles throughout the trans-Mississippi West in behalf of a road-improvement program.[35] The widely scattered sample road construction was especially illuminating, for it led to local experimentations both in grading methods and use of road-building materials and improved machinery. In Louisiana there was experimentation with the mixing of sand and clay, in the Midwest, in the use of brick, in the Far West, in the use of oil for settling dust, and at one experimental station even steel was tried out as a possible major road ingredient.[36]

One development led to another. Before the century closed, the movement for good roads and the experimentation necessary to bring about road improvement had set in motion profound changes in road engineering techniques; these in turn called for the invention and employment of new road-making machinery. Throughout this era of inquiry and experimentation nothing happened to dispute John L. McAdam's principle, basic to all road building, that a dry soil foundation will carry any load. Road engineers had agreed that there were two requisites for a good road—hardness and smoothness. Their major problem, and one in which they had been assisted by the Office of Road Inquiry, was how best, with the means at hand, to achieve these two objectives. Necessary in the construction of a good, hard road was a drainage system that would overcome the eroding action of water and frost. If thereby a firm, dry road foundation were established, then one of a variety of surfacing materials, such as gravel, stone, and even clay (hard pan) could be used to good effect in producing highly satisfactory wagon roads.[37]

The implementation of these basic road-making principles required new or improved equipment. Post-war road-building projects in the West still employed the same types of horse-drawn drags, scrapers, and dirt-hauling vehicles used in the early nineteenth century. But a succession of inventions important to the business were fast being made. In 1856 L. du Pont pioneered in the manufacture of blasting powder that greatly facilitated the rock-crushing process, which was in turn speeded up by Eli Whitney Blake's invention of the so-called "jaw rock crusher" and the simultaneous introduction of the dump wagon. These inventions were accompanied by the introduction of stump extractors, power rollers, and other devices and machines. Then with the manufacture of Portland cement, begun in the United States in 1871, the day was not far off when concrete was to be used in the making of the ideal hard-surfaced, dustless highways. Even steam engines made their appearance on some projects. Long hauls of rock, sand, and other materials were greatly augmented by railroad transportation, as were newly discovered petroleum products that were being utilized on some road projects within the trans-Mississippi West. The use of these new devices and methods in road building, however, did not overnight transform primitive, frontier trails into high standard roads.

Not until 1904 did anyone possess specific knowledge of the over-all road situation in the United States. At that time the United States Office of Public Roads (successor to the Office of Road Inquiry) made a thorough survey of road mileages (improved and unimproved) and expenditures for roads in each of the states and territories. This was probably the first complete inventory of road assets ever made in the nation and, among other things, it revealed the startling fact that within the trans-Mississippi West there were only 28,568 miles (2.51 per cent) of improved roads out of a total mileage of 1,050,635 within that region. As might have been expected, the average percentage of the improved western roads, namely 2.51, was considerably less than the national average of 7.14 percent indicated on the table on the opposite page.[38]

*B*RIDGE CONSTRUCTION as a means of improving upon primitive frontier methods of crossing streams, such as ferrying, rafting, fording, wading, swimming, and pickaback, was also a matter of importance. With the advent of the covered wagon migrations to the Far West, enterprising persons hastened to provide ferrying (in some instances, steamboat) services at many major crossings that included the Mississippi and Missouri rivers. Migrants frequently alluded in the diaries and journals to the availability of rope ferries and also to exorbitant tolls exacted by ferry operators. In one instance toll was posted at five dollars per head, "biped or quadruped."[39]

The building and operation of bridges likewise lay within the domain of private entrepreneurship, but in due course such fixed structures became increasingly the property and responsibility of the general public. Earlier bridges within the trans-Mississippi West, whether privately or publicly owned, were at best of simple wood construction. Poor engineering and neglect often caused such bridges either to be washed away during high water or to rot away. Even when public officials undertook

Public-Road Mileage and Expenditures in the Trans-Mississippi West in 1904

State or territory	Total mileage	Population per mile of road	Total miles of improved road *†	Percentage improved	Total dollars spent on roads	Dollars spent per mile	Dollars spent per inhabitant
Arizona	5987	20	217	3.62	109,309	18.25	0.89
Arkansas	36,445	36	236	0.64	1,395,343	38.28	1.06
California	46,653	31	8803	18.87	2,157,396	46.24	1.45
Colorado	30,214	17	178	0.58	707,224	23.40	1.31
Idaho	18,163	9	212	1.16	311,588	17.15	1.92
Iowa	102,448	21	1664	1.62	3,106,607	30.32	1.39
Kansas	101,196	14	273	1.26	1,232,817	12.18	0.83
Louisiana	24,897	55	34	0.13	951,873	38.23	0.68
Minnesota	79,324	22	6247	7.87	1,961,629	24.72	1.12
Missouri	108,133	28	2733	2.52	2,368,973	21.90	0.76
Montana	22,419	10	65	0.28	404,098	18.02	1.66
Nebraska	79,462	13	23	0.02	878,547	11.05	0.82
Nevada	12,585	3	64	0.50	46,876	3.72	1.10
New Mexico	15,326	12	2	0.01	165,652	10.80	0.84
North Dakota	59,332	5	212	0.35	550,341	9.28	1.72
Oklahoma	43,554	9	0	0.0	774,776	17.79	1.94
Oregon	34,258	12	2589	7.55	796,376	23.24	1.92
South Dakota	59,295	7	151	0.25	383,283	6.46	0.95
Texas	121,409	25	2128	1.75	4,138,157	34.08	1.35
Utah	7090	39	608	8.57	218,676	30.84	0.79
Washington	31,998	16	1976	6.17	1,436,070	44.88	2.77
Wyoming	10,447	8	153	1.46	345,932	9.45	1.04
Trans-Mississippi West	1,050,635	13	28,568	2.51	24,441,543	22.29	1.29
United States	2,151,570	35	153,662	7.14	79,771,418	37.07	1.05

* Data compiled by the United States Department of Agriculture, Office of Public Roads, *Public-Road Mileage* by Maurice O. Eldridge, Bulletin No. 32 (Washington, D.C., 1907), pp. 8–9.
† Surfaced with gravel, stone, brick, oil, or other topping materials.

bridge construction, preference was at first shown for cheap, readily available local materials. Iron bridges, infinitely superior but more costly than wooden ones, made their appearance in the West during the 1870s, but public acceptance of them was slow.

Gradually different kinds of bridges were constructed, and each type represented a distinctive principle and design. Most of the smaller bridges were the simple beam type achieved by throwing two parallel logs across a stream bed and covering them with planking. When the length involved was too great for use of single unsupported beams, cantilever, arch, suspension, or truss principles were successfully employed. Of all these common types, the truss alone was a modern invention. It employed simple beams supported by a connected superstructure of framework. The supports (one on each side) took the form of an upright angle. An iron rod extending from the apex of the angle down and through the horizontal beam, fastened at both ends, provided the needed support. To add protection from the weather such bridges were frequently covered and as such lent a distinctive touch to the countryside.[40] Regardless of principle employed, the construction of a bridge in the pioneer West was hailed with glee. When, for example, a wagon and foot bridge was built across the Rio Grande at Albuquerque in 1865, the New Mexico *Press* noted that henceforth pedestrians could safely walk across the river, horsemen could avoid quicksand, carriages avoid delay; "it will bring Albuquerque in communication with all the West."[41]

Important as bridges were to wagon traffic, the catalyst in major bridge construction in the West was the railroad. ". . . the railway has produced an epoch in the affairs of mankind," wrote John B. Jervis in an 1857 report on the feasibility of constructing a railroad bridge across the Mississippi River, and "its progress will be onward."[42] By passage of a River and Harbor Act in 1866 Congress appropriated funds for an army survey and report upon Mississippi River bridge construction between St. Paul and St. Louis. In making a belated 1878 report to the Secretary of War, the army engineers pointed out that during the period of the army's leisurely survey, 1866–1878, a total of eleven railroad and wagon drawbridges (or combinations of the two) had been constructed across the Mississippi River, and that still others had been authorized.[43] While the army engineers looked askance upon bridges that would obstruct river navigation, they placed no limit upon high spans. This same 1878 report observed that the loftiest steamer stack on the river, that of the *James Howard*, towered 69 feet above the pilot house, 104 feet above water; and that, presumably, bridge spans should be built to exceed in height this latter figure. In view of this it is perhaps not surprising that when the time came to consider spanning the Mississippi at St. Louis—the first bridge below the mouth of the Missouri—the preference was for wide arches resting upon high piers.

*B*UT THE DECISION to span the mighty Mississippi at this point involved much more than bridge engineering. It was an ideological triumph of east-west oriented commercial interests over those who clung tenaciously to the belief that neither railroads nor highways could possibly undermine the trade and traffic on the greatest "God-given" water artery of the world. And, moreover, a bridge at St. Louis would be, as the *Missouri Democrat* phrased it, this city's answer to an ebullient, crass Chicago out "to grasp the entire trade of the Far West."[44] Such a bridge had been considered initially as early as 1839, but the first major step leading to construction of a St. Louis bridge was passage of enabling legislation by Congress during 1866. The entire effort was destined to be a mighty one.

Appointed to direct the project as chief engineer was Captain James B. Eads, who was distinguished for his Union army services as a marine engineer. Once the basic matters had been resolved, the work of building began. The bridge was to be two-storied and was to be built to accommodate pedestrian and vehicular as well as railroad traffic. Giant caissons were erected on the river bed, piles sunk to underlying bedrock, two stone masonry piers built up from 91 and 127 feet respectively below high water. On these and on the embankments three huge steel arches were erected to provide the support for what in finished form was a double-decked, 75-foot–wide bridge 2225 feet in length.[45] At the time of its completion this bridge was regarded as one of the world's greatest engineering feats and another of the many great achievements of Captain Eads. It had taken seven years to construct. In the process of erection, workmen had encountered wrecks of sunken ships, the structure had been hit by a devastating tornado, and the engineers had confronted innumerable other problems new to their profession.

The official completion on July 4, 1874 of the new bridge sparked what was allegedly the greatest celebration since the winning of Independence. A crowd estimated at three hundred thousand gathered from all parts of the country to witness the "christening" of the Eads Bridge, as it was fittingly named, and to enjoy the Fourth of July in traditional western fashion. People came by train, in boats, carriages, on horseback, and on foot. At eight o'clock in the morning bands began to play; then came a fifteen-mile long parade featuring the "waffle king and queen," Druids, Sons of Hermann, the Temperance Society, the Ancient Order of Hibernians, marching workers, and units of the United States Army. All of this, reported the *Republican*, seemed to stretch out like "the vision of Macbeth"—"to crack of doom." Added highlights were a one-hundred gun salute and fireworks.[46] As night came, weary celebrants crowded into hotels, billiard halls, and saloons where, according to reports, all available beds, chairs, barber chairs, and benches were utilized as places for sleeping off the effects of the day.

The Eads Bridge was not the first major river span in the West; nor was it to be the last. Earlier bridge crossings of the Mississippi had been made, first at Minneapolis in 1854, and then at Rock Island in 1856; and within the next decade and a half at Hannibal, Missouri; Quincy, Illinois; Burlington, Keokuk, and Dubuque, Iowa; Winona and Hastings, Minnesota; and at Louisiana, Missouri. Preceding the Eads by two years was the completion of the vital Missouri River Bridge linking Omaha and Council Bluffs, and following the Eads structure were vital spans across the Colorado, the Green, Columbia, and other river barriers to rail, horsedrawn, and pedestrian transportation. Several of these bridges served rail traffic only; some were designed to serve horse-drawn vehicles and pedestrians only; still others met all transportation requirements.

For the period 1850–1900, however, nothing symbolizes either so clearly or so dramatically the passing of the transportation frontier in the Mississippi-Missouri area as did the completion of the Eads Bridge. For the citizens of St. Louis this event marked what a local historian called "the strife for commercial dominion"—the eclipse of outdated steamboat interests by the infinitely more efficient and fast-moving railroads.

*R*EGARDLESS of the merits of this particular observation, certain clear trends within the trans-Mississippi West prevailed during the closing quarter of the nineteenth century. This was an area of fast transition not only from steamboats to rails but also from body-shaking horse-drawn stagecoaches and lumbering freight wagons to speeding railroad trains. It was a period, too, that saw at least the beginnings of a movement from bad roads to good roads and from fords and ferries to great bridges across mighty rivers.

Those who on differing dates witnessed the arrival of a railroad in their home town, observed the construction of an improved road past their homes, and who saw sturdy bridges built across river barriers realized that the transportation frontier had given way to a new, fast-paced, and highly mobile order of things.[47] Even so, the opening of the twentieth century ushered in an improved public attitude toward road improvement and a consciousness that a new administrative and technological revolution was just then getting under way. Yet, by 1900 it was not yet possible to turn to a map showing long stretches of well-engineered, top-quality thoroughfares in the trans-Mississippi West. At best road building in this area was far below European standards. In 1897 a Los Angeles newspaper estimated that it would take four thousand dollars per mile to macadamize the thousands of miles that needed to be rebuilt.[48]

Nevertheless, the realization of goals set by those calling for better roads came faster than had been anticipated, due to the invention of "the touring car," capable, as the *Scientific American* stated, of traveling "sixty to seventy miles a day" even over ordinary roads. A hundred dollar contribution in 1908 by one automaker, Henry Ford, and additional contributions from auto owners for the good roads movement were at least an indication of the fact that automobile manufacturers and auto users were about to carry on the work ambitiously begun three decades earlier by the League of American Wheelmen.[49]

NOTES

Brackets indicate author is unknown

Chapter 1: The Transportation Frontier, 1865

[1] A. J. Leach, *A History of Antelope County, Nebraska* (Chicago, 1909), p. 19; Annadore F. Gregory, *Pioneer Days in Crete, Nebraska* (Chadron, Nebr., 1937), p. 20.

[2] There exists a wide assortment of source materials on western civilian roads and trails. Specific references to these will appear in subsequent footnotes. For United States government surveys and road-building operations see such standard works as W. Turrentine Jackson, *Wagon Roads West: A Study of Federal Road Surveys and Construction in the Trans-Mississippi West, 1846–1869* (Berkeley, Calif., 1952); William H. Goetzmann, *Army Exploration in the American West, 1803–1863* (New Haven, Conn., 1959).

[3] See for example the endpaper map in William Wadsworth, *The National Wagon Road Guide* (San Francisco, 1858), p. 73; S. W. Burt and E. L. Berthoud, *The Rocky Mountain Gold Regions* (Denver, 1861), pp. 16, 61; J. L. Campbell, *Idaho: Six Months in the New Gold Diggings. The Emmigrant's Guide Overland* (New York, 1864), pp. 42, 44–45; Edward H. Hall, *The Great West: Travellers', and Miners', and Emigrants' Guide and Hand-Book* (New York, 1865), p. 16.

[4] Hall, *The Great West*, p. 15; Burt and Berthoud, *The Rocky Mountain Gold Regions*, pp. 61–64.

[5] Campbell, *Idaho*, pp. 44–45.

[6] William C. Jolly, "Across the Plains in Days of Hostile Indians," *Nebraska Territorial Pioneers Association: Reminiscences and Proceedings*, 2 vols. (Lincoln, Nebr., 1923), II, 46.

[7] Frank A. Root and William E. Connelley, *The Overland Stage to California* (Topeka, Kan., 1901), p. 71.

[8] Campbell, *Idaho*, p. 51.

[9] Root and Connelley, *The Overland Stage to California*, p. 19.

[10] See list in *ibid.*, p. 398.

[11] G. S. McCain, "A Trip from Atchison, Kansas, to Laurette, Colorado," *Colorado Magazine*, XXVII (April 1950), p. 98.

[12] [   ], "A Stage Ride to Colorado," *Harper's New Monthly Magazine*, XXXV (July 1867), p. 137. Hereafter cited as *Harper's*. See also *Collections of the Kansas State Historical Society, 1926–1928* (Topeka, 1928), XVII, 190–191.

[13] Tables of distances from Kansas City to most of these distant forts, as well as to numerous other places en route, referred to as "[General James H.] Carleton's Distance Tables," appear in Hall, *The Great West*, pp. 163–170.

[14] Captain William Banning and George Hugh Banning, *Six Horses* (New York, 1930); Oscar Osburn Winther, "The Southern Overland Mail and Stagecoach Line, 1857–1861," *New Mexico Historical Review*, XXXII (April 1957), pp. 81–106. A discussion of the Butterfield concern appears in Chapter IV.

[15] The history of these government road projects is fully developed in Jackson, *Wagon Roads West*, chaps. 17–19. See also *The War of the Rebellion: A Compilation of the Official Records of the Union and Confederate Armies* (Washington, D.C., 1896), Ser. I, XLVIII, Pt. I, p. 341. Hereafter cited as *Official Records*. See also Merrill G. Burlingame, "The Influence of the Military in the Building of Montana," *Pacific Northwest Quarterly*, XXIX (April 1938), pp. 141–143.

[16] Oscar Osburn Winther, *Old Oregon Country: A History of Frontier Trade, Transportation, and Travel* (Stanford University, 1950), chaps. 2–3, maps.

[17] See [Sterling M. Holdredge, publ.], *State, Territorial and Ocean Guide Book to the Pacific* (San Francisco, 1865), map opp. p. 136, xliv. J. Ross Browne, "A Tour through Arizona," *Harper's*, XXX (March 1865), pp. 419, 692.

[18] Major General Grenville M. Dodge to Lieutenant Colonel Joseph McC. Bell, November 1, 1865, *Official Records*, Ser. I, XLVIII, Pt. I, pp. 341–343.

[19] For the best description and analysis of the advancing frontier line, see *Report on Population of the United States at the Eleventh Census: 1890* (Washington, D.C., 1895), Pt. I, pp. xxiv–xxv. Hereafter cited as *Eleventh Census.*

[20] *Ibid.*, p. xxv.

[21] *Ibid.*, pp. xxv–xxvi.

[22] *Ibid.*, pp. xviii, xxviii. The estimate on the number of floaters comes from the observant Frank A. Root in Root and Connelley, *The Overland Stage to California*, p. 314.

[23] Raymond L. Welty, "The Western Army Frontier, 1860–1870," Ph.D. dissertation, State University of Iowa, Iowa City, 1924, p. 15.

[24] *Population of the United States in 1860 . . . The Eighth Census* (Washington, D.C., 1864), p. iv. At the prevailing rate of growth it may be presumed that the trans-Mississippi West population as of 1865 was approximately five and one-half million. Hereafter cited as *Eighth Census.*

[25] *Ibid.*, p. xxxi. Published estimates for 1865 appear in various places, but they are at best estimates. See for example Hall, *The Great West,* and Henry G. Langley, comp., *The Pacific Coast Business Directory for 1867* (San Francisco, 1867), pp. 106–155, *passim.*

[26] *Eighth Census,* p. xxix.

[27] *Eleventh Census,* op. p. xxv.

[28] *Eighth Census,* p. xxvii. This census offers no figures on dwellings for Colorado and Nevada.

[29] Horace Greeley, *An Overland Journey . . . 1859* (New York, 1860), p. 128.

[30] One good but far from complete map showing urban centers, posts, major roads, and trails (but not ranches) is *Atlas to Accompany the Official Records of the Union and Confederate Armies,* 2 vols. (Washington, D.C., 1891–1895), II, plate CLXXI.

[31] The 1860 census accords St. Louis a population of 160,773. See *Eighth Census,* p. 297. By the end of the Civil War the city had, according to George H. Morgan's *Annual Statement of the Trade and Commerce of St. Louis . . . 1865* (St. Louis, 1866), p. 2, jumped to an estimated 204,327.

[32] [John Francis Campbell], *A Short American Tramp* (Edinburgh, 1865), p. 313.

[33] St. Louis *Daily Missouri Democrat,* January 31, 1867. Alex D. Anderson, *The Mississippi and Its Forty-Four Navigable Tributaries* (Washington, D.C., 1890), p. 10. The separately published Senate document gives the total navigable mileage of the Mississippi River system as 16,090 by 1890.

[34] J. Milton Mackie, *From Cape Cod to Dixie and the Tropics* (New York, 1864), pp. 157–158; *Duncan & Co's New Orleans Business Directory for 1865* (New Orleans, 1865), p. 1.

[35] Henry Latham, *Black and White* (London, 1867), p. 192, recounts firsthand observations; so too does Ellis P. Oberholtzer, *A History of the United States,* 5 vols., (New York, 1917–1937), I, 59. Captain Willard Glazier, *Peculiarities of American Cities* (Philadelphia, 1885), pp. 279–280, when visiting New Orleans in the mid-1880s, was impressed with the city's revival as a commercial port.

[36] Ossian E. Dodge, *Fourth Annual Report to the St. Paul Chamber of Commerce for 1870* (St. Paul, 1871), pp. 12–14. For St. Paul's prerail role, see Christopher C Andrews, *History of St. Paul, Minn.* (Syracuse, N.Y., 1890), pp. 402–406.

[37] [The Western Historical Company], *History of the State of Nebraska* (Chicago, 1882), p. 197.

[38] J[unius] E. Wharton and D. O. Wilhelm, *History of the City of Denver . . .* (Denver, 1866), p. 3.

[39] George J. Holyoake, *Travels in Search of a Settler's Guide-Book of America and Canada* (London, 1884), p. 78.

[40] Langley, *The Pacific Coast Business Directory for 1867*, p. 155.

[41] *Helena, Montana's Pioneer Directory* (Helena, Mont., 1868), p. 91.

[42] John A. Beadle, *The Undeveloped West; or Five Years in the Territories* (Philadelphia, 1873), pp. 452–453.

[43] Browne, "A Tour through Arizona," pp. 24, 559.

[44] T. Addison Richards, ed., *Appletons' Companion Hand-Book of Travel* (New York, 1866), pp. 210–211.

[45] A special census was taken in Portland in 1865. See S. J. McCormick, *The Portland Directory* (Portland, Ore., 1865), p. 9.

[46] Winther, *The Old Oregon Country*, chap. 15.

Chapter 2: The Persistence of the Overlanders

[1] Root and Connelley, *The Overland Stage to California*, p. 314.

[2] Horace Greeley, "The Plains, as I Crossed Them Ten Years Ago," *Harper's*, XXXVIII (May 1869), p. 790.

[3] Maj. Gen. John Pope to Col. R. M. Sawyer, August 1, 1865, *Official Records*, Ser. I, XLVIII, Pt. II, p. 1150.

[4] Maj. Gen. Grenville M. Dodge to Maj. Gen. John Pope, August 2, 1865, *ibid.*, p. 1158.

[5] Demas Barnes, *From the Atlantic to the Pacific, Overland: A Series of Letters* (New York, 1866), p. 24.

[6] James F. Meline, *Two Thousand Miles on Horseback: Santa Fé and Back* (New York, 1867), p. 22. Fort Kearny has reference to the second post by this name, the one located eight miles south and east of present Kearney, Nebraska. Much of the Oregon-California Trail traffic merged at this point. See Lyle E. Mantor, "Fort Kearny and the Westward Movement," *Nebraska History Magazine*, XXIX (September 1948), pp. 175–207.

[7] Mrs. James D. Agnew, "Idaho Pioneer of 1864," *Washington Historical Quarterly*, XV (January 1924), p. 45.

[8] Sarah R. Herndon, *Days on the Road: Crossing the Plains in 1865* (New York, 1902), pp. 123, 125.

[9] McCain, "A Trip from Atchison, Kansas, to Laurette, Colorado," pp. 96–97.

[10] Frank M. Mills, "Early Commercial Traveling in Iowa," *Annals of Iowa*, XI, ser. 3 (April 1914), p. 335; Bayard Taylor, *Colorado: A Summer Trip* (New York, 1867), p. 155.

[11] Hall, *The Great West*, pp. 156–157; [Col. Henry McCormick], *Across the Continent in 1865* (Harrisburg, Pa., 1937), p. 21.

[12] Ernest Snell, "Transportation during the Homestead Era," MS., Kansas State Historical Society Library, Topeka, Kansas; Walker D. Wyman, "Council Bluffs and the Westward Movement," *Iowa Journal of History*, XLVII (April 1949), p. 11.

[13] A good account of the mass migrations across Iowa and into the trans-Missouri region is in *ibid.*, pp. 113–118. Among the numerous accounts describing conditions

of prairie schooner travel are Frances C. Peabody, "Across the Plains Deluxe in 1865," *Colorado Magazine*, XVIII (March 1941), pp. 71–72; Robert G. Athearn, ed., "Across the Plains in 1863: The Diary of Peter Winne," *Iowa Journal of History*, XLIX (July 1951), pp. 223, 238.

[14] Meline, *Two Thousand Miles on Horseback*, p. 22.

[15] William T. Sherman to General Headquarters, *Senate Executive Documents*, 40 Cong., 1 sess., doc. 2, pp. 1–3; Athearn, "Across the Plains in 1863: The Diary of Peter Winne," p. 235.

[16] At Fort Benton the Fiske Trail connected with the Mullan Road and thereby established a new transcontinental route, this one in the far northern portion of the nation.

[17] Walter M. Underhill, "The Northern Overland Route to Montana," *Washington Historical Quarterly*, XXIII (July 1932), pp. 177–195; C. S. Kingston, ed., "The Northern Overland Route in 1867," *Pacific Northwest Quarterly*, XLI (July 1950), p. 235. A total of about 1400 persons traveled the Fiske Trail from 1863 to 1866. See Jackson, *Wagon Roads West*, p. 276.

[18] "Niobrara-Virginia City Wagon Road: Report of Col. James A. Sawyers, Superintendent," *South Dakota Historical Review*, II (October 1936), pp. 3–44. This is a reprint of the report published in *House Executive Documents*, 39 Cong., 1 sess., no. 58, pp. 10–32. See also Jackson, *Wagon Roads West*, chap. 17; Alice V. Myers, "Wagon Roads West: The Sawyers Expeditions of 1865, 1866," *Annals of Iowa*, XXIII, ser. 3 (January 1942), pp. 213–237.

[19] Lloyd McFarling, "A Trip to the Black Hills in 1876," *Annals of Wyoming*, XXVII (April 1955), pp. 35–42. Another interesting account is Clyde C. Walton, ed., *An Illinois Gold Hunter in the Black Hills: The Diary of Jerry Bryan, March 13 to August 20, 1876* (Springfield, Ill., 1960).

[20] Walker D. Wyman, "Freighting: A Big Business on the Santa Fe Trail," *Kansas Historical Quarterly*, I (November 1931), p. 26. The statistics from the Emporia *News* appear in this article.

[21] P. G. Scott, "Diary of a Frighting Trip From Kit Carson to Trinidad in 1870," *Colorado Magazine*, VIII (July 1931), p. 154.

[22] T. S. Hudson, *A Scamper through America* (London, 1882), p. 198. See also the interesting guidebook by Richard C. McCormick, *Arizona* (New York, 1865), pp. 21–22; Meline, *Two Thousand Miles on Horseback*, p. 271.

[23] Ralph P. Bieber, "Some Aspects of the Santa Fe Trail, 1848–1880," *Chronicles of Oklahoma*, II (March 1924), pp. 5–7. See also Walker D. Wyman, "The Military Phase of Santa Fe Freighting, 1846–1865," *Kansas Historical Quarterly*, I (November 1932), p. 428; also Victor Westphall, "Albuquerque in the 1870's," *New Mexico Historical Review*, XXIII (October 1948), pp. 253, 258.

[24] J. R. Johnson, "Nebraska in the Seventies," *Nebraska History*, XXXVII (June 1956), p. 79 ff.

[25] J. Allen Hosmer, "A Trip to the States," *South Dakota Historical Review*, I (July 1936), p. 184 ff. Another account of a return trip, this one in 1889, is I. W. Bond, comp., "Old Trails in Reverse," *Colorado Magazine*, XXXII (July 1955), pp. 225–233.

[26] Albert D. Richardson, *Beyond the Mississippi* (Hartford, Conn., 1867), p. 78.

[27] [Mr. Socrates Hyacinth], "After Romance—Reality," *The Overland Monthly*, II (May 1869), p. 463.

[28] J. Orin Oliphant, ed., "In a Prairie Schooner, 1878," by Mrs. Lucy Ide, *Washington Historical Quarterly*, XVIII (April 1927), pp. 122–125.

[29] *Ibid.* (October 1927), pp. 126, 191, 195, *passim;* 277, 285, 288, *passim.*

[30] Cass G. Barnes, *The Sod House* (Madison, Nebr., 1930), p. 31.

[31] See, for example, Reginald Aldridge, *Life on a Ranch* (New York, 1884), p. 6.

[32] James H. Cook, *Fifty Years on the Old Frontier* (New Haven, Conn., 1923), pp. 154–155.

[33] James H. Kyner, *End of Track* (Lincoln, Nebr., 1960), p. 170.

[34] The Eccles reminiscence was gathered by interview and published as Maurice Howe, "The Great West: Two Interviews," *The Frontier* and *Midland*, XVII (Winter 1936–1937), p. 146.

[35] Hudson, *A Scamper through America*, pp. 93–94. For an 1890 view of the Southwest, see also Susie C. Clark, *The Round Trip from the Hub to the Golden Gate* (New York, 1890), p. 16. For a comment on this transition, especially on the northern plains, see comment by J. Orin Oliphant in Ide, "In a Prairie Schooner, 1878," (April 1927), p. 122.

Chapter 3: Teamsters on the Frontier

[1] Nick Eggenhofer, *Wagons, Mules and Men* (New York, 1961), pp. 35–42. See also Oscar Osburn Winther, *The Story of the Conestoga* (New York, 1954).

[2] The history of the Russell, Majors and Waddell freighting firm is told in Raymond W. Settle and Mary Lund Settle, *Empire on Wheels* (Stanford University, Calif., 1949), chaps. 1–3.

[3] Matthew Quigg, comp., *Atchison City Directory, and Business Mirror for 1865* (n.p., 1865), pp. 8–9. [Millison and Heil, publs.], *Topeka City Directory and Business Mirror for 1868–69* (Topeka, 1868), p. 31. See also Wyman, "Freighting: A Big Business on the Santa Fe Trail," pp. 17–27. Due mainly to extremely highly transportation costs in the West, wagon freight volume and rates were stated in pounds rather than in tons.

[4] Quigg, *Atchison City Directory*, pp. 10–11; [George A. Crofutt and Company], *Great Trans-Continental Railroad Guide* by Bill Dadd, the Scribe (New York, 1869), p. 27.

[5] Figures on this trade appear in Morgan, *Annual Statement of the Trade and Commerce of St. Louis*, p. 35. See also [Crofutt], *Guide*, pp. 27–28; Welty, "The Western Army Frontier," pp. 298–299.

[6] Meline, *Two Thousand Miles on Horseback*, pp. 10, 22; Wyman, "Freighting: A Big Business on the Santa Fe Trail," pp. 26–27; also by Meline, "The Military Phase of Santa Fe Freighting," pp. 427–428. Charles F. Lummis, "Pioneer Transportation in America," *McClure's Magazine*, XXV (November 1905), pp. 84–85, also cites some figures on the volume of western wagon freighting. See also R. D. Holt, "Old Texas Wagon Trains," *Frontier Times*, XXV (September 1948), pp. 269–272. See also William A. Bell, *New Tracks in North America*, 2 vols. (London, 1869), I, 26.

[7] Richardson, *Beyond the Mississippi*, p. 329. See also Maj. Gen. Grenville M. Dodge to Maj. Gen. John Pope, August 2, 1865, *Official Records*, Ser. I, XLVIII, Pt. II, p. 1158; Richardson, *Beyond the Mississippi*, p. 329.

[8] Paul Morton, "Early Freighting Days in the West," *Santa Fe Employees' Magazine*, III (August 1909), p. 1013. See, for example, Beadle, *The Undeveloped West*, p. 98; Richardson, *Beyond the Mississippi*, p. 330; Richard E. Owen and E. T. Cox, *Report on the Mines of New Mexico* (Washington, D.C., 1865), p. 45.

[9] As construction of the Central Pacific Railroad pushed eastward, the wagon-

freighting lines were shortened correspondingly. See Hubert H. Bancroft, *History of Nevada, Colorado, and Wyoming, 1540–1888* (San Francisco, 1890), p. 235.

[10] Virginia City *Montana Post*, April 29, 1865; February 3, 1866. See also John W. Hakola, "Samuel T. Hauser and the Economic Development of Montana," Ph.D. dissertation, Indiana University, Bloomington, Ind., 1961, pp. 125–129. See also Hubert H. Bancroft, *History of Washington, Idaho, and Montana, 1845–1889* (San Francisco, 1890), pp. 729–730n. For a detailed discussion of wagon freighting in the so-called inland empire, see Winther, *Old Oregon Country*, chap. 15. Idaho trade is also discussed in some detail in Arthur L. Throckmorton, *Oregon Argonauts* (Portland, 1961), chap. 12.

[11] This practice is discussed in a pioneer account by Holt, "Old Texas Wagon Trains," p. 269. Newspaper advertisements and local directories also indicate that freighters doing short-haul operations were numerous.

[12] William F. Hooker, *The Prairie Schooner* (Chicago, 1918), p. 33. Hooker, who served for a time as a freighter for the Union Pacific Railroad, knew the economics of the freighting business well. Atchison *Daily Globe*, July 16, 1894.

[13] E. Neil Mattson, *Red River Carts Trek: Historic Pembina Trail* (n.p., n.d.), pp. 3–6. See also Andrews, *St. Paul*, pp. 406–407.

[14] Mattson, *Red River Carts*, p. 14; Andrews, *St. Paul*, p. 408. The Pembina carts are also discussed in scholarly manner by Harold E. Briggs, "Early Freight and Stage Lines in Dakota," *North Dakota Historical Quarterly*, III (July 1929), pp. 229–232.

[15] Emily Ann O'Neil, "Joseph Murphy's Contribution to Development of the Great American West," M.A. thesis, St. Louis University, St. Louis, 1947, provides a biographical sketch of Joseph Murphy, the St. Louis wagon maker, and it contains also sketchy information on J. Murphy wagons. Studebaker Brothers Manufacturing Company issued many illustrated catalogs, one an *Illustrated Catalogue of Wagons, Buggies and Carriages*, World's Fair Edition (South Bend, Ind., 1892). See also Welty, "The Western Army Frontier," p. 287; [Maj. George A. Lawrence], *Silverland* (London, 1873), p. 171. Although first made in St. Louis, the J. Murphy wagon was later manufactured in Chicago and Indianapolis, and subsequently became known as the "Bain." See also D. P. Rolfe, "Overland Freighting from Nebraska City," *Proceedings and Collections*, Nebraska State Historical Society, ser. 2 (Lincoln, Nebr., 1902), V, p. 281.

[16] Information on wagons comes in tidbits from such scattered sources as J. M. Hutchings, *In the Heart of the Sierras* (Oakland, Calif., 1886), p. 209; Emerson Hough, "A Study in Transportation: The Settlement of the West," *Century*, n.s., XLI (November 1901), p. 212; Samuel Bowles, *Across the Continent: A Summer's Journey* (Springfield, Mass., 1865), pp. 266–267.

[17] William Henry Jackson, *Time Exposure: An Autobiography* (New York, 1940), p. 108, makes the point that the so-called long trains, those numbered in the hundreds, were really in units of twenty-five. Demas Barnes, who wrote on-the-scene letters during an overland trip in 1865, commented interestingly about freighting on the plains in his book *From the Atlantic to the Pacific*, p. 23. A good reminiscent account appears in Atchison *Daily Globe*, July 16, 1894.

[18] [William F. Cody], *The Life of William F. Cody* (Hartford, Conn., [1879]), p. 66. Settle and Settle, *Empire on Wheels*, chap. 4, have described very well the pattern-setting Russell, Majors and Waddell methods; for the later period a suitable reference is Lummis, "Pioneer Transportation in America," p. 81. See also Rolfe, "Overland Freighting from Nebraska City," p. 282.

[19] T. S. Garrett, "Some Recollections of an Old Freighter," *Annals of Wyoming*, III (July 1925), pp. 86–93.

[20] The observant English traveler T. S. Hudson took special note of wagon trains; see his *A Scamper through America*, pp. 177–178. J. A. Filcher, *Untold Tales of California* (n.p., 1903), pp. 75–79, *passim*, has made teamsters a principal subject for discussion. And among a great variety of additional references are: Barnes, *The Sod House*, pp. 197–198; Holt, "Old Texas Wagon Trains," pp. 269, 276; Jesse Brown, "The Freighter in Early Days," *Annals of Wyoming*, XIX (July 1947), pp. 113–114; also T. H. McGee, "Early Days in the West," *Quarterly Bulletin*, Wyoming Historical Department, I (April 15, 1924), p. 15; William F. Hooker, "The Frontier Freight Train Wagon-boss of the 1870's," *The Union Pacific Magazine*, IV (November 1925), pp. 9–10. For the California scene, especially as it prevailed during the Gold Rush and later Comstock era, see the commendable work of Joseph A. McGowan, "Freighting to the Mines in California, 1849–1859," Ph.D. dissertation, University of California, Berkeley, 1949, pp. 279–280. The conditions described by this author prevailed in post-Civil War California and Nevada. See also Atchison *Daily Globe*, July 16, 1894.

[21] For the diatribe against mules see Sam P. Ridings, *The Chisholm Trail* (Guthrie, Okla., 1936), p. 399; Root and Connelley, *The Overland Stage to California*, p. 304. Chapter 13 in this valuable source is devoted to overland freighting. Most ardent in praise of mules for use in the southwestern desert were Owen and Cox, *Report on the Mines of New Mexico*, pp. 28–29. See also Holt, "Old Texas Wagon Trains," p. 272; *Agriculture of the United States in 1860 . . . The Eighth Census* (Washington, D.C., 1864), p. cxiii; Capt. John Mullan, *Miners and Travels' Guide . . .* (New York, 1865), p. 9.

[22] Root and Connelley, *The Overland Stage to California*, p. 304; Holt, "Old Texas Wagon Trains," pp. 271–274; T. U. Taylor, "In the Days of Frontier Freighting," *Frontier Times*, II (January 1925), p. 12.

[23] McGowan, "Freighting to the Mines in California," pp. 279–290.

[24] James C. Olson, ed., "From Nebraska City to Montana, 1866; The Diary of Thomas Alfred Creigh," *Nebraska History*, XXIX (September 1948), pp. 212, 227.

[25] Holt, "Old Texas Wagon Trains," pp. 272–273. See also Barnes, *From the Atlantic to the Pacific*, p. 23; Welty, "The Western Army Frontier," p. 112; Brown, "The Freighter in Early Days," p. 113; William M. Street, "The Victory of the Plow," *Transactions of the Kansas State Historical Society* (Topeka, 1906), X, pp. 35–36; Charles Raber, "Personal Recollections of Life on the Plains from 1860 to 1868," *Collections of the Kansas State Historical Society, 1923–25* (Topeka, 1925), XVI, pp. 316–341.

[26] [Russell, Majors and Waddell], *Rules and Regulations for the Governing of Russell, Majors & Waddell's Outfit* (Nebraska City, 1859), pp. 1–8.

[27] Some of the most vivid, if not delicate, commentaries on freighter cooking are scattered through Scott, "Diary," pp. 146–154. Also informative are Taylor, "In the Days of Frontier Freighting," pp. 12–13; Brown, "The Freighter in Early Days," p. 112; and Barnes, *The Sod House*, p. 200.

[28] Scott, "Diary," pp. 147–149; Brown, "The Freighter in Early Days," p. 112.

[29] [Russell, Majors and Waddell], *Rules and Regulations*, pp. 5–6. See also Barnes, *From the Atlantic to the Pacific*, p. 23; Brown, "The Freighter in Early Days," pp. 112–113; Taylor, "In the Days of Frontier Freighting," p. 12. See also T. K. Tyson, "Freighting to Denver," *Proceedings and Collections of Nebraska State Historical Society*, ser. 2 (Lincoln, Nebr., 1902), V, pp. 255–260. Contrary to the Russell, Majors and Waddell manual, Jackson, *Time Exposure*, pp. 110–111, states that wagon tongues should be out-turned instead of in-turned. Either system was functional.

[30] Bowles, *Across the Continent*, pp. 14–15. A good description of this type of

scene is also found in George P. Marvin, "Bull-Whacking Days," *Proceedings and Collections of Nebraska State Historical Society*, ser. 2 (Lincoln, Nebr., 1902), V p. 227.

[31] Dagmar Mariager, "Camp and Travel in Colorado," *Overland*, n.s., XVI (October 1890), p. 347. See also McGowan, "Freighting to the Mines in California," pp. 269, 271; Maj. W. Shepherd, *Prairie Experiences* (London, 1884), p. 201.

[32] Col. George A. Armes, *Ups and Downs of an Army Officer* (Washington, D.C., 1900), p. 161; James Swisher, *How I Know* (Cincinnati, 1881), pp. 209–211.

[33] W. W. Watson, "Early History of Jefferson County Overland Route," *Proceedings and Collections of the Nebraska State Historical Society*, ser. 2 (Lincoln, Nebr., 1902), V, pp. 217–218; see also Swisher, *How I Know*, p. 167.

[34] Charles Raber, "Personal Recollections," p. 330.

[35] This point is brought home very emphatically by A. W. Haggard, an old-time Great Plains freighter, in "The Freighter Business," *Annals of Wyoming*, III (July 1925), pp. 85–86.

[36] Filcher, *Untold Tales of California*, pp. 78–79; Clarence King, *Mountaineering in the Sierra Nevada* (Boston, 1872), pp. 215–216.

[37] King, *Mountaineering in the Sierra Nevada*, pp. 214–215.

[38] Filcher, *Untold Tales of California*, p. 89. See also King, *Mountaineering in the Sierra Nevada*, pp. 213–214.

[39] Filcher, *Untold Tales of California*, pp. 105–115.

[40] Holt, "Old Texas Wagon Trains," p. 275.

[41] Elmer O. Davis, comp., *The First Five Years of the Railroad Era in Colorado* (n.p., 1948), p. 110.

[42] Swisher, *How I Know*, p. 166, among others, observed and commented upon the transition that had taken place in frontier freighting operations. See also N. S. Shaler, "Winter Journey in Colorado," *Atlantic Monthly*, XLVII (January 1881), p. 50.

Chapter 4: Stagecoaching as Frontier Enterprise

[1] Greeley, "The Plains, as I Crossed Them Ten Years Ago," p. 794.

[2] Kenneth E. Colton, "Stagecoach Travel in Iowa," *Annals of Iowa*, XXII (January 1940), p. 177.

[3] Orville F. Grahame, "Stagecoach Days," *The Palimpsest*, V (May 1924), pp. 176, 185.

[4] William S. Wallace, "Stagecoaching in Territorial New Mexico," *New Mexico Historical Review*, XXXII, 3d ser. (April 1957), p. 206. See also Hubert H. Bancroft, *History of Arizona and New Mexico* (San Francisco, 1889), p. 496.

[5] Salt Lake City *Daily Union Vedette*, July 15, 1865.

[6] Charles S. Potts, "Transportation in Texas," in *Texas History*, ed. by Eugene C. Barker (Dallas, 1929), p. 545. See also Hubert H. Bancroft, *History of the Northern Mexican States and Texas*, 2 vols. (San Francisco, 1889), II, 569–570.

[7] Arthur J. Larsen, "The Northwestern Express and Transportation Company," *North Dakota Historical Quarterly*, VI (October 1931), pp. 42, 47–48, 51; Roy P. Johnson, "Stagecoaching Days . . . ," *The Fargo Forum*, December 26, 1954 and January 23, 1955, in Scrapbook, Minnesota Historical Society Library, St. Paul.

[8] Andrews, *St. Paul*, p. 406. See also Arthur J. Larsen, "Roads and Trails in the Minnesota Triangle, 1849–1860," *Minnesota History*, XI (December 1930), pp. 401–407.

[9] Oscar Osburn Winther, *Express and Stagecoach Days in California* (Stanford University, Calif., 1936), pp. 81–91. For a discussion of staging in and out of the southern mines of California, see William H. Boyd, "The Stagecoach in the Southern San Joaquin Valley, 1854–1876," *Pacific Historical Review*, XXVI (November 1957), pp. 365–366.

[10] Winther, *Express and Stagecoach Days in California*, pp. 153–156.

[11] Winther, *Old Oregon Country*, pp. 255–257.

[12] LeRoy R. Hafen, *The Overland Mail, 1849–1869* (Cleveland, 1926), chap. 3. In this chapter the author traces the beginning of pioneer mails in the intermountain area of the Far West.

[13] Banning and Banning, *Six Horses*, pp. 92 ff.

[14] Rupert N. Richardson and Carl Coke Rister, *The Greater Southwest* (Glendale, Calif., 1935), pp. 232–233; Hafen, *The Overland Mail*, p. 83.

[15] *Congressional Globe*, 34 Cong., 1 sess., pt. 3, p. 2202.

[16] *Ibid.*, 34 Cong., 3 sess., Appendix, pp. 307, 308, 321.

[17] United States, *Statutes at Large*, 34–36 Congs., vol. XI, p. 190.

[18] Report of the Postmaster General, December 1, 1859, *Senate Executive Documents*, 35 Cong., 1 sess., pp. 987–988.

[19] *Ibid.*, pp. 989–993.

[20] Winther, "The Southern Overland Mail and Stagecoach Line," pp. 96–97.

[21] *Ibid.*, pp. 97–98.

[22] Lyle H. Wright and Josephine M. Bynum, eds., *The Butterfield Overland Mail by Waterman L. Ormsby* (San Marino, Calif., 1955), *passim*.

[23] Report of the Postmaster General, *Senate Executive Documents*, 35 Cong., 2 sess., vol. IV, p. 718.

[24] Quoted in Ray A. Billington, *The Far Western Frontier, 1830–1860* (New York, 1956), 279.

[25] Sacramento *Daily Union*, September 1, 1857.

[26] The last days on the Butterfield trail are told in Roscoe P. Conkling and Margaret B. Conkling, *The Butterfield Overland Mail, 1857–1869*, 3 vols. (Glendale, Calif., 1947), II, 325–344.

[27] Settle and Settle, *Empire on Wheels*, chap. 6; Margaret Lang, "The Route of the Leavenworth and Pike's Peak Express," *Colorado History*, XII (September 1935), pp. 186–194. See also George A. Root and Russell K. Hickman, "Pike's Peak Express Companies," *Kansas Historical Quarterly*, XIII (August 1944), pp. 163–195, 211–242; (August 1945), pp. 485–526; (February 1946), pp. 36–9.

[28] The story of the Pony Express is satisfactorily told in Arthur Chapman, *The Pony Express* (New York, 1932), but some additional materials are included in Raymond W. Settle and Mary Lund Settle, *Saddles and Spurs: The Pony Express Saga* (Harrisburg, Pa., 1955).

[29] Settle and Settle, *Empire on Wheels*, chap. 8.

[30] As one of the first steps taken in revamping his line, Holladay changed the hitherto-used Oregon Trail route along the North Platte and through South Pass to a more direct route leading to Denver and Salt Lake City. His new route, established in 1862, followed the South Platte and crossed the continental divide at Bridger Pass. See Edward Bliss, "Denver to Salt Lake by Overland Stage in 1862," *Colorado Magazine*, VIII (September 1931), p. 190, n.

[31] For the best treatment of overland mail service on the central route, see Hafen, *The Overland Mail*, chaps. 10, 12. On the Holladay organization, consult J. V. Frederick, *Ben Holladay: The Stagecoach King* (Glendale, Calif., 1940), pp. 71 ff. Winther, *Old Oregon Country*, chap. 18, discusses stagecoach operations in the inland empire.

[32] Root and Connelley, *The Overland Stage to California*, chap. 17; pp. 400–404. See also Quigg, *Atchison City Directory*, pp. 10–11, for a somewhat itemized account of the assets of this concern. Its relations with Holladay are discussed in Frederick, *Ben Holladay*, pp. 243–252.

[33] Root and Connelley, *The Overland Stage to California*, pp. 404–405.

[34] This tabulation has been made by Frederick, *Ben Holladay*, p. 259.

[35] *Ibid.*, p. 302. In *Senate Executive Documents*, 46 Cong., 2 sess., vol. V, no. 211, p. 1, there is a compilation of all contracts entered into between the Postmaster General and Holladay.

[36] For the historical background of Wells, Fargo and Company, see Winther, *Express and Stagecoach Days in California*, pp. 51–75, 141–150.

[37] Root and Connelley, *The Overland Stage to California*, p. 406.

[38] Frederick, *Ben Holladay*, pp. 260–262.

[39] A good over-all treatment of the stagecoach business in Dakota Territory is Briggs, "Early Freight and Stage Lines in Dakota," pp. 229–261. The Marquis de Mores' venture is specially told by Lewis F. Crawford, *The Medora-Deadwood Stage Line* (Bismarck, N.D., 1925), pp. 5–6, 8. And a thorough account of the Cheyenne-Black Hills operations is Agnes W. Spring, *The Cheyenne and Black Hills Stage and Express Routes* (Glendale, Calif., 1949), pp. 81–95.

[40] Louis Pfaller, "The Fort Keogh to Bismarck Stage Route," *North Dakota History*, XXI (July 1954), pp. 91–125.

Chapter 5: Overland by Stage

[1] According to Alexander Andrews, "Coaching," *Gentleman's Magazine*, VI, n.s. (May 1871), p. 677, the William Dugdale diary contains the first mention of coaching in England.

[2] The best accounts dealing with the Concord coach are Elmer M. Hunt, "Abbot-Downing and the Concord Coach," *Historical New Hampshire* (November 1945), pp. 1–20; and Eggenhofer, *Wagons, Mules and Men*, pp. 160–168. See also Edwin G. Burgum, "The Concord Coach," *Colorado Magazine*, XVI (September 1939), pp. 173–180. At one time Burgum painted ornamental work on Concord coaches for Abbot, Downing and Company.

[3] Conkling and Conkling, *The Butterfield Overland Mail*, I, 133. See also Johnson, "Stagecoaching Days"; and Colton, "Stagecoach Travel in Iowa," p. 186.

[4] Richardson, *Beyond the Mississippi*, p. 159.

[5] Quoted in J. L. Ringwalt, *Development of Transportation Systems in the United States* (Philadelphia, 1888), p. 65.

[6] Hudson, *A Scamper through America*, p. 152. Mule teams were not unknown in the staging business. See Root and Connelley, *The Overland Stage to California*, p. 72.

[7] William S. Wallace, "Short-Line Staging in New Mexico," *New Mexico Historical Review*, XXVI (April 1951), p. 98.

[8] *Ibid.*, pp. 99–100.

[9] Atchison *Daily Globe*, September 14, 1940, Souvenir edition; [   ], *Half Hours in the Wide West* (London, ca. 1872), p. 166.

[10] Hutchings, *Heart of the Sierras*, p. 212. See also John W. Boddam-Whetham, *Western Wanderings* (London, 1874), p. 144.

[11] Johnson, "Stagecoaching Days," A[lexander] K. McClure, *Three Thousand Miles through the Rocky Mountains* (Philadelphia, 1869), p. 133.

[12] Oliver W. Holmes, ed., "James A. Garfield's Diary of a Trip to Montana in 1872," *Frontier and Midland,* XV (Winter 1934–1935), p. 163.

[13] [   ], *Half Hours in the Wide West,* pp. 167–168. There are numerous accounts of imbibing drivers and passengers. See for example Judge O. W. Williams, "The Old Times Stage Driver's Disappointment," *Frontier Times,* XXIX (June 1952), p. 265.

[14] Boddam-Whetham, *Western Wanderings,* p. 144; also J. G. Player-Frowd, *Six Months in California* (London, 1872), p. 11.

[15] Root and Connelley, *The Overland Stage to California,* p. 66.

[16] Clemens, Samuel L. (Mark Twain), *Roughing It* (Hartford, Conn., 1888), p. 25.

[17] Edward M. Blougher, "Early Day Transportation in Western Kansas," MS, Kansas State Historical Society, Topeka, p. 1. About eight to twelve animals were kept at stations, and it required from forty to eighty tons of hay to feed this number of animals over a one-year period. See Root and Connelley, *The Overland Stage to California,* p. 74.

[18] Salt Lake City *Daily Union Vedette,* June 6, 1865; Root and Connelley, *The Overland Stage to California,* p. 240; Lyle E. Mantor, "Stage Coach and Freighter Days at Fort Kearny," *Nebraska History,* XXIX (December 1948), p. 325. A twenty-day schedule was prescribed for eight months of the year; twenty-three days were allowed during winter months.

[19] Quigg, *Atchison City Directory,* advertisement, pp. 22, 68; Winther, *Express and Stagecoach Days in California,* p. 100, advertisement facsimile, op. p. 95; Henry Castle, *History of St. Paul and Vicinity* (Chicago, 1912), p. 416; Root and Connelley, *The Overland Stage to California,* pp. 64–65.

[20] Taylor, *Colorado: A Summer Trip,* p. 31.

[21] W. Thornton Parker, *Personal Experiences among North American Indians from 1867 to 1885* (Northampton, Mass., 1913), p. 56. See also [   ], *Half Hours in the Wide West,* p. 129.

[22] McClure, *Three Thousand Miles through the Rockies,* pp. 144–145.

[23] *Ibid.,* pp. 191, 305–306.

[24] Taylor, *Colorado: A Summer Trip,* p. 19. See also J. Ross Browne, "Ride on the Frontier of Texas," *Overland Monthly,* I (August 1868), p. 161, for an intimate account of travel and life in the Southwest.

[25] J. D. Fauntleroy, "Old Stage Routes of Texas," *Frontier Times,* VI (July 1929), p. 422. See also Kansas City *Star,* November 20, 1890.

[26] Swisher, *How I Know,* p. 180. See also William H. Bishop, "Across Arizona," *Harper's,* LXVI (March 1883), p. 490.

[27] Williams, "The Old Times Stage Driver's Disappointment," p. 266.

[28] Mantor, "Stagecoach and Freighter Days at Fort Kearny," p. 325.

[29] Samuel Bowles, *Our New West* (New York, 1869), p. 38.

[30] Richardson, *Beyond the Mississippi,* p. 340.

[31] Theodore R. Davis, "A Stage Ride to Colorado," *Harper's,* XXXV (July 1867), p. 137; Salt Lake City *Daily Union Vedette,* June 6, 1865. Taylor, *Colorado: A Summer Trip,* p. 168, bemoaned the fact that stagecoaches were built on the presumption that American people are lean and of diminutive stature.

[32] Barnes, *From the Atlantic to the Pacific,* pp. 7–8. See also Root and Connelley, *The Overland Stage to California,* p. 69 ff.

[33] Taylor, *Colorado: A Summer Trip,* p. 170.

[34] *Ibid.,* p. 33; Davis, "A Stage Ride to Colorado," pp. 139–140.

[35] Raphael Pumpelly, *Across America and Asia* (New York, 1870), pp. 1–5.

[36] Bowles, *Across the Continent,* pp. 15–16.

³⁷ Beadle, *The Undeveloped West*, p. 755; [   ], *Half Hours in the Wide West*, p. 251.

³⁸ Boddam-Whetham, *Western Wanderings*, p. 106.

³⁹ [Charles Beadle], *A Trip to the United States in 1887* (n.p., ca. 1888), p. 116. See also Wallis Nash, *Oregon, There and Back in 1877* (London, 1878), p. 101; John M. Murphy, *Rambles in North-Western America from the Pacific Ocean to the Rocky Mountains* (London, 1879), p. 76.

⁴⁰ Browne, "A Tour through Arizona," p. 419. See also Wallace, "Stagecoaching in Territorial New Mexico," pp. 204–208.

⁴¹ J[ohn] Codman, "Through Utah," *Galaxy*, XX (September 1875), p. 790.

⁴² [   ], *Half Hours in the Wide West*, pp. 198–201.

⁴³ McClure, *Three Thousand Miles through the Rocky Mountains*, pp. 431–432; Johnson, "Stagecoaching Days."

⁴⁴ Carie J. Crouch, "The Old Butterfield Stage," *National Republican*, XVII (March 1930), p. 21.

⁴⁵ Davis, *The First Five Years of the Railroad in Colorado*, p. 112. See also Topeka *Daily Commonwealth*, January 30, 1886.

⁴⁶ Dodge City *Globe*, October 22, 1930.

Chapter 6: Steamboats on a Vanishing Frontier

¹ This shift is clearly represented by figures on boat arrivals at the capital river port of New Orleans. In 1846 flatboat arrivals, totaling 2792, had hit a peak; at the onset of the Civil War the annual number had dropped to about five hundred. Steamboat arrivals at New Orleans for the approximate corresponding period numbered 2770 in 1846, but by 1860 the number of arrivals had reached their high-water mark of 3566. Precise tonnage figures are unfortunately not available. See Frank H. Dixon, *A Traffic History of the Mississippi River System*, National Waterways Commission Report (Washington, D.C., 1909), doc. 11, pp. 14–15.

² This is discussed in detail in George Dangerfield, *Chancellor Robert R. Livingston of New York, 1746–1813* (New York, 1960), pp. 415–417.

³ *Ibid.*, p. 15; Louis C. Hunter, *Steamboats on the Western Rivers* (Cambridge, Mass., 1949), Table 25, p. 662. The discrepancy in totals between those of Dixon and Hunter are minimal.

⁴ Dixon, *A Traffic History of the Mississippi River System*, p. 24. This crucial role played by St. Louis is well set forth in the St. Louis *Dispatch*, June 30, 1865. St. Louis is located 848 miles below St. Anthony Falls, the headwaters of Mississippi River steamboat transportation, 182 miles north of the mouth of the Ohio River, and 1242 miles above New Orleans. The mileage of navigable streams was subsequently increased by river clearance operations and use of improved shallow-water craft.

⁵ Dixon, *A Traffic History of the Mississippi River System*, p. 24; L. U. Reavis, *St. Louis: The Commercial Metropolis of the Mississippi Valley* (St. Louis, 1874), p. 14.

⁶ [Bureau of Railway Economics], *An Economic Survey of Inland Waterway Transportation in the United States* (Washington, D.C., 1930), doc. 56, p. 36. See also William L. Heckman, *Steamboating Sixty-five Years on Missouri's Rivers* (Kansas City, Mo., 1950), p. 29.

⁷ [Denson and Nelson], *New Orleans and Mississippi Valley Business Directory and River Guide for 1866 and '67* (St. Louis, 1866), p. 195.

⁸ Frederick Way, Jr., comp., *Way's Steamboat Directory* (Sewickley, Pa., [1944]),

p. 1. See also St. Louis *Daily Missouri Democrat*, March 10, 1869; Hunter, *Steamboats on the Western Rivers*, Table 25, p. 662. The leading postwar concerns were the St. Louis and New Orleans Packet Company (later the Merchant's Southern Line Packet Company), Chalmette Packet Company (which ranged widely over the Mississippi River system), the Crescent City Packet Company (going as far as Cariola, Arkansas), the Mississippi Packet Company, and many others. See Ella Rictor, "Transportation," in *Standard History of New Orleans, Louisiana*, Henry Rictor, ed. (Chicago, 1900), p. 290.

[9] A complete listing with navigable mileages appears in Anderson, *The Mississippi and Its Forty-Four Navigable Tributaries*, p. 10. This publication, a Senate document, lists the mileage of the navigable portions of the Mississippi system.

[10] Muriel H. Wright, "Early Navigation and Commerce along the Arkansas and Red Rivers in Oklahoma," *Chronicles of Oklahoma*, VIII (March 1930), pp. 65–88. For a complete list of steamboats on this river, see N. Philip Norman, "The Red River to the South . . . with a Tabulated List of Steamboats . . . ," *Louisiana Historical Quarterly*, XXV (April 1942), pp. 403–535.

[11] Wright, "Early Navigation and Commerce along the Arkansas and Red Rivers in Oklahoma," pp. 65–71. See also Edgar Langsdorf, "A Review of Early Navigation on the Kansas River," *Kansas Historical Quarterly*, XVIII (May 1950), p. 144.

[12] T. C. Purdy, "Report on Steam Navigation in the United States," in *Report on the Agencies of Transportation in the United States, Tenth Census* (Washington, D.C., 1883), IV, 16–17. See also St. Paul *Weekly Pioneer and Democrat*, November 18, 1864. Steamboating was also developed above St. Anthony Falls, but St. Paul remained the headwater port for the Mississippi River steamboat trade. St. Paul's navigation season opened about the last week in March or in early April; it usually closed between November 20 and December 10. Thus the days during which steamboats could operate in this area ranged from 200 to 250 days.

[13] Andrews, *History of St. Paul, Minn.*, p. 323. See also Ruth Bristow, "Early Steamboat and Packet Lines," *La Crosse County Historical Sketches* (La Crosse, Wis., 1931), Ser. 1, pp. 32–33.

[14] William J. Petersen, "Steamboating in the Upper Mississippi Fur Trade," *Minnesota History*, XIII (September 1932), p. 241. The upper Mississippi led to the Minnesota River, and a portage at the headwaters of this stream led in turn to the Red, or vice versa.

[15] St. Louis *Daily Missouri Democrat*, March 11, 1869; Fred A. Bill, "Early Steamboating on the Red River," *North Dakota Historical Quarterly*, IX (January 1942), pp. 77, 79–81. See also Marion H. Herriot, "Steamboat Transportation on the Red River," *Minnesota History*, XXI (September 1940), pp. 245–271.

[16] Alsop Brothers Freight Line Papers, MSS., Minnesota Historical Society, St. Paul.

[17] William J. Petersen, *Steamboating on the Upper Mississippi: The Water Way to Iowa* (Iowa City, 1937), p. 300.

[18] Andrews, *History of St. Paul, Minn.*, p. 400.

[19] St. Paul *Weekly Pioneer and Democrat*, July 7, 1865; Petersen, *Steamboating on the Upper Mississippi*, p. 300.

[20] [Diamond Jo Line Steamers], *Along the Mississippi* (St. Louis, 1906). William J. Petersen, "The Diamond Jo Line," *Palimpsest*, XXIV (July 1943), pp. 215–221. See also by the same author, "Good Times on the Diamond Jo," in *ibid.*, pp. 222–236.

[21] Anderson, *The Mississippi and Its Forty-Four Navigable Tributaries*, p. 10. Great Falls, thirty-five miles above Fort Benton, marked the true navigational headwaters of the Missouri River, and light craft could reach this point. Given mileages

vary. Army engineers who measure across the bends instead of along the middle of the river bed, place the distance from Fort Benton to the mouth at 2285 miles. See William E. Lass, *A History of Steamboating on the Upper Missouri River* (Lincoln, Nebr., 1962), p. 2.

²² Philip E. Chappell, "Floods in the Missouri River," *Transactions of the Kansas Historical Society, 1907–1908* (Topeka, 1908), X, pp. 536–558.

²³ Heckman, *Steamboating Sixty-five Years on Missouri's Rivers*, p. 19.

²⁴ Hiram M. Chittenden, *The American Fur Trade of the Far West*, 3 vols. (New York, 1902), I, 337–341. See also Lass, *Steamboating on the Upper Missouri River*, pp. 8–11.

²⁵ Purdy, "Report on Steam Navigation," p. 21; Hiram M. Chittenden, *History of Early Steamboat Navigation on the Missouri River*, 2 vols. (New York, 1903), I, 218–219. See also Hunter, *Steamboats on the Western Rivers*, pp. 47–49.

²⁶ Edgar A. Holt, "Missouri River Transportation in the Expansion of the West," *Missouri Historical Review*, XX (April 1926), pp. 380–381.

²⁷ An excellent report on Missouri River navigation entitled "Improvement on the Missouri River," prepared by Maj. C. W. Howell, army engineer, appears in *House Executive Documents*, 40 Cong., 2 sess., no. 136. See also St. Louis *Daily Missouri Democrat*, June 17, 1865.

²⁸ *House Exec. Docs.*, 39 Cong., 2 sess., no. 23, p. 48. Maj. Howell in his abovementioned report, "Improvement on the Missouri River," p. 9, estimates the 1867 passenger receipts at $1,500,000. Other aspects of this subject are discussed by William J. Petersen, "Steamboating on the Missouri River," *Iowa Journal of History*, LIII (April 1955), pp. 97–120. See also Chittenden, *History of Early Steamboat Navigation on the Missouri River*, I, 217, 237–238; II, 273; Winther, *Old Oregon Country*, p. 224; Purdy, "Report on Steam Navigation," p. 21.

²⁹ Alton B. Oviatt, "Steamboat Traffic on the Upper Missouri River, 1859–1869," *Pacific Northwest Quarterly*, XL (April 1949), pp. 99–100.

³⁰ St. Louis *Dispatch*, July 1, 1865.

³¹ Oviatt, "Steamboat Traffic on the Upper Missouri River," pp. 102–103.

³² Chittenden, *History of Early Steamboat Navigation on the Missouri River*, II, 419. See also William J. Petersen, "A Century of River Traffic," *The Palimpsest*, XVII (October 1946), pp. 296–297. Continued passenger service on the lower Missouri took the form of a brief resurgence during the late 1880s. During 1889, 332,218 passengers were carried on the lower Missouri, great numbers of them being excursionists. See War Department, "Report of the Chief Engineers," *Annual Reports*, vol. II, pt. 6, p. 3337. See also Lass, *Steamboating on the Upper Missouri River*, pp. 57–58.

³³ *Ibid.*, pp. 89–92; chap. 9.

³⁴ Anderson, *The Mississippi and Its Forty-Four Navigable Tributaries*, pp. 10, 18.

³⁵ William P. Frye, "South-Western Commerce and Gulf Harbors," *Forum*, XI (May 1891), p. 291; *The American Settler*, April 30, 1881.

³⁶ Purdy, "Report on Steam Navigation," pp. 22–25.

³⁷ *Ibid.*, pp. 26–27. For a detailed account of steamboats on the Colorado River, see Francis H. Leavitt, "Steam Navigation on the Colorado River," California Historical Society *Quarterly*, XII (March and June 1943), pp. 1–19, 151–174, and Hazel E. Mills, "The Arizona Fleet," *The American Neptune*, I (1941), pp. 255–274.

³⁸ W. Kaye Lamb, "The Advent of the 'Beaver,'" *The British Columbia Historical Quarterly*, II (July 1938), pp. 163–184.

³⁹ Purdy, "Report on Steam Navigation," pp. 27–31; Winther, *Old Oregon Country*, chap. 12.

[40] Dorothy O. Johansen, "Capitalism on the Far-Western Frontier: The Oregon Steam Navigation Company," Ph.D. dissertation, University of Washington, Seattle, 1941; Winther, *Old Oregon Country*, chap. 16.

[41] Hunter, *Steamboats on the Western Rivers*, pp. 565–567.

[42] Dixon, *A Traffic History of the Mississippi River System*, pp. 52–70; Anderson, *The Mississippi and Its Forty-Four Navigable Tributaries*, pp. 14–18.

[43] Purdy, "Report on Steam Navigation," pp. 41–43.

[44] *Ibid.*, pp. 36–37, 42.

[45] Hunter, *Steamboats on the Western Rivers*, pp. 564–567, 638, Table 22, points out that steamboat operations in and out of St. Louis and New Orleans declined roughly 20 percent and 29 percent respectively between 1860 and 1880.

[46] Mildred L. Hartsough, *From Canoe to Steel Barge* (Minneapolis, Minn.: 1934), p. 148. See also John Leng, *America in 1876: Pencillings During a Tour in the Centennial Year* (Dundee, 1877), p. 98, who tells of a visit aboard such a vessel while in dock at St. Louis.

[47] For precise figures on tonnages, lengths, and widths, see Hunter, *Steamboats on the Western Rivers*, p. 74, Table 4. Chapter 2 of this work is an excellent treatment of the structural evolution of the river steamboat.

[48] For a description of such a boat, see Mackie, *From Cape Cod to Dixie and the Tropics*, pp. 172–173; for another, consult Julian Ralph, *Dixie; or Southern Scenes and Sketches* (New York, 1896), pp. 1–5.

[49] Ralph, *Dixie*, p. 7.

[50] Mackie, *From Cape Cod to Dixie and the Tropics*, pp. 172–173.

[51] The literature on palace steamboats is not lacking in quantity, sentiment, and imagination. A classic is Samuel L. Clemens (pseud., Mark Twain), *Life on the Mississippi* (any edition). See also Petersen, *Steamboating on the Upper Mississippi*, in which Chapter 33 is entitled "Mid Pleasures on Palaces"; Garnett L. Eskew, *The Pageant of the Packets* (New York, 1929), gives considerable attention to the social history of steamboating. The menu mentioned is reproduced opp. p. 206. See also Fred E. Dayton, *Steamboat Days* (New York, 1925), pp. 351–352; and, lastly, Charles van Ravenswaay, "Old Man River," *American Heritage*, II, n.s. (Autumn 1950), p. 50.

[52] Alfred Falk, *Trans-Pacific Sketches: A Tour through the United States and Canada* (Melbourne, 1877), p. 258.

[53] [Beadle], *A Trip to the United States in 1878*, p. 61.

[54] George T. Borrett, *Letters from Canada and the United States* (London, 1865), p. 147.

[55] Browne, "Ride on the Frontier of Texas," p. 158. See also Cornelius O'Keefe, "Rides through Montana," *Harper's*, XXXV (September 1867), p. 569.

[56] An itemized list of individual ship losses up to 1868 is contained in William M. Lytle, comp., *Merchant Steam Vessels of the United States, 1807–1868* (Mystic, Conn., 1952), List B, pp. 209–277; other data are scattered.

[57] *Ibid.*

[58] Valuable information on the subject may be obtained from Works Progress Administration of Louisiana, "Navigation Casualties, 1866–1910," MS, Howard-Tilton Memorial Library, New Orleans. See also Hiram M. Chittenden, "Report on Steamboat Wrecks on Missouri River," *Nebraska History Magazine*, VIII (January–March 1925), pp. 20–26; *The Old Franklin Almanac for 1867* (Philadelphia, [1867]), pp. 35–37. Losses of this nature are confirmed by Morgan, *Annual Statement of the Trade and Commerce of St. Louis*, p. 12.

[59] A record of ships' losses appears in E. W. Wright, ed., *Lewis & Dryden's Marine History of the Pacific Northwest* (Portland, Ore., 1895).

[60] St. Louis *Daily Globe*, July 14, 1873.

⁶¹ San Francisco *Daily Alta California*, September 21, 1877.

⁶² Log of the *Lillie Martin* by H. Jacobs, MS, Missouri Historical Society, St. Louis.

⁶³ William M. Tompkins, Jr. to wife, April 1, 1866, La Beaume Papers, MSS, Missouri Historical Society, St. Louis.

⁶⁴ Browne, "Ride on the Frontier of Texas," p. 158.

⁶⁵ New Orleans *Daily Picayune*, June 3, 1866.

⁶⁶ *Ibid.*, October 4, 1889.

⁶⁷ *Ibid.*, April 25, 1875.

⁶⁸ New Orleans *Times*, June 16, 1865.

⁶⁹ Works Progress Administration, "Navigational Casualties."

⁷⁰ St. Louis *Globe-Democrat*, August 12, 1930. Upstream navigation at night in low water was extremely hazardous and under such conditions steamboat captains invariably tied up to avoid snags and sandbars.

⁷¹ Bristow, "Early Steamboat and Packet Lines," p. 35. See also Marie E. Meyer, "River Towns," *Palimpsest*, VII (December 1926), pp. 381–389; Charles P. Deatherage, *Steamboating on the Missouri in the Sixties* (n.p., 1924), p. 11. See also St. Louis *Globe-Democrat*, November 21, 1921; February 28, 1932.

⁷² Sam T. Bratton, "Inefficiency of Water Transportation in Missouri—A Geographical Factor in the Development of Railroads," *Missouri Historical Review*, XIV (October 1919), pp. 82–83.

Chapter 7: Railroads Blanket the West

¹ Seymour Dunbar, *A History of Travel in America* (New York, 1937), chaps. 42–44.

² William P. Smith, *The Book of the Great Railway Celebrations of 1857* (New York, 1858), pp. 210–211.

³ The instate railroad mileages in 1865 were as follows: Missouri, 925; Iowa, 891; Texas, 465; Louisiana (entire), 335; California, 214; Minnesota (entire), 213; Nebraska Territory, 122; Kansas, 40; Arkansas, 38; and Oregon, 19. Henry V. Poor, *Manual of the Railroads of the United States, for 1872–73* (New York, 1872), pp. xxxii–xxxiii. There are some discrepancies in figures between Poor's and, for example, [Carlton, publ.], *The Railroad and Insurance Almanac for 1865* (New York, 1865) and [   ], *Bradshaw's Railway Manual . . . for 1866* (London, 1866).

⁴ [   ], "Railroads in 1865," *Bankers' Magazine*, XV (October 1865), p. 319. For an informative account of intercity rivalry, see Wyatt W. Belcher, *The Economic Rivalry between St. Louis and Chicago, 1850–1880* (New York, 1947).

⁵ [   ], "Railroads in 1865." For a survey of railroad development in Missouri see Paul W. Gates, "The Railroads of Missouri," *Missouri Historical Review*, XXVI (January 1932), pp. 126–141.

⁶ The six were: Mississippi and Missouri; Burlington and Missouri; Cedar Rapids and Missouri; Chicago, Iowa and Nebraska; Dubuque and Pacific; Keokuk, Fort Des Moines and Minnesota. The lesser four were: Dubuque, Marion and Western; Keokuk, Mt. Pleasant and Muscatine; Mahaska County; McGregor Western. See [   ], "Railroads in 1865," p. 319.

⁷ An adequate summary of early Iowa railroad history is Cyrenus Cole, *Iowa through the Years* (Iowa City, Iowa, 1940), chap. 50. See also B. L. Wick, "John I. Blair and His Associates in Railway Building in Iowa," *Annals of Iowa*, XI, ser. 3 (October 1914), pp. 489–491; William J. Peterson, "Transportation by Land," *Palimpsest*, XXVII (October 1946), p. 309.

⁸ S. G. Reed, *A History of the Texas Railroads* (Houston, Tex., 1941), pp. 10, 57. See also Ira G. Clark, *Then Came the Railroads* (Norman, Okla., 1958), p. 27.

⁹ [   ], "Railroads in 1865," p. 324; Reed, *A History of the Texas Railroads*, 1–12, *passim.*; P. Briscoe, "The First Texas Railroad," *Quarterly of the Texas State Historical Association,* VII (April 1904), pp. 279–282.

¹⁰ Walter Prichard, ed., "A Forgotten Louisiana Engineer: G. W. R. Bayley and His 'History of the Railroads of Louisiana,'" *Louisiana Historical Quarterly,* XXX (October 1947), p. 1325. Bayley's work is here republished in full.

¹¹ Stephen E. Wood, "The Development of Arkansas Railroads," *Arkansas Historical Quarterly,* VII (Summer 1948), pp. 103–140, 155–193. See also [   ], "Railroads in 1865," p. 319.

¹² William W. Folwell, *A History of Minnesota,* 4 vols. (St. Paul, Minn., 1924), I, 327 ff.; II, 37 ff.; Poor, *Manual . . . for 1872–73,* p. xxxiii.

¹³ Richard L. Douglas, "A History of Manufactures in the Kansas District," *Collections of the Kansas State Historical Society, 1909–1910* (Topeka, Kan., 1910), XI 99–100.

¹⁴ Two company pamphlets give interesting highlights on California's first tracks: [Southern Pacific Company], *First in the West: Sacramento Valley Railroad* (San Francisco, 1955), p. 3; [Southern Pacific Company], *Southern Pacific's First Century* (San Francisco, 1955). See also John W. Caughey, *California* (New York, 1940), pp. 425–438; and for Pacific Northwest beginnings see Winther, *Old Oregon Country,* pp. 293–294.

¹⁵ By 1860 railroads radiating from the Great Lakes touched the Mississippi at ten places. See Henry M. Flint, *The Railroads of the United States: Their History and Statistics* (Philadelphia, 1868), p. 45.

¹⁶ Isaac F. Redfield, *The Laws of Railways,* 2 vols. (Boston, 1867), I.

¹⁷ Frederick A. Cleveland and Fred W. Powell, *Railroad Promotion and Capitalization in the United States* (New York, 1909), chap. 13.

¹⁸ A good case study of local aid is Earl S. Beard, "Local Aid to Railroads in Iowa," *Iowa Journal of History,* L (January 1952), pp. 1–34.

¹⁹ Robert S. Cotterill, "Early Agitation for a Pacific Railroad, 1845–1850," *Mississippi Valley Historical Review,* V (March 1919), pp. 396–409. See also Paul W. Glad, "Projected Railroads to the Pacific Northwest," M.A. thesis, Indiana University, Bloomington, Ind., 1949.

²⁰ Goetzman, *Army Exploration in the American West, 1803–1863,* chap. 7.

²¹ For the completed legislation, see *Laws of the United States of America . . . of the Thirty Eighth Congress, 1863–1864* (Washington, D.C., 1864), Public Law No. 185, pp. 367–376. Many books on western railroads contain summaries of these acts. One of the best of these is Lewis H. Haney, *A Congressional History of Railroads,* 2 vols. (Madison, Wisc., 1910), II, 63–75. Haney not only explains the acts but presents a section-by-section summary of both the 1862 and 1864 acts. See also John B. Sanborn, *Congressional Grants of Land in Aid of Railways* (Madison, Wisc., 1899), pp. 119–120. It is of importance to note that these acts actually made a point on the hundredth meridian the "initial" place from which the Pacific railroad would build westward. The acts stated that there would be a four-pronged system emanating at the Missouri River and converging on this point, which happened to be near Fort Kearny. The pronged line reaching this juncture could be designated as the one officially authorized to proceed westward to join the Central Pacific. One of the hopeful contenders for this privilege was the originally chartered Leavenworth, Pawnee and Western (later the Union Pacific Eastern Division), with Leavenworth as its eastern terminus. It failed to meet official specifications and therefore lost out to its rival, the Union Pacific. However, with its name changed in 1869 to the Kansas Pacific Railroad, this line

proceeded westward across the Smoky Hill Valley of Kansas, and ultimately reached Denver. From there, under the name Denver Pacific, the Kansas Pacific joined the Union Pacific at Cheyenne. By a pooling arrangement controlled by Jay Gould, the Kansas Pacific in 1878 became a part of the Union Pacific railroad system. The best summary account of these developments is Waldo Crippen, "The Kansas Pacific Railroad: A Cross Section of an Age of Railroad Building," M.A. thesis, University of Chicago, Chicago, 1932. See also Leonard W. Thompson, "The History of Railway Development in Kansas," Ph.D. dissertation, State University of Iowa, Iowa City, 1942.

[22] *Laws of the United States of America . . . 1863–1864*, Public Law No. 186, pp. 376–383. See also Poor, *Manual . . . 1872–73*, p. 328.

[23] There are, of course, numerous specialized treatises on each of these rail lines. For a summary discussion see Oscar Osburn Winther, *The Great Northwest* (New York, 1950), chap. 16. See also John F. Stover, *American Railroads* (Chicago, 1961), chap. 4.

[24] Actually the Atlantic and Pacific Railroad had its origins in a Missouri company called the Southwestern Pacific, first chartered in 1849 and later sold to John C. Frémont who played an important role in the formation of the Atlantic and Pacific Railroad. Unfortunately the company encountered financial difficulties, and following some organizational reshuffling re-emerged as a subsidiary of the St. Louis and San Francisco, or Frisco Line. See William S. Grever, "Railway Development in the Southwest," *New Mexico Historical Review*, XXXII (April 1957), pp. 153–154.

[25] Lindsay Campbell and Earle Heath, "From Trail to Rail," Southern Pacific Railroad Company *Bulletin,* Photostatic copy of this serialized history, Scrapbook, Southern Pacific Railroad Company Office, San Francisco, p. 55, hereafter cited as "From Trail to Rail." On August 14, 1884, under the laws of the state of Kentucky, the Southern Pacific Company was chartered, which in turn acquired control of the Southern Pacific Railroad Company, the Central Pacific, the Oregon and California Railroad, and assorted other holdings. See Henry V. Poor and H. W. Poor, *Poor's Manual of the Railroads of the United States: 1900* (New York, 1901), pp. 611–612. Hereafter cited as *Poor's Manual of the Railroads . . . 1900*. Land grants respecting southwestern projects are described in Sanborn, *Congressional Grants of Land in Aid of Railways*, pp. 114–126, *passim*.

[26] Haney, *A Congressional History of Railways*, II, pp. 128–133; Campbell and Heath, "From Trail to Rail," p. 91; Sanborn, *Congressional Grants of Land in Aid of Railways*, pp. 114–119 ff.

[27] While not a transcontinental railroad, the Denver and Rio Grande was nevertheless an important and unique rail development in the West. This was well expressed in the first annual report by its president, General William J. Palmer: ". . . it was the idea of constructing a North-South railway along the eastern base of the Rocky Mountains." See Denver and Rio Grande Railway, *First Annual Report . . . of the Denver and Rio Grande Railway . . . April 1st, 1873* (Philadelphia, 1873), p. 5. See also George L. Anderson, *General William J. Palmer: A Decade of Colorado Railroad Building, 1870–1880* (Colorado Springs, Colo., 1936). See also Robert G. Athearn, *Rebel of the Rockies: A History of the Denver and Rio Grande Western Railroad* (New Haven, Conn., 1962).

[28] An excellent resumé of this company's activities is Joseph Weidel, comp., "The Atchison, Topeka and Santa Fe Railway System: Excerpts from the President's Annual Reports to stockholders with Special Reference to the Construction History of the System Lines, 1873–1916," MS., vol. I, Henry E. Huntington Library, San Marino, Calif. See also Poor, *Manual . . . for 1872–73*, p. 196. For a comprehensive account see L. L. Waters, *Steel Trails to Santa Fe* (Lawrence, Kan., 1950), chaps. 3–4.

[29] A good comprehensive treatment of Gould's railroad financing is Julius Grodin-

sky, *Jay Gould: His Business Career* (Philadelphia, 1957), and by the same author, *Transcontinental Railway Strategy, 1869–1893* (Philadelphia, 1962). See also Clark, *Then Came The Railroads*, chap. 16.

[30] Bell, "Federal Legislation Concerning the Disposition of Grazing Lands (1862–1900)," p. 4. See also John B. Rae, *The Development of Rail Land Subsidy Policy in the United States*, Ph.D. dissertation abstract, University of Michigan, Ann Arbor, 1939, p. 1; Poor, *Manual . . . for 1872–73*, pp. 539–540. Depending somewhat upon definition of land grands, it might be contended that congressional land grant aid began as far back as 1830. See Cleveland and Powell, *Railroad Promotion and Capitalization*, chap. 17. Acreage figures on these grants, administration-by-administration, appear in Haney, *A Congressional History of Railways in the United States*, I, 123–124, 129–131; II, 14. See also *Eleventh Census: 1890. Report on Transportation Business in the United States . . .* by Henry C. Adams (Washington, D.C., 1895), p. 4.

[31] The contemporary literature pertaining to the railroad problem in the West and, in particular, to grievances against the railroads is extensive. One of the better accounts is William Larrabee, *The Railroad Question* (Chicago, 1893), pp. 131–133.

[32] *Report of the Proceedings of the Trans-Mississippi Congress . . . 1891* (Omaha, Nebr., 1892), p. 10.

Chapter 8: Laying the Track

[1] Thomas C. Clarke, "The Building of a Railroad," *The American Railway* (New York, 1889), p. 10.

[2] *Poor's Manual of the Railroads . . . 1900*, p. xliv. It is recalled that 3272 miles of rail line existed in the trans-Mississippi West in 1865. Therefore, the total mileage extant in 1890 was 72,473, as previously stated.

[3] Grenville M. Dodge, "How We Built the Union Pacific Railway," Senate Documents, 61 Cong., 2 sess. (Washington, D.C., 1910), doc. 447, pp. 11–14, 31. See also Grenville M. Dodge, *Romantic Realities: The Story of the Building of the Pacific Roads* (Omaha, Nebr., 1889), p. 15; C. H. Middleton, "Railroad Surveys—Camp and Field Life on the Union Pacific," *Scientific American Supplement*, No. 653, XXVI (July 7, 1888), pp. 10427–10428: Welty, "The Western Army Frontier," p. 111. An enlightening account by a member of a Northern Pacific surveying party is [Robert Ridgeway], *Robert Ridgeway* (New York, 1940), pp. 25–44.

[4] Dodge, "How We Built the Union Pacific Railway," p. 39. Dodge's reference to the absence of timber is not entirely correct. Local cottonwoods and cedars were used in making ties.

[5] [The Western Historical Company], *History of the State of Nebraska*, p. 192.

[6] Dodge, "How We Built the Union Pacific Railway," p. 31; Hubert H. Bancroft, *History of Utah, 1540–1886* (San Francisco, 1889), pp. 753–754.

[7] [Central Pacific Railroad Company], *Central Pacific Railroad* (New York, 1867), p. 3. See also John D. Galloway, *The First Transcontinental Railroad* (New York, 1950), pp. 77, 96.

[8] Campbell and Heath, "From Trail to Rail," p. 15.

[9] This appears as a quotation from the Sacramento *Union* in the Virginia City (Nevada) *Daily Union*, January 24, 1865. For an account concerning Central Pacific supplies see Galloway, *The First Transcontinental Road*, pp. 141–142.

[10] Robert L. Fulton, *Epic of the Overland* (San Francisco, 1924), p. 39; Edwin L. Sabin, *Building the Pacific Railway* (Philadelphia, 1919), pp. 111, 114: see also Sacramento *Daily Bee*, July 28, 1866.

[11] Fulton, *Epic of the Overland*, p. 37.

[12] See Virginia City (Nevada) *Daily Territorial Enterprise*, March 21, 1869, for some interesting figures on the Central Pacific Line.

[13] William C. Hoad, "Some Episodes in the History of the Santa Fe Railroad," MS, Kansas State Historical Society Library, Topeka. See also G. W. Rafter, "Railroad Building on the Texas Frontier," *Engineering Magazine*, II (October 1891), p. 36; W. R. Armstrong, "Railroad Construction," *Railway Review*, LV (July 18, 1914), p. 69; William S. Kennedy, *Wonders and Curiosities of the Railway* (Chicago, 1884), p. 78.

[14] Some newspaper commentaries, especially those favorable to the company, were compiled and published. See [Union Pacific Railroad Company], *Progress of the Union Pacific Railroad* (New York, 1868), p. 7.

[15] [The Western Historical Company], *History of the State of Nebraska*, pp. 107, 195. See also Marshall M. Kirkman, *Science of Railways* (New York, 1903), pp. 175, 180.

[16] Sidney Dillon, "Historic Moments: Driving the Last Spike of the Union Pacific," *Scribner's Magazine*, XII (August 1892), p. 257. This process is described in Davis, *The First Five Years of the Railroad Era in Colorado*, p. 5. It is also vividly described in [Union Pacific Railroad Company], *Progress of the Union Pacific Railroad*, pp. 9–10.

[17] J. S. Casement Letters, MSS, Henry E. Huntington Library, San Marino, California.

[18] [Union Pacific Railroad Company], *Progress of the Union Pacific Railroad*, pp. 9–10.

[19] Kyner, *End of Track*, p. 151.

[20] O. P. Byers, "When Railroading Outdid the Wild West Stories," *Collections of the Kansas State Historical Society, 1926–1928* (Topeka, 1928), XVII, 342, 344.

[21] Beadle, *The Undeveloped West*, p. 120; George W. Pine, *Beyond the West* (Utica, N.Y., 1870), p. 344.

[22] Ripley Hitchcock, "At the Head of the Rails," *Chautauquan*, IX (June 1889), pp. 540–543.

[23] Sacramento *Daily Bee*, April 29, 1869; December 18, 1869.

[24] J. N. Bowman, "Driving the Last Spike at Promontory Point, 1869," California Historical Society *Quarterly*, XXXVI (June 1957), pp. 97–106; (September 1957), pp. 263–274, is a carefully prepared, detailed, and documented account of the "last spike" ceremony.

[25] *Ibid.*, pp. 98–101, 104; (September 1957), pp. 266–272. See also Robert M. Utley, "The Dash to Promontory," *Utah Historical Quarterly*, XXIX (April 1961), pp. 114–117. A good and precise account of this ceremony, but one written in 1892, is by Sidney Dillon, one-time president of the Union Pacific Railroad Company. See Dillon, "Historic Moments," pp. 253–259. See also Campbell and Heath, "From Trail to Rail," p. 31.

[26] Salt Lake City *Deseret Evening News*, May 12, 1869.

[27] Sacramento *Daily Bee*, May 13, 1869. It was quite clear even then that the boxcar "city" of Promontory would not long remain the junction of the two roads; as it turned out, this was to be Ogden, Utah.

[28] San Francisco *Call*, May 8, 9, 1869; Campbell and Heath, "From Trail to Rail," pp. 30–31; Virginia City (Nevada) *Daily Territorial Enterprise*, May 8, 11, 1869.

[29] Chicago *Tribune*, May 11, 1869.

[30] *Ibid.*, May 10, 1869.

[31] St. Louis *Missouri Democrat*, May 10, 1869.

[32] St. Paul *Pioneer Press*, September 9, 1883.

[33] Andrews, *St. Paul*, p. 577. See also other interesting reports on the preparade festivities in St. Paul *Pioneer Press*, September 1–4, 1883. See also Eugene V. Smalley, *History of the Northern Pacific Railroad* (New York, 1883), on the over-all construction of the Northern Pacific Railroad.

[34] George N. Hillman, *Driving the Golden Spike* (St. Paul, Minn., [1932]), p. 21. Hillman was a court reporter who took notes on this occasion.

Chapter 9: Travel by Rail

[1] H. Hussey Vivian, *Notes of a Tour in America* (London, 1878), p. 85; Charles B. George, *Forty Years on the Rail* (Chicago, 1887), p. 72. Others also ascribed to Chicago such terms as the "garden city" and the "queen city of the West." See, for example, William Robertson and W. F. Robertson, *Our American Tour . . . in the Autumn of 1869* (Edinburgh, 1871), p. 94. It must, however, be kept in mind that travelers also reached Omaha by other routes; many of them used Missouri River steamers.

[2] [   ], *Half Hours in the Wide West*, p. 104.

[3] The first line to reach Omaha from Chicago was the Chicago and North Western; the date, 1867.

[4] During the preceding winter, trains had actually crossed the Missouri on a temporary pile bridge partly supported by ice, but the spring thaw made further use of the bridge unsafe.

[5] W. F. Rae, *Westward by Rail: A Journey to San Francisco and Back and a Visit to the Mormons* (London, 1871), pp. 65–66; McClure, *Three Thousand Miles through the Rocky Mountains*, pp. 29–34; Flint, *The Railroads of the United States*, p. 408.

[6] Vivian, *Notes of a Tour in America*, p. 101.

[7] Henrik Cavling, *Fra Amerika*, 2 vols. (Copenhagen, 1897), I, 320–31. Similar observations were made by H. Buss, *Wanderings in the West, during the Year 1870* (London, 1871), pp. 10–11. See also Lady Duffus Hardy, *Through Cities and Prairie Lands: Sketches of an American Tour* (London, 1881), pp. 78, 80. The French traveler, A. Édouard Portalis, in his book *Les États-Unis* (Paris, 1869), chap. 2, shared the view of other foreign travelers that Omaha was for him the beginning of the West. A good descriptive account of Omaha as seen by a passenger on one of the first through trains from the West appears in the Sacramento *Daily Bee*, June 19, 1869.

[8] Clarence Pullen, "Overland Route to the Pacific," *Harper's Weekly*, XXXV (February 14, 1891), p. 126. See also H. Andreasen, *Amerika: Seet fra et Lanbostandpunkt* (Copenhagen, 1884), p. 161.

[9] [American Social Science Association], *Handbook for Immigrants* (New York, 1871), p. 17.

[10] George M. Pullman, a New Yorker who moved to Chicago, conceived the idea that sleeping cars could be greatly improved and with funds he accumulated as an industrial contractor he proceeded in 1855 to develop what ten years later became the first "Pullman car." Pullman's "Pioneer" cost roughly twenty thousand dollars fully equipped. It was the first genuinely successful sleeping car. The car received its first nation-wide notice when attached to the funeral train carrying the body of President Abraham Lincoln from Chicago to Springfield. In 1867 the Pullman Palace Car Company was organized and south Chicago became the location of the company's factory. Pullman cars became widely used on railroad lines throughout the nation. See Joseph Husband, *The Story of the Pullman Car* (Chicago, 1917), chap. 2. See also [London

Times], *A Visit to the United States* (London, 1887), pp. 364–365; Ruth Wolfe, *Pioneering in Ways of Travel* (n.p., n.d.), p. 161.

[11] Susan Coolidge, "A Few Hints on the California Journey," *Scribner's Monthly,* VI (May 1873), p. 28.

[12] Beadle, *The Undeveloped West*, pp. 166, 743.

[13] [London *Times*], *A Visit to the United States,* pp. 364, 390. See also Robertson and Robertson, *Our American Tour,* p. 92; [A London Parson], *To San Francisco and Back* (London, ca. 1870), p. 43. A good description of a Union Pacific Pullman sleeper also appears in [Helen Hunt Jackson], *Bits of Travel at Home* (Boston, 1887), p. 5.

[14] [Lawrence], *Silverland*, p. 109. Each year witnessed some refinements and improvements in Pullman cars, but basically they did not change much from year to year. See *American Settler,* June 23, 1883. Complete sample Union Pacific menus appear in W. G. Marshall, *Through America; or Nine Months in the United States* (London, 1881), pp. 108–109. The first dining car, named "Delmonico," was placed in service on the Chicago and Alton Railroad in 1868. See Horace Porter, "Railway Passenger Travel," in *The American Railway* (New York, 1889), pp. 242–244. For a Frenchman's view on the sleeping cars, see Portalis, *Les États-Unis,* p. 50.

[15] Coach fare during the period under review ranged from about two and a half to three cents per mile, depending on the distance traveled. H. G. Prout, "Railroad Travel in England and America," *Scribner's Magazine,* XVI (October 1894), pp. 402–404, 418.

[16] Robert Louis Stevenson, "Across the Plains," *Living Age,* CLVIII (August 4, 1883), p. 312. See also Wolfe, "Pioneering in Ways of Travel," p. 16.

[17] [G. F. Byron], "The Overland Emigrant," *The Cornhill Magazine,* XVIII, n.s. (June 1892), p. 640.

[18] Such places were often referred to as "breakfast," "lunch," or "supper," stations. Josephine J. Clifford, "To Texas, and by the Way," *Overland,* VII (September 1871), p. 271.

[19] Coolidge, "A Few Hints on the California Journey," p. 27.

[20] Hudson, *A Scamper through America,* p. 199.

[21] Robert V. Hine, ed., *William Andrew Spalding, Los Angeles Newspaperman: An Autobiographical Account* (San Marino, Calif., 1961), pp. 3–4; Robert Louis Stevenson, *Across the Plains* (London, 1892), pp. 27–29; [Byron], "The Overland Emigrant," p. 637.

[22] Howe, "The Great West," p. 146.

[23] [A London Parson], *To San Francisco and Back,* p. 35.

[24] Stevenson, *Across the Plains,* pp. 35, 47.

[25] Hine, *William Andrew Spalding,* pp. 4–5; Clifford, "To Texas, and by the Way," p. 271.

[26] Hine, *William Andrew Spalding,* p. 3. See also good accounts in Hudson, *A Scamper through America,* p. 199; B. Kroupa, *An Artist's Tour* (London, 1890), pp. 4–5.

[27] George, *Forty Years on the Railroad,* pp. 230–231.

[28] M. M. Shaw, *Nine Thousand Miles on a Pullman Train . . .* (Philadelphia, 1898), pp. 138–145.

[29] [Byron], "The Overland Emigrant," p. 641.

[30] George, *Forty Years on the Rail,* pp. 221–222. An amusing and very satirical commentary on the free pass situation is Auguste Faure, *Passes; or the Beauties of Transportation* (Baltimore, 1900).

[31] Bob Ford to president of the Wabash, St. Louis and Pacific Railroad, October 14, 1882. Railroad Papers, MSS., Missouri Historical Society, St. Louis.

[32] [Crofutt], *Guide*. Also a widely consulted guide was Richards, ed., *Appletons' Companion Hand-Book of Travel*. Scores of other guides appeared on the market before the end of the century.

[33] In 1882 Crofutt stated that the aggregate sale of his guides had reached five hundred thousand copies, in spite, he said, of thirty-one "imitators." The principal item designed for those making special side trips was George A. Crofutt, *Crofutt's Overland Tours* (Chicago, 1888).

[34] Marshall, *Through America*, p. 123.

[35] Rae, *Westward by Rail*, p. 63.

[36] *American Settler*, November 12, 1881; March 24, 1883; Marshall, *Through America*, pp. 124–125.

[37] [Crofutt], *Guide*, p. 45.

[38] Buss, *Wanderings in the West*, pp. 24–27.

[39] *Ibid.*; W. W. Ross, *10,000 Miles by Land and Sea* (Toronto, 1876), pp. 38, 42.

[40] [Crofutt], *Guide*, pp. 52–60. Guidebooks serving the subsequently constructed Pacific rail lines follow a similar pattern. Moreover, travelers reacted in similar fashion to points of interest along the route.

[41] Until completion of the Utah Central Railroad, Ogden to Salt Lake City, stopover passengers traveled to the Mormon capital by stagecoach. Later, tourists traveling the Denver and Rio Grande could reach Salt Lake City directly from Denver. See Bancroft, *History of Utah*, pp. 756, 756n, 759.

[42] Ernest J. Moyne, trans. and ed., *Alexandra Gripenberg's A Half Year in the New World* (Newark, Del., 1954), p. 186. See, for a skeptical view, Rae, *Westward by Rail*, pp. 105–128, 178–181.

[43] Marshall, *Through America*, p. 163. For a comparable view see also Edward Pierrepont, *Fifth Avenue to Alaska* (London, 1885), p. 20.

[44] Hardy, *Through Cities and Prairie Lands*, p. 128. For an earlier account by an American—a newspaperman—see (signed by "O'L"), Sacramento *Daily Bee*, May 12, 1869.

[45] John E. Lester, *The Atlantic to the Pacific* (Boston, 1873), pp. 78–82, 257. See also Falk, *Trans-Pacific Sketches*, p. 25; T. C. Porter, *Impressions of America* (London, 1899), pp. 144–145; Rae, *Westward by Rail*, p. 282.

[46] Samuel Bowles, *The Pacific Railroad—Open; How to Go; What to See; Guide to and through Western America* (Boston, 1869), p. 5.

[47] James W. Steele, *Rand, McNally & Co.'s New Guide to the Pacific Coast: Santa Fe Route* (Chicago, 1893). Numerous published company brochures and travelers' guides would depict in glamorous terms and in illustrated form the scenic attractions of the respective routes.

[48] *American Settler*, March 3, 1883.

[49] St. Louis *Daily Missouri Democrat*, January 27, 1865.

[50] Edwin Muller, "The Epic of the Santa Fe," *Reader's Digest*, XXXIX (December 1941), p. 103.

[51] [B. R. C.], *A Trip to the Rockies* (New York, 1889), pp. 40–46, 62.

[52] A. J. Ryan, *Greatest Fruit . . . : A Lively Representation of the Great State of Kansas* (Topeka, 1870), pp. 45–46. See also E. Douglas Branch, *The Hunting of the Buffalo* (New York, 1929), pp. 129-132.

[53] [Jackson], *Bits of Travel at Home*, p. 4.

[54] *American Settler*, August 14, 1880.

[55] William Minturn, *Travels West* (London, 1877), pp. 373–378.

[56] Porter, *Impressions of America*, p. 24.

[57] Bess Carroll, "The Coming of the Railroads," *Frontier Times*, V (October 1927), p. 43.

[58] Samuel Storey, *To the Golden Land: Sketches of a Trip to Southern California* (London, 1889), pp. 86–87.

[59] *American Settler*, November 8, 1884. Some ranchers were reported to have tied their more "scraggy, worn-out" animals to the tracks so that they would be struck by trains.

[60] Frederick S. Williams, *Our Iron Roads* (London, 1885), pp. 492–493.

[61] *American Settler*, January 17, 1885.

[62] H. G. Prout, "Safety in Railroad Travel," in *The American Railway* (New York, 1889), p. 191. See also M. G. Cunniff, "Comforts of Railroad Travel," *World's Work*, VI (June 1903), p. 3577.

[63] Porter, "Railway Passenger Travel," p. 250.

[64] *American Settler*, June 26, 1886.

Chapter 10: Indians, Outlaws, and Wayfarers

[1] *Official Records*, Ser. I, XLVIII, pt. II, pp. 1157–1158. See also Grenville M. Dodge, *The Indian Campaign of Winter of 1864–65* ([Denver, 1907]), p. 3. The tribes involved were mainly the Cheyenne, Arapaho, Kiowa, portions of the Sioux, and Blackfeet.

[2] Dodge, *The Indian Campaign of Winter of 1864–65*, p. 11; Mantor, "Stagecoach and Freighter Days at Fort Kearny," pp. 327–328; Root and Connelley, *The Overland Stage to California*, p. 256.

[3] *Official Records*, Ser. I, XLVIII, pt. I, p. 41.

[4] Salt Lake City *Daily Union Vedette*, June 20, 1865. See also Herndon, *Days on the Road*, pp. 86, 144, 152; also [McCormick], *Across the Continent in 1865*, p. 7.

[5] *Official Records*, Ser. I, XLVIII, pt. I, p. 338. For an account of the Sioux attack, see August Mencken, *The Railroad Passenger Car* (Baltimore, 1957).

[6] Henry Tisdale, "Travel by Stage in the Early Days," *Transactions of the Kansas State Historical Society, 1901–1902* (Topeka, 1902), VII, p. 463.

[7] Davis, "A Stage Ride to Colorado," pp. 143–146.

[8] *Official Records*, Ser. I, XLVIII, pt. I, pp. 315–316, 997–998.

[9] *Ibid.*, Ser. I, XLVIII, pt. II, p. 1243.

[10] *Ibid.*, Ser. I, XLVIII, pt. I, p. 91.

[11] Dodge, *The Indian Campaign of Winter of 1864–65*, p. 5.

[12] Root and Connelley, *The Overland Stage to California*, p. 373.

[13] *Official Records*, Ser. I, XLVIII, pt. II, p. 1045.

[14] Barnes, *From the Atlantic to the Pacific*, p. 16; [Mc Cormick], *Across the Continent in 1865*, p. 7.

[15] McClure, *Three Thousand Miles through the Rocky Mountains*, pp. 51, 58–68.

[16] Welty, "The Western Army Frontier, 1860–1870," p. 125.

[17] Dodge, "How We Built the Union Pacific," pp. 29–30.

[18] Byers, "When Railroading Outdid the Wild West Stories," p. 243.

[19] Galloway, *The First Transcontinental Railroad*, p. 296.

[20] Boddam-Whetham, *Western Wanderings*, p. 64.

[21] "Log of the Steamer *Abeona*, 1867," MS, Missouri Historical Society, St. Louis. See also Chittenden, *History of Early Steamboat Navigation on the Missouri River*, I, 123.

[22] Captain Willard Glazier, *Ocean to Ocean on Horseback* (Philadelphia, 1899), chap. 26.

²³ Hafen, *The Overland Mail*, pp. 320–323.

²⁴ William A. Pinkerton, *Train Robberies, Train Robbers, and the "Holdup" Men* (Chicago, 1907), pp. 52–54.

²⁵ [Wells, Fargo and Company], *Report of Jas. B. Hume and Jno. N. Thacker . . . Giving Losses by Train Robbers, Stage Robbers and Burglaries . . .* (San Francisco, 1885), pp. 3, 18. Varying figures are given on the number of holdups credited to Black Bart, but the figure used here is taken from this formal Report.

²⁶ [Wells, Fargo and Company], *Wells, Fargo & Co.'s Express: Instructions for Use of Agents and Employees Only, 1882* (San Francisco, 1882), p. 47.

²⁷ Thomas J. Dimsdale, *The Vigilantes of Montana . . .* (Helena, Mont., n.d.) is the classic and standard record of these events.

²⁸ Spring, *The Cheyenne and Black Hills Stage and Express Routes*, pp. 199 ff.

²⁹ Santa Fe *Rocky Mountain Sentinel*, April 3, 1879.

³⁰ Rivaling William A. Pinkerton as a detective was General D. J. Cook, Chief of the Rocky Mountain Detective Agency. Exploits by road agents are related by him in John W. Cook, comp., *Hands-Up; or Five Years of Detective Life in the Mountains and on the Plains: Reminiscences of General D. J. Cook . . .* (Denver, 1897), pp. 13–26.

³¹ *Ibid.*, pp. 36–40.

³² *Dictionary of American Biography* (New York, 1929), II, 35–36; Pinkerton, *Train Robberies, Train Robbers, and the "Holdup" Men*, pp. 31–33.

³³ I. E. Solomon, "Stages Held Up on Black Canyon Route," *Arizona Historical Review*, I (October 1928), pp. 50–53. For a general account, see Cook, *Hands Up; or Five Years of Detective Life in the Mountains and on the Plains*, pp. 237–238. Typical individual accounts are these: [   ], "Stage Hold-Up at Pegleg in 1877," *Frontier Times*, IV (February 1927), pp. 49–51; Mrs. A. W. Koock, "Early Day Stage Robbery in Llano County [Texas]," *Frontier Times*, IV (July 1927), pp. 38–39; Donald McCarthy, "Bill Brazelton, Stage Robber," *Frontier Times*, XXVII (June 1950), pp. 250–253; J. Marvin Hunter, "Arrest of the Balcones Stage Robbers," *Frontier Times*, XV (May 1938), pp. 365–368.

³⁴ Johnson, "Stagecoaching Days."

³⁵ Pinkerton, *Train Robberies, Train Robbers, and the "Holdup" Men*, pp. 22–24. The literature on the James brothers is massive. One book by James D. Horan, *Desperate Men* (New York, 1949), is based in part on complete Pinkerton Detective files according to Robert A. Pinkerton II. See Horan, *Desperate Men*, pp. 67–68. See also Cook, *Hands-Up; or Five Years of Detective Life in the Mountains and on the Plains*, pp. 238–240.

³⁶ Pinkerton, *Train Robberies, Train Robbers, and the "Holdup" Men*, pp. 24–27.

³⁷ *Ibid.*, pp. 11, 84; Alvin Harlow, "Bandits," *Dictionary of American History* (New York, 1940), I, 152.

³⁸ [One Who Knows], *The Spider and the Fly; or, Tricks, Traps, and Pitfalls of City Life* (New York, 1873), p. 51.

³⁹ B. E. Lloyd, *Lights and Shades in San Francisco* (San Francisco, 1876), pp. 79–84.

⁴⁰ Colon Smith, *Out West* (London, 1884), pp. 65, 76–77.

⁴¹ [By Himself], *The Gallynipper in Yankeeland* (London, 1882), p. 53.

⁴² John Morris, *Wanderings of a Vagabond: An Autobiography* (New York, 1873), pp. 234–241, 413–432. This is one of many contemporary accounts dealing with gambling in the West.

Chapter 11: Good Roads and the Passing
of the Transportation Frontier

[1] [   ], *Prize Essays on Roads and Road Making: 1870* (Boston, 1870), p. 84.

[2] For a scholarly treatment of federal road construction to 1869, see Jackson, *Wagon Roads West*. See also J. E. Pennybacker, *State Management of Public Roads: Its Development and Trends* (Washington, D.C., 1915), which is an informative item; also L. W. Page, "Roads and Canals," *Cyclopaedia of American Agriculture* (New York, 1917), IV, p. 322; [Commissioner of Agriculture], "County Roads and Road Laws," *Report of the Commissioner of Agriculture . . . 1868* (Washington, D.C., 1868), p. 348.

[3] [Commissioner of Agriculture], "County Roads and Road Laws," p. 353. See also Albert A. Pope, *Wagon Roads as Feeders to Railways* (Boston, 1892), p. 11.

[4] George R. Chatburn, *Highways and Highway Transportation* (New York, 1923), pp. 126–127. See also Arthur J. Larsen, "The Development of the Minnesota Road System," Ph.D. dissertation, University of Minnesota, Minneapolis, 1938, p. 282; G. C. Clemens, *A Manual of the Law of Roads and Highways in the State of Kansas* (Topeka, 1885), p. 22.

[5] Clemens, *A Manual of the Laws,* pp. 52, 54. For a good summary of state road laws, see United States Department of Agriculture Office of Road Inquiry, *State Laws Relating to the Management of Roads Enacted in 1894–95,* Roy Stone, comp., Bulletin No. 18 (Washington, D.C., 1895).

[6] E. W. Herendeen, "Road Making," in *Rural Affairs* (Albany, N.Y., 1868), IV, p. 56.

[7] Larsen, "Development of the Minnesota Road System," pp. 295–299.

[8] *Proceedings of the Seventh Annual Meeting of the Missouri Road Improvement Association . . . , December 15, 1898* (Columbia, Mo., 1899), pp. 29–30.

[9] Larsen, "Development of the Minnesota Road System," p. 300.

[10] [Commissioner of Agriculture], "County Roads and Road Laws," pp. 348–350, 352. Plank roads first came into wide use in the 1840s. They were usually constructed by laying planks across stringers, or sleepers. Corduroy roads were built by laying logs or slabs transversely along a simply prepared road bed.

[11] Taylor, *Colorado: A Summer Trip,* p. 158.

[12] United States, *Twelfth Census . . . 1900: Manufactures* (Washington, D.C., 1902), vol. X, pt. IV, pp. 325–331. See also Rose, "The Highway from the Railroad to the Automobile," in Labatat and Lane, *Highways,* pp. 84, 86.

[13] *The Wheelman,* I (October 1882), p. 24. See also *Outing,* I (June 1882), p. 10.

[14] *Outing,* II (May 1883), p. 7.

[15] A directory of wheelmen appears in Lyman Hotchkiss Bagg (pseud., Karl Kron), *Ten Thousand Miles on a Bicycle* (New York, 1887), Chap. 40.

[16] *Ibid.,* Chap. 37, entitled "Literature of the Wheel," lists twenty-two cycling journals, also numerous cycling books, pamphlets, and guides. See also Fred C. Kelly, "The Great Bicycle Craze," *American Heritage,* VIII (December 1956), p. 69. In 1897 the membership of the wheelmen reached 102,636. In that year California had 948 members; Minnesota, 674; Colorado, 582; Idaho had only 3 members. Membership, of course, bulked in the eastern states. For a complete breakdown on membership by states, see Philip P. Mason, "The League of American Wheelmen and the Good Roads Movement, 1880–1905," Ph.D. dissertation, University of Michigan, Ann Arbor, 1957, p. 50.

[17] [League of American Wheelmen], *Road and Hand-Book* (Columbia, Mo., 1895). See also, for example, California Associated Cycling Clubs, *Touring Guide and Road Book* (San Francisco, 1898).

[18] Bagg, *Ten Thousand Miles on a Bicycle,* pp. 473–484.

[19] *Ibid.,* pp. 472–480. As indicated, part of the Stevens story is related secondhand by Bagg; other parts are quoted directly from the original narrative. Portions of Stevens' narrative were also published in installments in *Outing* magazine.

[20] [League of American Wheelmen], *Road and Hand-Book,* pp. 64–67. See also California Associated Cycling Clubs, *Touring Guide and Road Book,* pp. 84, 87.

[21] *The Wheelman,* I (October 1882), p. 41; Kelly, "The Great Bicycle Craze," p. 69.

[22] Mason, "The League of American Wheelmen and the Good Roads Movement," pp. 64 ff.

[23] Chatburn, *Highways and Highway Transportation,* p. 133.

[24] Pope, *Wagon Roads as Feeders to Railways,* p. 8.

[25] *Ibid.,* p. 3; see also Roy Stone, "Good Roads," *Overland,* XXV, 2 ser. (March 1895), pp. 235–236; *New York Times,* September 11, 1892.

[26] Reprinted in *New York Times,* September 11, 1892.

[27] *The Wheelman,* I (October 1882), p. 42.

[28] *New York Times,* September 11, 1892.

[29] [Missouri State Board of Agriculture], *Report of the Roads Improvement Convention and First Annual Meeting of the Missouri State Roads Improvement Association* . . . (Columbia, Mo., 1893), pp. 12, 24.

[30] *The State's Duty* (a special convention issue), XII (September 1900), pp. 10–18.

[31] Chatburn, *Highways and Highway Transportation,* p. 132. See also Stone, "Good Roads," pp. 234–235.

[32] Arthur J. Larsen, "Development of the Minnesota Road System," p. 350.

[33] Miller, "History of the Modern Highway," p. 90; Wayne E. Fuller, "Good Roads and Rural Free Delivery of Mail," *Mississippi Valley Historical Review,* XLII (June 1955), p. 69; Chatburn, *Highways and Highway Transportation,* p. 138.

[34] *Congressional Record,* 52 Cong., 2 sess., XXIV, pt. 2, p. 883.

[35] The United States Department of Agriculture Office of Road Inquiry issued forty bulletins, published in Washington, D.C., 1894–1911. See also *Annual Reports of the Department of Agriculture* . . . *1901* (Washington, D.C., 1901), pp. xcix–ci. See also Maurice O. Eldridge, "Progress in Road Building in the United States," *Yearbook of the United States Department of Agriculture: 1899* (Washington, D.C., 1900).

[36] *Annual Reports of the Department of Agriculture* . . . *1899* (Washington, D.C., 1899), pp. xi, 281; *Annual Reports of the Department of Agriculture* . . . *1900* (Washington, D.C., 1900), pp. 281–286.

[37] Herendeen, "Road Making," pp. 59–60. See also Albert A. Pope, *The Movement for Better Roads* (Boston, 1892), pp. 23–24; *The Wheelman,* II (September 1883), p. 468.

[38] United States Office of Public Roads, *Public-Road Mileage, Revenues, and Expenditures in the United States in 1904,* Maurice O. Eldridge, comp., Bulletin No. 32 (Washington, D.C., 1907), pp. 8–9.

[39] The Mormons were enterprising ferry operators in the West. See Bancroft, *History of Utah,* p. 247. See also Harold E. Briggs, *Frontiers of the Northwest* (New York, 1940), pp. 356–357; and Lloyd Lewis and Stanley Pargellis, *Grange Country* (Boston, 1949), no pagination.

[40] Larsen, "Development of the Minnesota Road System," pp. 305–307. The first iron bridge was built in 1839. See also Wilbur J. Watson, *Bridge Architecture* (New York, 1927), pp. 1–4, 19–21.

[41] New Mexico *Press,* February 7, 1865.

[42] John B. Jervis, *Report . . . Railroad Bridge over the Mississippi River, at Rock Island* (New York, 1857), pp. 9–10.

[43] Maj. Gen. G. K. Warren, *Report on Bridging the Mississippi River between St. Paul, Minn., and St. Louis, Mo.* (Washington, D.C., 1878). By 1868 four railroad bridges had been completed across the Mississippi at Hannibal, Missouri; Quincy, Illinois; and Burlington and Dubuque, Iowa. Railroad bridges that followed were at Winona, Minnesota (1870); Hastings, Minnesota (1871); Keokuk, Iowa (1873); and Louisiana, Missouri (1873). See John A. Bryan, "Bridging the Mississippi at St. Louis," MS, St. Louis Public Library, p. 6.

[44] St. Louis *Daily Missouri Democrat,* February 14, 1865.

[45] Bryan, "Bridging the Mississippi at St. Louis," pp. 3–6. See also M. M. Yeakle, *The City of St. Louis of To-Day* (St. Louis, 1889), pp. 251–253. The most comprehensive history of the entire St. Louis bridge project is C. M. Woodward, *A History of the St. Louis Bridge* (St. Louis, 1881).

[46] St. Louis *Republican,* July 5, 1874.

[47] Reavis, *St. Louis: The Commercial Metropolis of the Mississippi Valley,* p. 111.

[48] [Los Angeles *Times-Mirror*], *The Los Angeles Times Almanac* (Los Angeles, 1897), p. 452.

[49] Letter to Henry Ford, May 27, 1908, Ford Archives, Dearborn, Michigan.

BIBLIOGRAPHICAL NOTES

The Transportation Frontier, 1865

A mass of material pertaining to the stirring events West of the Mississippi River during or shortly after the Civil War has been examined here with reference to transportation. There exist no special treatises on this particular subject. The interested student or researcher will find his grist scattered profusely in such primary sources as that gold mine of information, *The War of the Rebellion: A Compilation of the Official Records of the Union and Confederate Armies* (Washington, D.C., 1896), especially in Ser. I, XLVIII, pts. I–II, and in the accompanying *Atlas to Accompany the Official Records of the Union and Confederate Armies,* 2 vols. (Washington, D.C., 1891–1895). The *Official Records* contain valuable on-the-spot reports of the Indian situation, movements, people, and the location and condition of roads or trails. Only a few maps in the *Atlas* are of the trans-Mississippi West in 1865. Roads shown on these maps are in the main accurate, but only a limited number of the routes of travel are shown. The Eighth and Ninth United States censuses also yield useful basic material, but it must be remembered that these pertain specifically to the years 1860 and 1870, not to in-between dates.

An extremely illuminating body of primary material focusing on a given period such as 1865 or thereabouts consists of published guides and city and town directories. Some of these have been cited here, namely: Edward H. Hall, *The Great West: Travellers', Miners', and Emigrants' Guide and Handbook* (New York, 1865); J. L. Campbell, *Idaho: Six Months in the New Gold Diggings. The Emigrants' Guide Overland* (New York, 1864); Henry G. Langley, comp., *The Pacific Coast Business Directory for 1867* (San Francisco, 1867), T. Addison Richards, ed., *Appleton's Companion Hand-Book of Travel* (New York, 1866, and later editions); and S. J. McCormick, *The Portland Directory* (Portland, Ore., 1865). Other useful items in this category are F. Fry, comp., *Fry's Travelers' Guide and Descriptive Journal of the Great North-Western Territories* (Cincinnati, 1865); David M. Gazlay, comp., *Gazlay's Business Directory . . . 1864, 1865: California and Oregon* (San Francisco, 1864); *Duncan & Co's New Orleans Business Directory for 1865* (New Orleans, 1865); Matthew Quigg, comp., *Atchison City Directory, and Business Mirror for 1865* (n.p., [1865]); and Capt. John Mullan, *Miners and Travelers' Guide . . .* (New York, 1865). Captain Mullan was a sharp, accurate observer, and his *Guide* is one of the more reliable ones. The facts, figures, and general information contained in items of this nature are not always scrupulously accurate, but in many instances they constitute the only record of a given place at a given period of time. The Henry E. Huntington Library, San Marino, California, has a good and separately catalogued collection of directories. Others are scattered in major libraries throughout the West. Directories and guides, along with available contemporary newspapers and published eye-witness travel accounts, provide one with a fruitful combination of sources throwing light on such topics as the transportation frontier in 1865.

Reminiscent accounts of the frontier transportation situation after the Civil War ended are plentiful, and certain ones, shored up by critical editorial pens, are both respectable and useful. A standard item of this character is Frank A. Root and William E. Connelley, *The Overland Stage to California* (Topeka, 1901). Root, the major author of this book, was an express and post office agent on the Kansas-Nebraska frontiers, whereas Connelley, as Secretary of the Kansas State Historical Society and author of several works, served mainly as an editor of this informative, well-indexed volume. It was reprinted by *Long's* College Book Company (Columbus, Ohio, 1950).

Two now standard works on federal government-sponsored explorations and trail and road building in the West during the midcentury decades are William H. Goetzmann, *Army Exploration in the American West, 1803–1863* (New Haven, Conn., 1959) and W. Turrentine Jackson, *Wagon Roads West: A Study of Federal Road Surveys and Construction in the Trans-Mississippi West, 1846–1869* (Berkeley, Calif., 1952). Both works are significant contributions to the scholarship on the subjects indicated.

Articles and profuse information on this and the other chapters scattered throughout western historical journals may be found by consulting the author's *A Classified Bibliography of the Periodical Literature of the Trans-Mississippi West, 1811–1957* (Bloomington, Ind., 1961).

The Persistence of the Overlanders

The literature of the overlanders, namely diaries, journals, and reminiscences pertaining mainly to crossings of the trans-Missouri West, is for the most part identified with the period 1840–1865. The secondary literature of the covered wagon migrations relates largely to this same quarter-century period. The overland literature, either original or secondary, is relatively scarce for the post-Civil War period, but the fact remains that heavy overland migrations persisted between the years 1865–1890, and support for this contention is to be found. Again one turns to *Official Records of the Union and Confederate Armies* (Washington, D.C., 1896), Ser. I, XLVIII, pts. I–II, for reports and references to the influx of Civil War veterans and strictly civilian families heading west in wagon caravans during and after 1865.

General descriptions of the migrations based on personal observations come from travelers. Two of the best books by Americans offering precise information are James F. Meline, *Two Thousand Miles on Horseback: Santa Fé and Back* (New York, 1867) and Demas Barnes, *From the Atlantic to the Pacific, Overland: A Series of Letters* (New York, 1866). Easily the most vivid and graphic book-length account is Sarah R. Herndon, *Days on the Road: Crossing the Plains in 1865* (New York, 1902). Snatches of information are to be found in several contemporary and reminiscent accounts printed in book form. One such is James H. Kyner, *End of Track* (Lincoln, Nebr.,

1960). Kyner was a railroad engineer in the postwar West and he observed firsthand wagon trains westward bound. Also presenting pertinent sketches of migrant families is a western classic, Albert D. Richardson, *Beyond the Mississippi* (Hartford, Conn., 1867). Another observation is an Englishman's account, T. S. Hudson, *A Scamper through America* (London, 1882). A reliable and ably written book on migration over the central route is W. J. Ghent, *The Road to Oregon: A Chronicle of the Great Emigrant Trail* (New York, 1934). The last chapter of Ghent's book discusses the decline of the trail.

A highly significant and ably edited book-length diary relating to this particular subject is Andrew F. Rolle, ed., *The Road to Virginia City: The Diary of James Knox Polk Miller* (Norman, Okla., 1960). Miller traveled from Chicago to Virginia City, M.T., via Salt Lake City and returned East by way of Fort Benton. The very literate author of this diary covers the years 1864–1867. Several accounts by participants in the post-Civil War migrations have been published in historical periodicals. Vivid Oregon Trail accounts by women are Mrs. James D. Agnew, "Idaho Pioneer of 1864," *Washington Historical Quarterly*, XV (1924), 44–48, and J. Orin Oliphant, ed., "In a Prairie Schooner, 1878," by Mrs. Lucy Ide, *Washington Historical Quarterly*, XVIII (1927), 122–131, 191–198, 277–288. Mrs. Agnew's destination was Idaho, Mrs. Ide's, Washington Territory. An enlightening account of a plains crossing is G. S. McCain, "A Trip from Atchison, Kansas, to Laurette, Colorado," *Colorado Magazine*, XXVII (1950), 95–102; so too are Frances C. Peabody, "Across the Plains DeLuxe in 1865," *Colorado Magazine*, XVIII (1941), 71–76; and James C. Olson, ed., "From Nebraska City to Montana, 1866: The Diary of Thomas Alfred Creigh," *Nebraska History Magazine*, XXIX (1948), 208–237. An interesting wartime account is "Across the Plains in 1863: The Diary of Peter Winne," edited by Robert G. Athearn, *Iowa Journal of History*, XLIX (1951), 221–240. Some unusual observations on migrants recorded by a teamster appear in P. G. Scott, "Diary of a Freighting Trip from Kit Carson to Trinidad in 1870," *Colorado Magazine*, VIII (1931), 146–154. Easily the most wittily written exposition is [Mr. Socrates Hyacinth], "After Romance—Reality," *The Overland Monthly*, II (1869), 463–468. One of the rare West to East accounts was written by the son of a Montana justice: it is J. Allen Hosmer, "A Trip to the States," *South Dakota Historical Review*, I (1936), 179–224.

One of the strong holdings in items relating to post-Civil War overlanders is the privately held Everett D. Graff collection of western Americana, Chicago.

Teamsters on the Frontier

No comprehensive study of wagon freighting in the trans-Mississippi West has yet been published. Early freighting on the plains as conducted by the freighting firm of Russell, Majors and Waddell has, however, been competently treated in Raymond W. Settle and Mary Lund Settle, *Empire on Wheels* (Stanford University, Calif., 1949). This book is based heavily upon manuscript sources, such as the Waddell Collection, Henry E. Huntington Library,

San Marino, California. An excellent companion book comprising an original source is the reminiscences of one of the freighting partners, Alexander Majors, *Seventy Years on the Frontier* (Chicago, 1893).

Several books have been written on the Santa Fe Trail and trade—likewise representing the beginning phases of freighting on the plains. The most readable and reasonably accurate book on this subject is R. L. Duffus, *The Santa Fe Trail* (New York, 1930), and an excellent companion source item for this general history is Max L. Moorhead, ed., *Commerce of the Prairies* by Josiah Gregg (Norman, Okla., 1954). Special studies of wagon freighting on the Santa Fe Trail have appeared in article form. Two such items are Walker D. Wyman, "Freighting: A Big Business on the Santa Fe Trail," *Kansas Historical Quarterly*, I (1931), 17–27, and, by the same author, "The Military Phase of Santa Fe Freighting, 1846–1865," *Kansas Historical Quarterly*, I (1932), 415–428. These articles were the product of the author's "Freighting on the Santa Fe Trail, 1843–1866," M.A. thesis, Iowa State University, Iowa City, 1931.

Information on wagon freighting on the plains after 1865 is more fragmentary. A brief but captivating description of early western transportation, of which freighting was a part, is Charles F. Lummis, "Pioneer Transportation in America," *McClure's Magazine*, XXV (1905), 561–573; XXVI (1905), 81–94. Accounts of wagon freighting emanating from given Missouri River towns appear in the appropriate city or town directories, for example, Mathew Quigg, comp., *Atchison City Directory, and Business Mirror for 1865* (n.p., [1865]); [Millison and Heil, publs.], *Topeka City Directory and Business Mirror for 1868–69* (Topeka, 1868). For valuable data on wagon freighting linked with steamboat freighting operations in and out of St. Louis, see George H. Morgan, *Annual Statement of the Trade and Commerce of St. Louis . . . 1865* (St. Louis, 1866). The role of the military in western wagon freighting is thoroughly presented in Raymond L. Welty, "The Western Army Frontier, 1860–1870," Ph.D. dissertation, State University of Iowa, Iowa City, 1924. For the Pacific and Rocky Mountain areas, Hubert H. Bancroft, *Works*, 39 vols. (San Francisco, 1874–1890), in particular the volumes pertaining to regions and states concerned, usually contain accurately chronicled accounts on wagon freighting as well as other forms of transportation. A considerable portion of Oscar Osburn Winther, *The Old Oregon Country* (Stanford University, Calif., 1950) deals with freighting in the Pacific Northwest as does also Arthur L. Throckmorton, *Oregon Argonauts* (Portland, Ore., 1961), a scholarly study of merchant adventurers on the Oregon frontier. Joseph A. McGowan, "Freighting to the Mines in California, 1849–1859," Ph.D. dissertation, University of California, Berkeley, 1949, is an exhaustive study of the California area for the years indicated, but it leaves the important postmining period untouched.

The distinctive character of the Red River cart trade is best treated in Harold E. Briggs, "Early Freight and Stage Lines in Dakota," *North Dakota Historical Quarterly*, III (1929), 229–261. Also, much local information on this subject is available in Christopher C. Andrews, *History of St. Paul, Minn.* (Syracuse, N.Y., 1890).

The truly rough, frontier life of teamsters, their wagons, and their art of mule skinning and bull whacking are re-created from a body of varied source material ranging from newspapers to diaries, reminiscences, and accounts by observing travelers. Simple, but authentic, are William F. Hooker, "The Frontier Freight Train Wagon-boss of the 1870's," *The Union Pacific Magazine*, IV (1925), 9–10, and by the same author, *The Prairie Schooner* (Chicago, 1918). Also of a reminiscent, but informative, nature are T. K. Tyson, "Freighting to Denver," *Proceedings and Collections of Nebraska State Historical Society*, ser. 2 (Lincoln, Nebr., 1902), V; D. P. Rolfe, "Overland Freighting from Nebraska City," *Proceedings and Collections*, Nebraska State Historical Society, ser. 2 (Lincoln, Nebr., 1902), V, 281; and T. S. Garrett, "Some Recollections of an Old Freighter," *Annals of Wyoming*, III (1925), 86–93. Among several excellent articles growing out of a Ph.D. dissertation is one dealing particularly with ox-team operations; it is Walker D. Wyman, "Bullwhacking: A Prosaic Profession Peculiar to the Great Plains," *New Mexico Historical Review*, VII (1932), 297–310. Some of the flavor and folklore associated with freighting, especially in the mountainous West, is contained in J. A. Filcher, *Untold Tales of California* (n.p., 1903); James Swisher, *How I Know* (Cincinnati, 1881); and in parts of Clarence King, *Mountaineering in the Sierra Nevada* (Boston, 1872). The story of western wagon makers is yet to be written. Emily Ann O'Neal, "Joseph Murphy's Contribution to the Great American West," M.A. thesis, St. Louis University, St. Louis, 1947, is based largely upon Murphy's account books, but it falls short of being an adequate treatment of the widely and extensively used J. Murphy wagons.

Stagecoaching as Frontier Enterprise

Both stagecoaching as a business enterprise and the social history of coaching have received more attention from professional and amateur historians than have other forms of prerailroad transportation within the trans-Mississippi West. A very readable trade book on stagecoaching, and unique in its treatment of James E. Birch as a pioneer in overland staging, is Captain William Banning and George Hugh Banning, *Six Horses* (New York, 1930). The history of the Butterfield Overland Mail, for example, has been accorded a three-volume work, Roscoe P. Conkling and Margaret B. Conkling, *The Butterfield Overland Mail, 1857–1869*, 3 vols. (Glendale, Calif., 1947). This work contains a detailed description of the Oxbow, section-by-section. The third volume contains plates and maps exclusively. A standard and very ably prepared history of the development of stagecoach-carrying mail services in the West is now unfortunately scarce, LeRoy R. Hafen, *The Overland Mail, 1849–1869* (Cleveland, 1926). A classic volume, basically a source book, devoted to staging enterprises on the Great Plains is Frank A. Root and William E. Connelley, *The Overland Stage to California* (Topeka, 1901). Supplementing this valuable work and based on available documentary material (at best limited) is J. V. Frederick, *Ben Holladay: The Stagecoach King* (Glendale, Calif., 1940). Still another good book of a regional character is Agnes W. Spring, *The Cheyenne and Black Hills Stage and Express Routes* (Glendale, Calif., 1949). Also, two books by the author, *Express and Stagecoach Days in California* (Stanford University, Calif., 1936) and *The Old Oregon Country* (Stanford University, Calif., 1950), relate stagecoaching operations in the Pacific coast area.

Comprehensive as are the books on this subject, some segments remain for treatment in article form. Arthur J. Larsen, "The Northwestern Express and Transportation Company," *North Dakota Historical Quarterly*, VI (1931), 42–62, helps to fill a gap pertaining to Minnesota as does Harold E. Briggs, "Early Freight and Stage Lines in Dakota," *North Dakota Historical Quarterly*, III (1929), 229–261, for Dakota Territory, and Kenneth E. Colton, "Stagecoach Travel in Iowa," *Annals of Iowa*, XXII (1940), 3–53, for Iowa. Comparable studies relating to the Southwest are two by William S. Wallace: "Short-Line Staging in New Mexico," *New Mexico Historical Review*, XXVI (1951), 89–100, and "Stagecoaching in Territorial New Mexico," *New Mexico Historical Review*, XXXII, 3d ser. (1957), 204–210; Charles S. Potts, "Transportation in Texas," in *Texas History*, Eugene C. Barker, ed. (Dallas, 1929); and for Montana, Paul F. Sharp, "Whoop-up Trail: International Highway on the Great Plains," *Pacific Historical Review*, XXI (1952), 129–144. Then, dealing more specifically with one given company rather than with the staging business within an area are two informative articles, namely, Margaret Long, "The Route of the Leavenworth and Pike's Peak Express," *Colorado Magazine*, XII (1935), 186–194, and George A. Root and Russell K. Hickman, "Pike's Peak Express Companies," *Kansas Historical Quarterly*, XIII (1944), 163–195, 211–242, 485–526; XIV (1946), 36–92.

The most available and also most valuable source materials on the staging business pertain to postal contracts and are therefore embodied in the published United States government executive documents covering the years concerned. This document series is available in most research libraries.

Overland by Stage

Bibliographical references on stagecoach travel differ markedly from those related to staging as a business enterprise, although some items deal with both aspects of the subject. Published accounts by travelers, notably British, who crossed the West by stagecoach, provide abundant, and, on the whole, interesting and amusing reading.

A delightful travel account of this nature is John W. Boddam-Whetham, *Western Wanderings* (London, 1874). The author comments vividly and at times sardonically on stage drivers in the mountainous West coast region and also on roads. Wallis Nash, *Oregon, There and Back in 1877* (London, 1878) and John M. Murphy, *Rambles in North-Western America from the Pacific Ocean to the Rocky Mountains* (London, 1879) also describe staging in this same area but do so in a more serious and more irritable vein. Other British accounts are T. S. Hudson, *A Scamper through America* (London, 1882), a generally informative item; Raphael Pumpelly, *Across America and Asia* (New York, 1870), the opening chapter of which deals with the overland coach with particular reference to the Southwest; and a chapter in Volume I of William H. Dixon, *New America*, 2 vols. (London, 1867), which touches upon the perils of staging over the central route. Brief but pointed comments on some of the English stagecoach travelers appear in Robert G. Athearn, *Westward the Briton* (New York, 1953), Chap. 1.

Americans who traveled west of the Mississippi were by no means reticent about publishing their reactions to coaching. Indeed, some of the accounts are gems. Such, for example, is Samuel L. Clemens (pseud., Mark Twain), *Roughing It* (Hartford, Conn., 1888); also Samuel Bowles, *Our New West* (New York, 1869); Albert D. Richardson, *Beyond the Mississippi* (Hartford, Conn., 1867); John A. Beadle, *The Undeveloped West; or Five Years in the Territories* (Philadelphia, 1873); Horace Greeley, *An Overland Journey . . . 1859* (New York, 1860); and some of the writings of Bayard Taylor, for example, his *Colorado: A Summer Trip* (New York, 1867). Other travel accounts bearing significantly on this topic are A[lexander] K. McClure, *Three Thousand Miles through the Rocky Mountains* (Philadelphia, 1869) and Demas Barnes, *From the Atlantic to the Pacific, Overland: A Series of Letters* (New York, 1866). A rare and valuable item relating to staging on the oxbow route is Lyle H. Wright and Josephine M. Bynum, eds., *The Butterfield Overland Mail*, by Waterman L. Ormsby (San Marino, Calif., 1942). Staging in general is also treated in books of a secondary character such as Captain William Banning and George Hugh Banning, *Six Horses* (New York, 1930) and in a book by the author, *Via Western Express and Stagecoach* (Stanford University, Calif., 1945).

In addition to general regional references to staging, there are numerous articles and source items that pertain particularly to individual states or territories. Edward Vischer, "Stage Coach Days," *Quarterly of the Society of California Pioneers*, VII (1930), 51–53, pertains to California; Edward T. Bollinger, "Middle Park Stage Driving," *Colorado Magazine*, XXVIII (1951), 269–280, and Albert B. Sanford, ed., "Early Colorado Days," by Thomas T. Cornforth, *Colorado Magazine*, I (1924), 251–257. Both of these brief items pertain to the centennial state. Self-identifying is Kenneth E. Colton, "Stagecoach Travel in Iowa," *Annals of Iowa*, XXII (1939–1941), 175–200, as is also a reminiscent account by Cornelius O'Keefe, "Ride through Montana," *Harper's*, XXXV (1867), 568–585.

Steamboats on a Vanishing Frontier

A thorough, scholarly background book of steamboating, but one mainly concerned with the area of the Mississippi and eastward, is Louis C. Hunter, *Steamboats on the Western Rivers* (Cambridge, Mass., 1949). Also basic to any comprehensive study on steamboating is T. C. Purdy, "Report on Steam Navigation in the United States," in *Report on the Agencies of Transportation in the United States, Tenth Census* (Washington, D.C., 1883). Important, too, as a register of boats are Frederick Way, Jr., comp., *Way's Steamboat Directory*

(Sewickley, Pa., [1942]) and William M. Lytle, comp., *Merchant Steam Vessels of the United States, 1807–1868* (Mystic, Conn., 1952). Important as a regional catalogue of ships is a book edited by E. W. Wright, *Lewis & Dryden's Marine History of the Pacific Northwest* (Portland, Ore., 1895). A writer on steamboating, mainly on the Mississippi and the Missouri rivers, is William J. Petersen. His major, and standard, work is *Steamboating on the Upper Mississippi: The Water Way to Iowa* (Iowa City, Iowa, 1937). Important articles by him are "Steamboating in the Upper Mississippi Fur Trade," *Minnesota History*, XIII (1932), 221–243, and "Steamboating on the Missouri River," an article in *Iowa Journal of History*, LIII (1955), 97–120. Several of his other articles on the Diamond Jo Line are cited in the footnotes to this chapter. An interesting article by Theodore C. Blegen is "The 'Fashionable Tour' on the Upper Mississippi," *Minnesota History*, XX (1939), 377–396; another is Irving H. Hart, "Steamboating on the Mississippi Headwaters," *Minnesota History*, XXXIII (1952), 7–19. Each important western tributary of the Mississippi River has one or more historians. One of the earliest works on the Missouri is Hiram M. Chittenden, *History of Early Steamboat Navigation on the Missouri River*, 2 vols. (New York, 1903), I, whereas the most recent is William E. Lass, *A History of Steamboating on the Upper Missouri River* (Lincoln, Nebr., 1962). Lass has made use of manuscript materials not available to Chittenden, and, as the title indicates, the emphasis is upon the Upper Missouri River. Articles that treat in considerable detail steamboating operations on the Arkansas and Kansas rivers are Muriel H. Wright, "Early Navigation and Commerce along the Arkansas and Red Rivers in Oklahoma," *Chronicles of Oklahoma*, VIII (1930), 65–88; Edgar Langsdorf, "A Review of Early Navigation on the Kansas River," *Kansas Historical Quarterly*, XVIII (1950), 140–145; and Mattie Brown, "River Transportation in Arkansas, 1819–1890," *Arkansas Historical Quarterly*, I (1942), 342–354. Informative articles on steamboating on the Red River of the North are Fred A. Bill, "Early Steamboating on the Red River," *North Dakota Historical Quarterly*, IX (1942), 69–85, and Marion H. Herriot, "Steamboat Transportation on the Red River," *Minnesota History*, XXI (1940), 245–271.

Steamboating in California and the Southwest, and especially on the Colorado River, has been the subject of several readable and enlightening books and articles. Jerry MacMullen, *Paddle-Wheel Days in California* (Stanford University, Calif., 1944) relates a wide range of information concerning steamboats, their builders, operations, disasters, and the rivers over which the boats operated. There are two good references to steamboating on the Colorado: Francis H. Leavitt, "Steam Navigation on the Colorado River," California Historical Society *Quarterly*, XXII (1943), pp. 1–19, 151–174, and Hazel E. Mills, "The Arizona Fleet," *The American Neptune*, I (1941), 255–274. For the Pacific Northwest steamboating a readable and reasonably solid little book is Randall V. Mills, *Stern-Wheelers Up Columbia* (Palo Alto, Calif., 1947).

There are many more manuscript records extant on the subject of steamboating than on other forms of prerailroad transportation. These include mainly ship manufacturers' records, logs, journals, and a variety of personal correspondence and pictures. The historical society libraries of states that played important roles in the river trade have become the main depositories for such materials.

The Missouri Historical Society, St. Louis, for example, has a good collection of steamboat material.

Railroads Blanket the West

The subject of railroads in the trans-Mississippi West has many ramifications and the materials on it are as mountainous in quantity as they are broad in scope. The reader wishing a broad overview on western rails as a phenomenon of frontier enterprise is, nevertheless, limited as to choices of available books. One background book is Robert R. Russel, *Improvement of Communication with the Pacific Coast as an Issue in American Politics, 1783–1864* (Cedar Rapids, Iowa, 1948). Another background book is Robert E. Riegel, *The Story of the Western Railroads* (New York, 1926). It emphasizes the first Pacific railroad, but if used in conjunction with the more recent, ably executed Ira G. Clark, *Then Came the Railroad: The Century from Steam to Diesel in the Southwest* (Norman, Okla., 1958), a broader general coverage is obtained. A basis for post-Civil War developments is provided in another article by Robert E. Riegel, "Trans-Mississippi Railroads during the Fifties," *Mississippi Valley Historical Review*, X (1923), 153–172. A recent, readable, general history with chapters on the West is John F. Stover, *American Railroads* (Chicago, 1961). Available in most libraries is the disjointed, but nevertheless useful and well illustrated, general transportation reference, Seymour Dunbar, *A History of Travel in America*, 4 vols. (Indianapolis, Ind., 1915; one-volume ed., New York, 1937).

Federal railroad surveys in the West were the subject of special studies. Somewhat lacking in analysis but clear in presentation is George L. Albright, *Official Explorations for Pacific Railroads, 1853–1855* (Berkeley, Calif., 1921). A more critical approach to this subject is contained in Chapter 7 of William H. Goetzmann, *Army Exploration in the American West, 1803–1863* (New Haven, Conn., 1959).

Much pertinent information on the background surveys and general aspects of railroads west of the Mississippi River appears in periodicals. On proposals and surveys are Margaret L. Brown, "Asa Whitney and His Pacific Railroad Publicity Campaign," *Mississippi Valley Historical Review*, XX (1933–1934), 209–224; Robert S. Cotterill, "Early Agitation for a Pacific Railroad, 1845–1850," *Mississippi Valley Historical Review*, V (1918–1919), 396–414; George Wilkes, "Proposal for a National Rail-road to the Pacific Ocean, for the Purpose of Obtaining a Short Route to Oregon and the Indies," *Magazine of History* (Extra Numbers), XXXVI, 113–153; Paul W. Glad, "Frederick West Lander and the Pacific Railroad Movement," *Nebraska History Magazine*, XXXV (1954), 173–192; Robert W. Johannsen, ed., "Reporting a Pacific Railroad Survey: Isaac Stevens' Letters to Stephen A. Douglas," *Pacific Northwest Quarterly*, XLVII (1956), 97–106; S. D. Mock, "Colorado and the Surveys for a Pacific Railroad," *Colorado Magazine*, XVII (1940), 54–63; Pearl Russell, "Analysis of the Pacific Railroad Reports," *Washington Historical Quarterly*, X

(1919), 3–16. Those seeking data on individual lines will always find Henry V. Poor, *Manual of the Railroads in the United States* and its successor, Henry V. Poor and H. W. Poor, *Poor's Manual of Railroads in the United States*, published annually in New York, beginning in 1868, an invaluable reservoir of specific information. A remarkable single-volume item packed with significant financial information intended for English investors is Steven Frederick Van Oss, *American Railroads as Investments* (New York, 1893). Important books giving broad coverage of specific aspects of western railroad financing and construction are Frederick A. Cleveland and Fred W. Powell, *Railroad Promotion and Capitalization in the United States* (New York, 1909); Lewis H. Haney, *A Congressional History of Railways in the United States*, 2 vols. (Madison, Wisc., 1910); and John B. Sanborn, *Congressional Grants of Land in Aid of Railways* (Madison, Wisc., 1899), all older but useful works. Important articles dealing with financing (including land grants) are David Maldwyn Ellis, "The Forfeiture of Railroad Land Grants, 1867–1894," *Mississippi Valley Historical Review*, XXXIII (1946–1947), 27–60; and by the same author, "The Oregon and California Railroad Land Grant, 1866–1945," *Pacific Northwest Quarterly*, XXXIX (1948), 253–283; Paul W. Gates, "The Railroad Land-Grant Legend," *Journal of Economic History*, XIV (1954), 143–146; William S. Greever, "A Comparison of Railroad Land-Grant Policies," *Agricultural History*, XXV (1951), 83–90; Robert S. Henry, "The Railroad Land Grant Legend in American History Texts," *Mississippi Valley Historical Review*, XXXII (1945–1946), 171–194; John W. Johnston, "Railway Land Grants," *North American Review*, CXL (1885), 280–289; C. Clyde Jones, "The Burlington Railroad and Agricultural Policy in the 1920's," *Agricultural History*, XXXI (1957), No. 4, 67–74; George W. Julian, "Railway Influence in the Land Office," *North American Review*, CXXXVI (1883), 237–256; Ray H. Mattison, "The Burlington Tax Controversy in Nebraska over the Federal Land Grants," *Nebraska History Magazine*, XXVIII (1947), 110–131; John B. Rae, "The Great Northern's Land Grant," *Journal of Economic History*, XII (1952), 140–145; Ralph N. Traxler, Jr., "The Texas and Pacific Railroad Land Grants: A Comparison of Land Grant Policies of the United States and Texas," *Southwestern Historical Quarterly*, LXI (1958), 359–370.

A larger assortment of books is available on many of the individual railroad lines or systems. The most recent, readable, and valuable item in this category is Robert G. Athearn, *Rebel of the Rockies* (New Haven, Conn., 1962). The general histories of the Union Pacific are aged and inadequate, among them J. P. Davis, *The Union Pacific Railway* (Chicago, 1894) and Nelson Trottman, *History of the Union Pacific* (New York, 1923). Strangely, the Central Pacific does not have its general historian, although Oscar Lewis, *The Big Four* (New York, 1938) contains spirited, even gossipy, biographical sketches of the men who built the Central Pacific. A scholarly study giving insight into the operations of the builder of the Northern Pacific Railroad is James B. Hedges, *Henry Villard and the Railways of the Northwest* (New Haven, Conn., 1930). L. L. Waters, *Steel Trails to Santa Fe* (Lawrence, Kans., 1950) is a history of the Atchison, Topeka and Santa Fe Railroad and is based upon this company's records. A work similarly built, and solidly so, upon company archival materials is Richard C. Overton, *Burlington West* (Cambridge, Mass., 1941). There are several company-inspired and company-subsidized railroad histories of a purely journalistic variety, but these add little to the substantive character of railroad literature. An exception is one of the earliest books of this nature, E. V. Smalley, *History of the Northern Pacific Railroad* (New York, 1883). Smalley's volume relates, rather well, the construction story of the Northern Pacific Railroad. An exhaustive treatise on one of the West's most controversial figures is Julius Grodinsky, *Jay Gould: His Business Career* (Philadelphia, 1957). A dull, yet painstaking, biography of another leading railroad figure is G. T. Clark, *Leland Stanford* (Stanford University, Calif., 1931).

The so-called transcontinental railroads command a literature substantially different from that relating local rail-laying activities. Chroniclers of the smaller, local railroads have, for the most part, found their publication outlets in state and regional historical periodicals. The many articles on railroading in Missouri, for example, include such valuable articles as G. C. Broadhead, "Early Railroads in Missouri," *Missouri Historical Review*, VII (1912–1913), 149–150; Homer Clevenger, "The Buildings of the Hannibal and St. Joseph Railroad," *Missouri Historical Review* XXXVI (1941), 32–47; Homer Clevenger, "Railroads in Missouri Politics 1875–1887," *Missouri Historical Review*, XLIII (1949), 220–236; and by the same author, "The Buildings of the Hannibal and St. Joseph Railroad, *Missouri Historical Review*, XXXVI (1941), 32–47; Margaret Louise Fitzsimmons, "Missouri Railroads during the Civil War and Reconstruction," *Missouri Historical Review*, XXXV (1941), 188–206; Paul W. Gates, "The Railroads of Missouri, 1850–1870," *Missouri Historical Review*, XXVI (1931–1932), 126–141; R. B. Oliver, "Missouri's First Railroad," *Missouri Historical Review*, XXVI (1931–1932), 12–18; R. E. Riegel, "The Missouri Pacific Railroad to 1900," *Missouri Historical Review*, XVIII (1923–1924), 3–26, 173–196. The history of frontier railroading in Iowa is well covered in several worthwhile articles that include Dwight L. Agnew, "Iowa's First Railroad," *Iowa Journal of History*, XLVIII (1950), 1–26; and by the same author, "The Rock Island Railroad in Iowa," *Iowa Journal of History*, LII, the article entitled (1954), 203–222; see as well Earl S. Beard, "The Background of State Railroad Regulation in Iowa," *Iowa Journal of History*, L (1952), 1–34; and Sarah Ellen Groves, "The Coming of the Railroad," *Palimpsest*, II (1921), 240–243. Texas railroads, which led in the Southwest, are also subjects of several informative articles, among them P. Briscoe, "The First Texas Railroad," *Quarterly of the Texas State Historical Association*, VII (1903–1904), 279–285; S. S. McKay, "Texas and the Southern Pacific Railroad, 1848–1860," *Southwestern Historical Quarterly*, XXXV (1931–1932), 1–27; and S. G. Reed, "Land Grants and Other Aids to Texas Railroads," *Southwestern Historical Quarterly*, XLIX (1946), 518–523. For Minnesota see Harold F. Peterson, "Early Minnesota Railroads and the Quest for Settlers," *Minnesota History*, XIII (1932), 25–44; and a brief item, [   ], "Minnesota Railway System," *Hunt's Merchants' Magazine*, XLIII (1860), 758.

In general, and as one might expect, the periodical literature relating to any one state or territory is commensurate with the amount of railroading activity within such an area during the period under review. Thus for Arkansas there are relatively few pertinent articles. Some of them are W. A. Burgess, "Building the Frisco Roadbed in Northwest Arkansas," *Arkansas Historical Quarterly*, X (1951), 268–284; Walter Moffatt, "Transportation in Arkansas, 1819–1840," *Arkansas Historical Quarterly*, XV (1956), 187–201; and Stephen E. Wood, "The Development of Arkansas Railroads," *Arkansas Historical Quarterly*, VII (1948), 103–140, 155–193; for Oklahoma there is Homer S. Chambers, "Early-Day Railroad Building Operations in Western Oklahoma," *Chronicles of Oklahoma*, XXI (1943), 162–170; Dakota, Herbert S. Schell, "The Dakota Southern, A Frontier Railway Venture of Dakota Territory, *South Dakota Historical Review*, II (1936–1937), 99–125; Montana, Stoyan Christowe, "Montana Railroad Gang," *Atlantic Monthly*, CLXXIX (April 1947), 102–108, Flora Mae Bellefleur Isch, "The Importance of Railroads in the Development of Northwestern Montana," *Pacific Northwest Quarterly*, XLI (1950), 19–29, W. M. Underhill, "The Northern Overland Route to Montana," *Washington Historical Quarterly*, XXIII (1932), 177–195; for Arizona there is Lucile Anderson, "Railroad Transportation through Prescott. The Prescott and Arizona Central Railroad," *Arizona Historical Review*, VII (1936), 55–72; Utah, Robert L. Wrigley, Jr., "Utah and Northern Railway Co.: A Brief History," *Oregon Historical Quarterly*, XLVIII (1947), 245–253; Kansas, Lela Barnes, ed., "Letters of Cyrus Kurtz Holliday, 1854–1859," *Kansas Historical Quarterly*, VI (1937), 241–294; The Rev. Peter Beckman, O.S.B., "Atchison's First Railroad," *Kansas Historical Quarterly*, XXI (1954), 153–165; A. Bower Sageser, "Building the Main Line of the Missouri Pacific through Kansas," *Kansas Historical Quarterly*, XXI (1955), 326–330; and Colorado, William S. Jackson, "Railroad Conflicts in Colorado in the 'Eighties," *Colorado Magazine*, XXIII (1946), 7–25; S. D. Mock, "The Financing of Early Colorado Railroads," *Colorado Magazine*, XVIII (1941), 201–209; Nathaniel W. Sample, "Pioneer Railroading in Colorado," *Colorado Magazine*, XXIV (1947), 141–144, Henry Dudley Teetor, "First Railroad Built in Colorado," *Magazine of Western History*, IX (1888–1889), 566–568.

The Pacific coast region, where railroads weighed very heavily on public consciousness, has produced a plethora of articles that for California include Franklyn Hoyt, "San Diego's First Railroad: The California Southern," *Pacific Historical Review*, XXIII (1954), 133–145; Lewis B. Lesley, "The Entrance of the Santa Fé Railroad into California," *Pacific Historical Review*, VIII (1939), 89–96; Clarence M. Wooster, "More about Railroading in California in the Seventies: The Fire Train," California Historical Society *Quarterly*, XXII (1943), 178–180; [   ], "Building the Railroad down the San Joaquin in 1871; From the Reminiscences of Clarence M. Wooster," California Historical Society *Quarterly*, XVIII (1939), 22–31; Oregon, John Tilson Ganoe, "The History of the Oregon and California Railroad," *Quarterly of the Oregon Historical Society*, XXV (1924), 236–283, 330–352; Joseph Gaston, "The Genesis of the Oregon Railway System," *Quarterly of the Oregon Historical Society*, VII (1906), 105–132; and by the same author, "The Oregon Central Railroad," *Quarterly of the Oregon Historical Society*, III (1902), 315–326; Frank B. Gill, "Oregon's First Railway," *Quarterly of the Oregon His-*

torical Society, XXV (1924), 171–235; and, finally, Washington, W. W. Baker, "The Building of the Walla Walla & Columbia River Railroad," *Washington Historical Quarterly*, XIV (1923), 3–13; D. C. Corbin, "Recollections of a Pioneer Railroad Builder," *Washington Historical Quarterly*, I (January 1907), 43–46; Sol H. Lewis, "A History of the Railroads in Washington," *Washington Historical Quarterly*, III (1912), 186–197.

Laying the Track

Track laying as a frontier phenomenon has produced a literature distinct from that relating to the political and financial aspects of railroading. And as might well be expected, national and even world-wide interest in the Union Pacific-Central Pacific project accounts for the existence of a considerable array of materials pertaining to the construction of the first Pacific railroad. Closest to the operations themselves are the interesting and informative, though perhaps one-sided, accounts by construction officers, such as Grenville M. Dodge, "How We Built the Union Pacific Railroad," *Senate Documents*, 61 Cong., 2 sess. (Washington, D.C., 1910), doc. 447 (also published separately in book form); another book by Dodge, *Romantic Realities: The Story of the Pacific Roads* (Omaha, 1889) discussing the Union Pacific; and Robert L. Fulton, *Epic of the Overland* (San Francisco, 1924) relating the building of the Central Pacific. Another engineer's history of the Pacific railroad, and a useful one too, is John D. Galloway, *The First Transcontinental Railroad* (New York, 1950). A popular but nonetheless worthwhile item pertaining to the Southern Pacific Railroad Company's construction and early history is Lindsay Campbell and Earle Heath, "From Trail to Rail," Southern Pacific Railroad Company *Bulletin*, published in serialized form during the years 1926–1930. Serving in part, at least, as a construction history of the Northern Pacific Railroad is Eugene V. Smalley, *History of the Northern Pacific Railroad* (New York, 1883).

Both magazines and professional journals have likewise given space to track-laying literature, much of which is of a reminiscent character. Such an article is George H. Kelly, "Incidents of Building a Railroad—Bowie to Globe," *Arizona Historical Review*, I (1928), 68–73; and also George W. Rafter, "Railroad Building on the Texas Frontier," *Engineering Magazine*, II (October, 1891), 29–41; O. P. Byers, "When Railroading Outdid the Wild West Stories," *Collections of the Kansas State Historical Society, 1926–1928* (Topeka, 1928), 339–349. A brief but fascinating article by a wandering reporter is Ripley Hitchcock, "At the Head of the Rails," *Chautauquan*, IX (1889), 540–543. Less accessible to the general reader but rewarding to the researcher are the contemporary newspaper stories issued by the press. And most revealing of all are the official reports and general information contained in the published United States House and Senate Reports for the thirty-eighth to the fiftieth Congresses. Especially enlightening are the reports and correspondence of government directors and commissioners who passed upon the actual work of construction.

Track-finishing ceremonies, especially those attending the driving of the last spike at Promontory, Utah, have been the subject of many conflicting newspaper and magazine articles. The most recent and also the most thorough account of what took place at Promontory is J. N. Bowman, "Driving the Last Spike at Promontory Point, 1869," California Historical Society *Quarterly,* XXXVI (1957), 97–106, 263–274; also good, but less full in its treatment is Robert M. Utley, "The Dash to Promontory," *Utah Historical Quarterly,* XXIX (1961), 99–117. Still valuable, though subject to some modification, is Edwin L. Sabin, *Building the Pacific Railway* (Philadelphia, 1919). Sabin, who was an eye-witness at Promontory, wrote his book to help commemorate the fiftieth anniversary of the spike-driving ceremony.

Travel by Rail

Accounts by those who traveled by railroad in frontier portions of the trans-Mississippi West have for the most part been written by Americans and Britishers, but in this type of literature may be found as well observations by representatives of other nationalities such as Frenchmen, Scandinavians, Germans, Italians, Poles, and Japanese.

In addition to describing stagecoaching in the West A[lexander] K. McClure, *Three Thousand Miles through the Rocky Mountains* (Philadelphia, 1869) has something to say about early train travel in this region. A combination travel account and general observations on the West is Richard H. Davis, *The West from a Car-Window* (New York, 1892). Railroading as seen through the eyes of a conductor is M. M. Shaw, *Nine Thousand Miles on a Pullman Train* . . . (Philadelphia, 1898). Rich in useful detail and best of the western railroad guides are those published by George A. Crofutt and Company for travelers on the central route. There are many editions that follow the first *Great Trans-Continental Railroad Guide* by Bill Dadd, The Scribe (Chicago, 1869). Some of the most fascinating American travel accounts have been written by women; among them are Helen Hunt Jackson, *Bits of Travel at Home* (Boston, 1887); and Susan Coolidge, "A Few Hints on the California Journey," *Scribner's Monthly,* VI (May, 1873), 25–31. A reminiscent account of train travel in frontier days is Harvey Rice, "A Trip to California in 1869," *Magazine of Western History,* VII (1887–1888), 675–679; VIII (1888), 1–7.

Representative of scores of British accounts relating their reactions to train travel across the western prairies and mountains are T. S. Hudson, *A Scamper through America* (London, 1882) and Edward Money, *The Truth about America* (London, 1886), with a chapter on railroads. Written with a flair and profusely illustrated is George A. Sala, *America Revisited,* 2 vols. (London, 1882). Volume II, Chaps. 8–14, are especially good on Omaha and the train ride to San Francisco. Emily Faithfull, *Three Visits to America* (New

York, Edinburgh, 1884), discusses travel on the Denver and Rio Grande line. First, fresh impressions of the prairies appear in H. Hussey Vivian, *Notes of a Tour in America* (London, 1878) and in William Robertson and W. F. Robertson, *Our American Tour . . . in the Autumn of 1869* (Edinburgh, 1871); also in W. F. Rae, *Westward by Rail: A Journey to San Francisco and Back and a Visit to the Mormons* (London, 1871). A good observer and narrator of the western scene with one chapter, 26, devoted to railroads is L. P. Blouët (pseud., Max O'Rell), *Jonathan and His Continent* (New York, 1889). The impression of one Englishman who traveled widely by rail through the Middle West on over the central route is Frederick T. Townshend, *Ten Thousand Miles of Travel* (London, 1869). There is also W. G. Marshall, *Through America; or Nine Months in the United States* (London, 1881). Among the best, and a classic on this subject, is Robert Louis Stevenson, *Across the Plains* (London, 1892).

Among the non-English items that enliven this subject is one by the Dane, Henrik Cavling, *Fra Amerika,* 2 vols. (Copenhagen, 1897), who wrote wittily about his countrymen on the prairies while traveling by rail over both central and northern lines. And the Atchison, Topeka and Santa Fe as viewed also by a Dane, is H. Andreasen, *Amerika: Seet fra et Lanbostandpunkt* (Copenhagen, 1884). A Frenchman's reaction to Omaha and the Pacific railroad at the time of completion is A. Édouard Portalis, *Les États-Unis* (Paris, 1869) An absorbing account comes from the Polish author of *Quo Vadis,* Charles Morley, trans. and ed., *Portrait of America: Letters of Henry Sienkiewicz* (New York, 1959). The western travels of a Finnish countess are related in her journal, Ernest J. Moyne, ed. and trans., *Alexandra Gripenberg's A Half Year in the New World: Miscellaneous Sketches and Travels in the United States* (Newark, Del., 1954).

The researcher in the field of railroad history of the West—regardless of ramifications of the subject—must necessarily turn to the large collections of material available to him in the special transportation libraries. One of the largest collections, and one containing materials on most forms of transportation, is the Timothy Hopkins Transportation Library, Stanford University, California. Also large, with items running into the scores of thousands, is the Bureau of Railroad Economics Library of the Association of American Railroads, Washington, D.C. Both are world-wide in scope, but of the two collections the Hopkins is the stronger in western railroad materials. Relatively modest, but weighted in materials on the Great Northern Railroad is the James J. Hill Library, St. Paul. Fair, but not outstanding, are the railroad materials in the Library of Congress, Washington, D.C. The most impressive collection of archival materials available to scholars is the Burlington Railroad records on deposit at the Newberry Library, Chicago. Also a part of the Newberry's own holdings in rarities is its admirable collection of travel accounts. Many items are also to be found in the Henry E. Huntington Library. Most western state historical society libraries have good materials in varying quantities, as do the large university libraries—especially the Baker Library at Harvard, Cambridge, and the Bancroft Library at the University of California, Berkeley.

Indians, Outlaws, and Wayfarers

The most readily available and also most rewarding source of information on Indian attacks upon western transportation routes, at least during the height of such disturbances, is the monumental compilation *The War of the Rebellion: A Compilation of the Official Records of the Union and Confederate Armies* (Washington, D.C., 1896), Ser. I, XLVIII, pts. I–II. The army reports on both the general situation and on individual incidents are usually based upon on-the-spot observations rather than on hearsay evidence. These records do not attempt explanations of the causes of the Indian attacks, and the red men are dealt with coldly in these reports as "the enemy." Abundant, too, are accounts in the form of unpublished and published diaries, journals, and reminiscences of emigrants, teamsters, stagecoach drivers, and travelers who, like the army men, were close to the events themselves. Great numbers of these items—too numerous to mention here—contain some references to Indians, and some tell of actual encounters with the red men along their routes of travel. Still unpublished manuscript accounts are to be found in university and state historical society libraries. Grenville M. Dodge, whose numerous letters and dispatches appear in the *Official Records,* contributed as well the pamphlet, *The Indian Campaign of Winter of 1864–65* ([Denver, 1907]) bearing on this subject. Frank A. Root and William E. Connelley, *The Overland Stage to California* (Topeka, 1901). Root, writing from notes and recollections, is an excellent source. An interesting and pertinent travel account by an ex-Union officer and prolific writer on many features of the post-Civil War West is Captain Willard Glazier, *Ocean to Ocean on Horseback* (Philadelphia, 1899). Other items of value are Henry Tisdale, "Travel by Stage in the Early Days," *Transactions of the Kansas State Historical Society, 1901–1902* (Topeka, 1902); Demas Barnes, *From the Atlantic to the Pacific, Overland: A Series of Letters* (New York, 1866); and A[lexander] K. McClure, *Three Thousand Miles through the Rocky Mountains* (Philadelphia, 1869). A good, objectively written secondary treatment of this subject is LeRoy R. Hafen, *The Overland Mail, 1849–1869* (Cleveland, 1926); another is J. V. Frederick, *Ben Holladay: The Stagecoach King* (Glendale, Calif., 1940). Treating this subject on a somewhat broader basis but useful as general background material is Ellis P. Oberholtzer, *A History of the United States since the Civil War,* 5 vols. (New York, 1936), Vol. I, Chaps. 5–6. And highly pertinent, but less available, is Raymond L. Welty, "The Western Army Frontier, 1860–1870," Ph.D. dissertation, State University of Iowa, Iowa City, 1924.

Highwaymen appear to fascinate writers and readers, and the bad men of the West have been the subject of many books and articles. Classic detective accounts are James H. Cook, *Fifty Years on the Old Frontier* (New Haven, Conn., 1923) and William A. Pinkerton, *Train Robberies, Train Robbers, and the "Holdup" Men* (Chicago, 1907). Also a standard and favorite item in this category is Thomas Dimsdale, *The Vigilantes of Montana; or, Popular Justice in the Rocky Mountains* (any edition); another vigilante book is Stanton A. Coblentz, *Villains and Vigilantes* (New York, 1936). California road agents are well handled in Joseph H. Jackson, *Tintypes in Gold* (New York, 1939). Highway robbery in the Black Hills area is very adequately dealt with in Agnes W. Spring, *The Cheyenne and Black Hills Stage and Express Routes* (Glendale, Calif., 1949). The magazine *Frontier Times* is rich in reminiscent accounts, mostly by Texans, about highway robberies in the Southwest. Scattered articles appear in the state and regional periodical literature, for example: Will C. Barnes, "The Canyon Diablo Train Robbery," *Arizona Historical Review*, III (1) (1930–1931), 88–104; I. E. Solomon, "Stages Held up on Black Canyon Route," *Arizona Historical Review*, I (3) (1928), 50–53; John W. Clampitt, "The Vigilantes of California, Idaho, and Montana," *Harper's*, LXXXIII (1891), 442–451. And an interesting trade book is James D. Horan, *Desperate Men* (New York, 1949).

Information on confidence men and women and on gambling is garnered in bits here and there as indicated in the footnotes.

Good Roads and the Passing of the Transportation Frontier

The materials relating to this subject, especially those describing the plight of frontier roads, are not unrelated to those associated with Chapter 1, The Transportation Frontier.

The literature sparked by the wheelmen, or more specifically the League of American Wheelmen, found its outlet in the official publication of the League, *The Wheelman,* and such other monthly magazines as *Harper's, Overland Monthly, Scribner's, Leslie's,* and *Outing.* Useful in determining the location of roads and inns and in obtaining comments on the condition of roads and the general quality of inns are the many touring guides and handbooks issued by the League of American Wheelmen and other bicycle clubs. Very disorganized, but a mine of information on cycling, is Lyman Hotchkiss Bagg (pseud., Karl Kron), *Ten Thousand Miles on a Bicycle* (New York, 1887).

Rich in materials on roads and road improvement (but not too easily available) are the *Annual Reports of the Department of Agriculture* roughly for the period 1890–1905 published in Washington, D.C. Also published by the Department of Agriculture and rich in information, but more specifically by the Office of Road Inquiry, are forty bulletins (issued at irregular intervals during the period 1894–1911). Scattered but nevertheless available are also the proceedings of various good-roads conventions and conferences held in trans-Mississippi West states during this same period of time. Some of these proceedings are published as bulletins of the Office of Public Road Inquiry.

There are few books devoted especially to the subject of roads west of the Mississippi River, but many of those dealing with roads and road-making on a nation-wide scale contain much information welcome to the historian of the frontier. The booklets and pamphlets of Albert A. Pope, *The Movement for Better Roads* (Boston, 1892), and *Wagon Roads as Feeders to Railroads* (Boston, 1892) and others of a promotional character. Of a technical nature is E. W. Herendeen, "Road Making" in *Rural Affairs* (Albany, N.Y., 1868). And of a general nature, historical and descriptive, are such books as George R. Chatburn, *Highways and Highway Transportation* (New York, 1923) and Jean Labatat and Wheaton J. Lane, eds., *Highways in Our National Life* (Princeton, N.J., 1950). As yet unpublished, but worthy of print, is Philip P. Mason, "The League of American Wheelmen and the Good Roads Movement, 1880–1905," Ph.D. dissertation, University of Michigan, Ann Arbor, 1957.

INDEX